DÆDALUS

JOURNAL OF THE AMERICAN ACADEMY OF ARTS AND SCIENCES

America's Museums

Summer 1999

Issued as Volume 128, Number 3, of the
Proceedings of the American Academy of Arts and Sciences

Summer 1999, "America's Museums"
Issued as Volume 128, Number 3, of the Proceedings of the
American Academy of Arts and Sciences.
ISBN 0-87724-016-7

© 1999 by the American Academy of Arts and Sciences.

Library of Congress Catalog Number 12-30299.

Editorial Offices: Dædalus, Norton's Woods,
136 Irving Street, Cambridge, MA 02138.
Telephone: (617) 491-2600; Fax: (617) 576-5088;
Email: daedalus@amacad.org

Dædalus (ISSN 0011-5266) is published quarterly by the
American Academy of Arts and Sciences. U.S. subscription
rates: for individuals—$33, one year; $60.50, two years;
$82.50, three years; for institutions—$49.50, one year;
$82.50, two years; $110, three years. Canadian subscription
rates: for individuals—$42, one year; $78.75, two years;
$109.50, three years; for institutions—$60, one year; $102,
two years; $138.50, three years. All other foreign subscribers
must add $7.00 per year to the price of U.S. subscriptions.
Replacement copies for damaged or misrouted issues will be
sent free of charge up to six months from the date of original
publication. Thereafter, back copies are available for the
current cover price plus postage and handling. GST number:
14034 3229 RT.

All subscription orders, single-copy orders, and change-of-
address information must be sent in writing to the Dædalus
Business Office, 136 Irving Street, Suite 100, Cambridge, MA
02138, U.S.A.

Printed in the United States of America.
Printing Office: 2901 Byrdhill Road, Richmond, VA 23228.

U.S.A. newsstand distribution by Eastern News Distributors,
Inc., 2020 Superior Street, Sandusky, OH 44870 (Telephone:
800-221-3148).

Periodicals postage paid at Boston, MA, and at additional
mailing offices.

Postmaster: Send address changes to DÆDALUS,
136 Irving Street, Suite 100, Cambridge, MA 02138, U.S.A.

Contents

Preface to the Issue
"America's Museums"

A S THE TWENTIETH CENTURY APPROACHES its end, there is, understandably, a growing interest in how the world's major cultural institutions have fared in the last hundred years. While *Dædalus* has done a great deal to explore higher education, both in the United States and abroad, analyzing how colleges and universities have changed in what has incontestably been a chaotic and violent century memorable as much for its revolutions and wars as for its massive social transformations and technological innovations, on only one occasion has the Journal committed itself to an in-depth study of the world's libraries, so crucial to intellectual life in our time. The Fall 1996 *Dædalus* issue, "Books, Bricks, and Bytes," celebrating the centennial of the founding of the New York Public Library, may properly lay claim to providing the model for this issue on America's museums, but the differences between the two studies need to be acknowledged at once.

"America's Museums," as its name implies, is a study principally of museums in the United States. Very early in the deliberations that led to the commissioning of essays for this issue, a decision was made that it would deal only with American museums. Given that the interest of the group that planned the issue was never to dwell exclusively or principally on the nation's art museums—one of the objects of the exercise was to remind readers how diverse in fact is the contemporary universe of those institutions that agree to call themselves museums—a concentration on the thousands of museums of various types that exist in the United States alone seemed a reasonable strategy. A more broadly international perspective would only have diluted the elements of a narrative and an analysis that many thought merited close study precisely because so much has changed so recently.

To say this is not to suggest that American museum development in this century is in some sense *sui generis*, that its bears only very slight resemblance to what has happened abroad, in Europe and elsewhere. Still, it is useful to be reminded that while America's museums may lay claim to eighteenth- and early-nineteenth-century origins—one thinks of what is written in these pages about individuals as different as Peale, Barnum, and Smithson, for example—the story of America's museums is largely a post–Civil War tale. If private fortunes laid the foundations of some of the great American museums of late-nineteenth-century America, if the national government played a relatively minor role in their early creation and development, a situation very different from that of Europe, it was a small group of wealthy individuals in a pre-income-tax age who provided much of the capital for both the buildings and the collections that made Europeans for the first time take note of American museums. While many of the impressive "palaces" built for these collections, in their sober, classical, and dignified styles, resembled the more opulent royal and aristocratic palaces of Europe, where so many of the world's "treasures" were stored, the resemblances were always superficial. Whatever models the great museums of Europe—of Germany, the United Kingdom, and France—might provide, however much the wealthy of the New World might wish to imitate them in matters of taste, there was always some wish to move beyond the European example, to create something that expressed America's distinctiveness. America's democracy, as Tocqueville described it, and as Bryce rediscovered it toward the end of the nineteenth century, guaranteed a certain originality, and, in time, a greater involvement by the community, variously described and defined.

In the creation of a museum like the American Museum of Natural History in New York in 1869, it was significant that the city undertook to pay for the building and its maintenance costs while private donors agreed to support the scientific inquiry intended to take place within its walls. Just as European museums were moving away from conceiving of themselves simply as a "cabinet of treasures," accepting traditions common to the Italian Renaissance and the era of the Enlightenment, so American museums began to see themselves as more than storehouses of valuable or interesting and curious objects. The principle of "public responsibility" guaranteed that American museums would make education one of their principal purposes, but it was not immediately evident how these educational purposes could be realized. Indeed, that question remains a vital one even today.

To understand how American museums have changed in the last hundred years, to analyze the many new interests and forces that have been accommodated in this period, would be to write a social, economic, political, and cultural history of the nation. No one would be bold enough to suggest that this has been achieved in the present issue of *Dædalus*. Yet something of comparable importance has been accomplished, implicitly and explicitly; this issue raises questions about why and how American museums have been transformed, particularly in the last half-century. Political and social movements unknown in Franklin Roosevelt's America have surfaced to compel museums to hear arguments that were never previously uttered. It is not at all obvious that museums abroad have been compelled to cope with comparable pressures, which is not to suggest that they remain faithful to their "elitist" pasts while America's museums are increasingly subjected to populist yearnings. In the United States, as elsewhere, museums have become "popular," and the change cannot be ascribed simply to the development of mass tourism. The nation's history is being reconceived, and museums are cooperating in making such intellectual reconsideration possible.

If America's museums are vulnerable to public opinion today in ways that would have been quite inconceivable some decades ago, it becomes essential to understand how this has affected what museums choose to do, what they believe is necessary to exhibit, how, in short, they view themselves, and how their "publics" see them. If museums are recognized today to be community assets—providing income not otherwise available, helping to restore central cities, rescuing them from their ghetto status, giving confidence and self-esteem to individuals and groups previously marginalized—is the accompanying rapid "commercialization" of these institutions desirable, indeed inevitable? Are museums compromising their educational purposes, losing their primacy as centers of research and learning, by becoming emporia—"businesses" almost as well-known for their gift shops and restaurants as for their galleries and special exhibits? Or, given the competition they face, and the financial plight in which almost all find themselves, is there any alternative to this commercial strategy?

How are we to explain the fact that many of the new museums and the "wings" attached to existing ones have become the architectural "treasures" of our time, the "cathedrals" of popular culture, more frequented on Sundays than many of the half-empty churches that so recently appealed to vast numbers? Is the explanation to be found in a vivid concern with the arts of exhibition, a growing recognition of the importance of space, light, and mass, all perceived in new ways? Are museums, in their yearning to appeal to contemporary taste, able to accept innovation while so many other cultural institutions seem to lag, scarcely understanding what modern people wish to know and to experience?

How is authority perceived in today's American museums? What powers still adhere to directors, curators, and trustees? Has the generation of "founders" been effectively displaced by more qualified individuals, specifically trained for their museum tasks? Indeed, how are the professions thought to be responsible for museums, concerned with preservation, education, and conservation, perceiving their new roles? How are modern technologies transforming museums? Do they have effects comparable to what we discover in the nation's libraries? Who are tomorrow's museum "visitors" likely to be, and what will the character of their museum visits be? Is the whole concept of a "museum-worthy object" massively out of date? Indeed, what importance do objects of any kind have in many of the most-frequented museums? As new and exceedingly sensitive questions are being raised about personal and institutional property rights, how are such complex issues likely to be resolved in the future? What, in short, may we expect America's museums to be in the twenty-first century? Does their present character provide a hint of what they are likely to be, of the new social and intellectual powers that have achieved a certain renown in recent years, that many imagine will continue to be influential in the next century?

To ask these questions is to ask a more fundamental one. Of the many American museums created or vastly expanded in recent decades, which, if any, are likely to become models for others, yet to be conceived and constructed? This is another way of asking whether in 1929 when the Museum of Modern Art was created in New York, when later it moved to its very unconventional architectural quarters in 1939, there were very many who anticipated its potential influence, recognizing that it would become a model for modern art museums throughout the world, and not only because of its architecture, exhibition strategies, and collections. If that museum achieved its distinction early, not least as an educational institution, was it largely because of the exceptional qualities of its first two directors, Alfred H. Barr, Jr., and René d'Harnoncourt, or were other factors no less important? To pose that question is to raise an even more critical one: Who are likely to be tomorrow's patrons of America's museums? Will a new generation of very rich men and women consent to be as generous as those who have left such indelible marks on the country's museums? What kinds of support may be expected from corporations and municipal, state, and federal funding agencies, and are these likely to be moved principally by arguments that dwell on the economic advantages to be realized, or will they be concerned as much or even more with the cultural, social, and educational goals that may be achieved? Are historical museums, for example, destined to have a new life, and what will that life be?

What about science and technology museums, art museums, children's museums, not to speak of categories scarcely thought of today? In the 1930s, when the Chicago Museum of Science and Industry was rethinking its purposes—it had been founded in 1929—it spoke of the museum being "concerned in its final form as much with man as a social being as with his scientific discoveries and his industries." Will such objectives be even more apparent in the future, given what the new technologies are almost certain to be, further transforming the social fabric of the country? In short, what is the American museum legacy of the twentieth century likely to be, and how much will Americans choose to build on its own rich and various domestic models and how much are they likely to look for inspiration and example from abroad?

To raise these matters is to make explicit what many will discover in this issue, that the American museum world in the last several decades has been confronted by complex and divisive political and cultural issues. This has been a time of very considerable controversy, and to read some of the titles of the essays in this issue is to be made aware of how difficult it has been for museums to satisfy their critics. One thinks, for example, of "The Divided House of the American Art Museum" by Neil Harris, "On Museum Row: Aesthetics and the Politics of Exhibition" by Chon Noriega, "From Being *about* Something to Being *for* Somebody: The Ongoing Transformation of the American Museum" by Stephen Weil, "What is the Object of this Exercise? A Meandering Exploration of the Many Meanings of Objects in Museums" by Elaine Heumann Gurian, or "Museums as Centers of Controversy" by Willard Boyd, and one knows that this has not been an easy time for those who acknowledge that museums cannot accept today what they were satisfied to see as their principal roles until very recently. Indeed, it is precisely the range and variety of challenges that the museums of the country have been obliged to confront that has given them much of their vigor and novelty. To say this is not to suggest that American museums have been unique in their obligation to cope with political and cultural demands, and that museums outside the United States, in Europe, for example, have not confronted comparable situations. One has only to read the compelling study by Frances Spalding, *The Tate: A History*, to know that this remarkable gallery, a century after its founding, "still courts controversy and attracts criticism as well as praise." This is the condition of many of America's museums, and it is in no way surprising that this should be so.

When Maxwell Anderson writes of the need for museums to "harness their collective potential through new technologies," he sees this as enabling them to "serve their educational mandates while navigating through a world of diminishing attention span and free time." These are characteristic conditions of contemporary life that museums, like universities, libraries, publishers, and others seeking to reach wider audiences, must pay considerable attention to. While there is nothing intrinsically demeaning in seeking ever-larger audiences, and indeed in taking pride in breaking all existing records in respect to museum attendance, the television output of much of the developed world today suggests how easy it is to make market share the all-important criterion of success. If education is to be seen as a continuing museum obligation—to be perceived in wholly new ways, as John Falk, Emlyn Koster, and others argue—then it must be given very substantial priority, which is not to deny or reduce the importance of the many other purposes for which museums exist. Indeed, the very large issue of how museums are to be encouraged to continue to make major contributions to scholarship and to learning in a great variety of disciplines, so important for many who know the history of these institutions, must be seen as a continuing challenge.

When Harold Skramstad, in his essay "An Agenda for American Museums in the Twenty-First Century," speaks of the museum as "a new educational model," his purpose is not to diminish the importance of traditional schools, but only to suggest what museums can do for children that schools are not likely to do, what they are able to do also for the education of adults. When he speaks of the American museum as a "model community institution," he is addressing issues that Bonnie Pitman treats at very considerable length. If certain of the mass media pay attention only to the most prominent museums, to their special exhibitions that draw hundreds of thousands of visitors, there are many smaller museums, some of very recent origin, that enjoy no such national celebrity but are no less vital to their communities, expressing values that need to be recognized as essential to the American democracy. They express community aspirations that need to be taken as democratic assets. Skramstad's essay, like Pitman's, may be read as a celebration of diversity, which is not to suggest that either is wholly content with the conditions that now obtain.

Kathleen McLean, in writing about "Museum Exhibitions and the Dynamics of Dialogue," sees museums as both temples and forums and is as concerned with the second as an earlier generation of museum directors was with the first. When she writes of the role of artists in creating "interesting and challenging exhibitions," she is describing new actors, individuals who are very self-consciously challenging the curators in their role as the only ones who can speak with authority on what an exhibition ought to be. It is not an accident that this issue closes with essays on museum architecture. Susanna Sirefman, writing about contemporary museum architecture, sees it as essentially "welcoming," a "multicultural crossroads," seeking to be a link between the past and the present. It is the very complexity of the purposes that a museum seeks to fulfill that makes it such a challenging assignment for architects, that leads so many of the greatest renown to seek to design them.

When those who planned this issue first discussed it, the name of Cardinal Newman and his incomparable work *The Idea of a University* were mentioned. Several of the planners wondered whether it would not be useful to commission short essays on "The Idea of a Museum." It is significant, in my view, that those who in the end submitted brief essays—essentially memoranda—were individuals fundamentally concerned with architecture. That art, as much as the innovative content of the innumerable museums in the United States described in this issue, must be denominated as one of the glories of this century. We feel a great indebtedness to Victoria Newhouse, Charles Correa, and Bernard Tschumi for their insightful and provocative contributions.

Because we live at a time when institutions—cultural and intellectual but others as well—are inadequately studied, our knowledge of how these various bodies fared in the past is surprisingly limited. In these circumstances, it is easy to be dismissive of earlier achievements, to make too much of present accomplishments, and to dwell too uncritically on future ambitions. While an effort has been made to avoid these analytic shoals—so characteristic of our day—we recognize that we may not have always succeeded. More significantly, perhaps, some who read this issue may wonder whether sufficient attention has been given to the influence of mass tourism on museums, abetted by the museums themselves through their massive public relations and publicity campaigns. Are museums in danger of losing their reputations for encouraging study and contemplation by those who enter their portals? It is easy to mock the huge crowds attending special exhibitions scarcely able to see the treasures over the heads of others. Or, as in so many galleries abroad, the Vatican museums, for example, it sometimes appears that the crowds are more intent on searching for the red flag or green umbrella that reassures them that their guide is still there than in seeing what these rooms contain. Both in the United States and in Europe, it becomes ever more important to know the character of those who in fact are going to museums in such number, to understand more about what they are experiencing in these visits. The term "experience" figures prominently in these *Dædalus* pages; so, also, does the term "community." Both need to be looked at sympathetically but critically, precisely because they express ambitions that it would be churlish to dismiss or deny.

This issue owes a great deal to the Institute of Museum and Library Services, the National Endowment for the Arts, the National Endowment for the Humanities, the Pew Charitable Trusts, and the Rockefeller Foundation for their financial support. Because many who wrote for this issue wished to see it widely distributed in the museum community, several thousand copies were sent to directors, curators, trustees, public officials, and others who share responsibility for the nation's museums. The Institute of Museum and Library Services and the Pew Charitable Trusts provided funds for this purpose, as did Edwin McAmis and Lois and Georges de Menil, great and loyal friends of the Journal. We are very grateful for their help. Diane

Frankel, as much as anyone, deserves our thanks, not least for seeing the possibilities of this issue. In planning sessions held at the Institute of Museum and Library Services in Washington, D.C., and at the Huntington Library in San Marino, California, and at the authors' conference held at the Center for Advanced Study in the Behavioral Sciences in Stanford, California, the issues touched on in these essays were discussed and debated. It will surprise no one to learn that not all who attended these meetings were equally sanguine about America's museums at this time in the nation's history. No one, however, doubted the importance of these institutions and the need for seeing them in ways that would not have been considered some decades ago. As Bonnie Pitman says in the concluding paragraph to the essay that opens this issue, "While there are many problems facing museums now and in the future, we should focus not on the difficulties but on the incredible opportunities that will engage museums as entirely new audiences gain access to the information and ideas housed in their collections and exhibitions. Museums are working together to share services, expertise, and collections to increase their abilities to communicate with and actively engage the public."

S.R.G.

Bonnie Pitman

Muses, Museums, and Memories

I T IS COMMONLY REPORTED that museums are growing—more
people are visiting museums, great numbers of museums are
being created, and an even larger number are expanding.
Today, museums are identified as the most popular cultural
institutions visited by Americans.[1] The American Association
of Museums (AAM) estimates that in the decade of the 1990s,
attendance grew by over two hundred million visitors. What
are visitors to these institutions seeking? Is it an experience
with artifacts and objects—the real thing—at a time when
virtual reality is a growing phenomenon? Is it the need for
places that provide opportunities for educational and aesthetic
experiences, for discourse, for social gatherings?

Museums are more than the repositories of the past, with
memories and objects both rare and beautiful. Museums are
cultural, educational, and civic centers in our communities—
centers for exhibition, conservation, research, and interpretation; they are theaters and movie houses, job-training programs, schools and day-care centers, libraries and concert halls.
The notion of museums as quiet, contemplative places of learning where collections are studiously researched and cared for
by scholars has changed dramatically in recent decades. The
number of museums that offer this kind of experience is diminishing; museums increasingly serve as gathering places, as forums for their communities. The exhibitions presented and the
range of materials incorporated into collections reflect the multiple
voices, needs, and interests of individual communities.

Bonnie Pitman is executive director of the Bay Area Discovery Museum in Sausalito,
California.

The word "museum" comes from the Greek *mouseion*, which identified a temple dedicated to the Muses, the nine goddesses of inspiration, learning, and the arts. Among the most famous classical museums was the one in Alexandria founded around the third century B.C., destroyed in the third century A.D. The *mouseion* in Alexandria, a philosophical academy with scholars in residence, was fully supported by the state. There is a direct relationship between Alexandria's *mouseion* and the museums of today; both are gathering places of objects and ideas that assist individuals in understanding the world around them.

The use of the term *museum* was more broadly developed during the Renaissance, referring to the private collections of individual patrons. These "cabinets of curiosities," with antiquities, rare jewels, and other objects on display, reflected the pride of their owners. These museums were intended to provide pleasure to others as well as opportunities to discover, to learn. While not open to the public, these collections were available to the aristocracy, the clergy, and serious scholars. The establishment of the first museums in America owed much to individuals willing to share their personal collections and wealth in order to enhance the knowledge and education of the community.

While there are more than 8,300 institutions listed in the Official Museum Directory, estimates of the total number of museums range from 8,300 to more than 11,000. From art museums to zoos, the list includes children's museums, natural history museums, history museums, historic sites, science and technology centers, aquariums, and planetariums. Additionally, the definition embraces an expansive breadth of collections, with great variety in the size of the physical plant and the range of programs available to the public. To be accredited by the AAM, a museum must:

· be a legally organized not-for-profit institution or part of a not-for-profit institution or government entity;
· be essentially educational in nature;
· have a formal stated mission;
· have at least one full-time paid professional staff person who has museum knowledge and experience, and is delegated

authority and allocated financial resources sufficient to operate the museum effectively;

· present regularly scheduled programs and exhibits that use
and interpret objects for the public according to accepted
standards;

· have a formal and appropriate program of documentation,
care, and use of collections and/or tangible objects;

· have a formal and appropriate program of maintenance and
presentation of exhibits.[2]

The eight hundred museums accredited in the United States
represent the leading institutions, those willing to be judged by
the standards of the museum profession. The accredited museums represent approximately 10 percent of all the museums in
the country; they include all the major institutions in terms of
quality of collections, service to the community, and annual
budgets.

Today, America's museums face a variety of internal and
external challenges as they look for ways to communicate their
values to society; to take advantage of the new technologies
that create fundamental changes in the ways people access
information and view and use their collections; and to respond
to the changing demographic and economic shifts in both local
and regional communities. Throughout these challenges, their
search for new ways to fund their operations is perpetual.

A BRIEF HISTORY OF AMERICA'S MUSEUMS

Numerous books chronicle the history of museums in America.
Authors including Edward Alexander, Nathaniel Burt, Steven
Conn, Neil Harris, and Karl Meyer provide thoughtful over-
views of their development, of the complex transition from
private houses and "cabinets of curiosities" for the wealthy and
privileged to public institutions designed to serve the public
good. The chronicling of the history of museums, these gatherings of objects into collections for enjoyment and study, has a
long tradition. Botanical gardens and zoos were built by the
Assyrians as early as 2000 B.C. They were present at Karnak in
Egypt in 1500 B.C. and are amply documented in many texts.

Museums as we know them, however, were created in Europe during the Renaissance; they flourished in the eighteenth century.

Karl Meyer points out that "Even before the American Revolution the educated classes, made up of professional men, well-to-do merchants, and land owners, had begun to establish public galleries."[3] In 1773 the Charleston Library Society's decision to collect animals, plants, and minerals that represented the natural history of South Carolina marked the founding of the first museum in America. The tradition of historical societies began in 1791 with the establishment of the Massachusetts Historical Society, which included both a library and a public gallery. Historical societies encouraged the desire to promote learning, to chronicle the history of the nation. By 1876 there were seventy-eight historical societies, and the majority of these institutions included a museum with collections in art and history, boasting many kinds of documents.[4] The first historic house museum, Hasbrouck House, was acquired in 1850 in the state of New York. The headquarters for General Washington in Newburgh, Hasbrouck House was to be maintained in the condition characteristic of the time when he used it. Preservationists secured Mt. Vernon, which was then transferred to the Mt. Vernon Ladies' Association of the Union, a volunteer group dedicated to raising funds and preserving the site in the late 1850s. In 1926 America's first outdoor museum was opened, using an original site in Colonial Williamsburg; it was funded by John D. Rockefeller, Jr. In 1929, Henry Ford opened an outdoor museum that moved historical structures to the site of Henry Ford Museum & Greenfield Village in Michigan.

In Philadelphia, Charles Willson Peale, acknowledged for his civic leadership, moved his collection of art and natural history objects from his home to the Philosophical Hall of the American Philosophical Society in 1794, and from there to Independence Hall in 1802, where it was open to the public without charge. Later, Peale established branches of his museum in Baltimore and New York City, exhibiting his own paintings and those of members of his family as well as collections of mounted specimens of animals, birds, and insects. Peale's museums organized collections in an orderly fashion, competing with the "catchpenny" museums that were becoming increasingly popular, with their live performances and unique—though not always authentic—objects. In 1827, after the death of Peale, his museums closed, having gone bankrupt.

By the middle of the nineteenth century, there were essentially two types of museums in the United States. The first was a public gallery, part of a library, art academy, historical society, college, or private club; the second was generally called the "dime museum," established for commercial purposes, dedicated to entertainment. Many of the museums established in the mid-1800s were intended to help educate the growing immigrant populations in America's cities through displays of objects that conveyed a visual narrative. The growth of America's museums paralleled the growth of the cities and also the development of new communities around the country. The displays, illuminated by natural light, featuring rows of glass cases, carefully arranged to allow scientific examination, "serve[d] as windows onto the world."[5]

The influence of Phineas T. Barnum on featuring museums principally as entertainment, boasting large exhibitions, is often overlooked. Barnum, immensely interested in what attracted the public's interest, wished for people to be startled, to gasp with wonder at the world around them. In 1841, purchasing the collections from several museums, including Peale's museums, he created a collection of over six hundred thousand objects. His building was filled with attractions and curiosities both living and dead—including Siamese twins, Tom Thumb, and strange and rare objects, along with ancient relics (both genuine and fake) from around the world in spectacularly disordered presentation. Cities around the country, from Cincinnati to Chicago, developed this type of museum; these museums, associated with showmanship, theatricality, and publicity, are redolent in some respects of the "blockbuster" shows of today.

Museums created after the Civil War focused on presenting objects and ideas in a more orderly and systematic fashion. Specimens of exotic butterflies might well dazzle viewers in New York and Philadelphia, but their purpose, under glass, was to demonstrate that nature—even in her most exotic creations— had an essential order.[6] Through the end of the nineteenth and the beginning of the twentieth centuries, growth in the number of American museums paralleled the growth in knowledge, with discoveries about the universe perpetually celebrated.

In 1846, the Smithsonian Institution was founded with a gift to the United States government from James Smithson, an Englishman interested in "the increase and diffusion of knowledge."[7] In its early years, the Smithsonian focused principally on scientific research. The arrival in 1873 of George Brown Goode changed the direction of the Smithsonian; he focused on making it a national museum with collections in the arts and humanities as well as the natural sciences. The 1870s, following the years of Civil War, were a time of industrial and commercial expansion. During this period the Metropolitan Museum of Art, the American Museum of Natural History, the Museum of Fine Arts in Boston, and the Philadelphia Museum of Art were founded. Each, established with a different purpose, perceived its collections differently, but all sought support from the pubic and private sectors. Museums created during this period were dedicated to educating the public.

The first American zoo was founded in Central Park in Philadelphia in 1854. The concept of zoos as "menageries," with various animal specimens, changed dramatically after the 1870s. The New York Zoological Society began to display animals in natural surroundings, with large barless enclosures becoming common in the late 1890s. In the past thirty years, zoos have ceased to be places where wild and domestic animals live in captivity to become "bioparks" promoting conservation and education about all forms of animal and plant life.

A similar and equally dramatic trend has occurred in botanical gardens. The earliest American gardens were founded in Washington, D.C., in 1850, in St. Louis in 1859, and in New York City in 1895. Today, there are more than three hundred botanical gardens in the United States. The New York Botanical Garden in the Bronx, the largest in the country, includes public gardens, research facilities, and a major library. In recent years, the missions of zoos and botanical gardens have expanded greatly. Their concern is to address the destruction of natural habitats for animals and plants by humans in many parts of the world. Zoos and botanical gardens have become places of learning and sanctuaries to prevent the extinction of many endangered and threatened species. Conservation and education are at the forefront of their work.

Children's museums and science and technology centers have strong historic links to their educational mission. The Brooklyn Children's Museum, established in 1899, and the Boston Children's Museum, which opened in 1913, house collections of special interest to children—toys, artifacts from other cultures, children's costumes, and natural history collections. Focused on serving children, their families, and their caregivers, children's museums have strong ties to the communities they serve. Currently, children's museums represent one of the fastest-growing sectors of the museum community; there are over 350 children's museums in the country, with another hundred in the planning stages.

The interest in science and technology was influential in the founding of the Smithsonian and of the Philadelphia Centennial Exposition of 1876, which included five buildings dedicated to industrial exhibitions of all types. The collection of machines, implements, and all manner of innovations became the basis of the collections in the National Museum of American History, which embraces various technologies, including computers, and the National Air and Space Museum, which features the Wright Brothers' *Flyer* and Alan Shephard's *Mercury* capsule. The Museum of Science and Industry in Chicago, established in 1926 by Julius Rosenwald, head of Sears, Roebuck & Co., opened in 1933; the New York Museum of Science and Industry (now defunct) represents the arrival of science technology centers, founded without collections, that focus on their role as educational institutions to promote an understanding of scientific principles. These centers have grown rapidly in the past three decades. Since World War II, and in particular after the launch of *Sputnik*, America's desire to enhance opportunities for teaching and learning about science and technology has increased. Science museums and science technology centers, emphasizing the teaching of science, are today very prominent; they include the Pacific Science Center in Seattle, the Museum of Science in Boston, the Franklin Institute in Philadelphia, and the Exploratorium in San Francisco. Their exhibitions are designed to secure the active engagement of those who seek to learn about scientific principles. The Association of Science–Technology Centers (ASTC) estimates that one-quarter of its current members (which number over five hundred) opened their doors in the 1990s. The growing demand for children's and science museums reflects the public's increased understanding of how such organizations support opportunities for education and how they contribute to both school and family learning in their communities.

Yet today, as in the past, for many the idea of a museum brings to mind an art museum. Because art museums are frequently the most visible museums in a community, boasting powerful and wealthy boards of directors, enjoying frequent coverage in the press, and emphasizing the value of the art in their collections and on display, and because they are frequently represented in the advertising sections of newspapers with promotions of their current exhibitions, they are well known. The tradition of the art museums' star system, the powerful and influential people associated with them—not only those who sit on their boards of trustees, but also the artists whose works are exhibited, the architects who design their buildings, and the large crowds that are attracted to their special exhibitions—gives them their renown.

The power and wealth associated with an art museum's board may have its origins in the Metropolitan Museum of Art in New York and the Museum of Fine Arts in Boston; both were founded by groups of private citizens in 1870. The distinction of the Boston Museum of Fine Arts (as well as the Philadelphia Museum of Art) derived in part from its galleries for the display of art, but also from its early school for industrial design. As Steven Conn has said, these museums were not "palaces of fine art but functional places instead where art would be put to the service of industry." By contrast, "the Metropolitan Museum . . . was established to exhibit the objects d'art collected by its wealthy benefactors."[8] After the election of J. P. Morgan to the Metropolitan's board in 1888, he filled vacancies on the board with millionaires like himself, including Henry Clay Frick, Henry Walters, and others of comparable wealth. Other art museum boards followed this same model, including Chicago,

Detroit, San Francisco, and Washington. Another important reason that art museums have enjoyed such ample notice is that a number were established as gifts by individuals like Henry Frick and Isabella Stewart Gardner, who provided the entire contents of their private homes to be converted into museums and opened to the public. Paul Mellon funded the building of the National Gallery of Art in Washington, while J. Paul Getty's bequest created the museums that bear his name in Malibu and Los Angeles.

Tax law was immensely important in accommodating the needs of wealthy donors who wished to contribute to art museums:

> Two fiscal measures have been indispensable to the rise of the art museum in the United States: The Payne-Aldrich Tariff of 1909, which added to the duty free list the importation of original works of art that were more than twenty years old, and the charitable deduction provision in federal and state taxing income, estates and gifts. Without these legislative inducements, it is safe to say the museum explosion of this century could never have occurred.[9]

Money invested to construct buildings, purchase works of art, and create major exhibitions, not to speak of large individual gifts, attracts attention to art museums. One example of an individual donor's generosity is found in the $30 million donations to the Museum of Contemporary Art, San Diego, and the San Diego Museum of Art. Significant, also, is the economic impact on communities of the presentation of such "blockbuster" exhibitions as the tomb of King Tutankhamen, or the paintings of Monet, Van Gogh, or Jackson Pollock, which become major cultural and news events.

ACCREDITATION—STANDARDS OF EXCELLENCE

The AAM's Accreditation Program provides a formal review process of the country's museums, those that are willing to hold themselves publicly accountable for maintaining specific standards of performance and are committed to regular review and improvement. Today, there are over 750 museums that have achieved accreditation, and hundreds more are in the process of seeking this distinction. Accreditation provides a formal means for evaluating a museum's performance; it measures an institution against evolving standards in the field.

Over the years, the Accreditation Program has led to improvements in performance. In the 1970s, the accreditation reviews emphasized the need to upgrade fundamental organizational structures. This was a time for many museums to redefine and clarify their missions and operations, which many had never reviewed since their original founding. The focus of many accreditation reviews in the 1980s was more specifically on the care and management of collections. The 1990s have seen attention concentrated on the public dimension of museums. Museums accredited today do not just present information to the public; they seek to communicate with disparate audiences, demonstrate that they are well managed and that they care for their collections and their resources.

The definition of a museum, and the delineating of the characteristics of an accredited museum, have provided invaluable guidance to a broad range of museums that aspire to operate effectively and be publicly accountable. The roster of currently accredited museums includes organizations as diverse as the San Diego Zoo and Wild Animal Park; the Rogers Historical Museum in Rogers, Arkansas; the Brooklyn Children's Museum, celebrating its hundredth anniversary in 1999; the McFadden-Ward House in Beaumont, Texas; the Field Museum in Chicago; the Peabody Museum of Natural History at Yale University; and the Studio Museum of Harlem in New York City.

In the light of increased public scrutiny of the not-for-profit sector, the AAM Accreditation Program has set a goal of having 1,600 museums accredited in the next ten years. The accreditation program continues to be the centerpiece of AAM's efforts to motivate, foster, and recognize advancement and excellence in museum performance, accountability, and service to the public. Supported by the Museum Assessment Program and the Technical Information Service, museums have increased access to a comprehensive network of information to effect and manage change as they seek to meet the challenges of the new century.

THE DIVERSITY OF AMERICA'S MUSEUMS

The diversity of museums in the United States is indeed impressive. There are well over 8,300 museums in the country and more than 15,000 historic sites, with collections of very different sizes. Some museums boast no collections of any note, but use objects and ideas to provide instruction. The decade-old study *Museums Count,* a report by the American Association of Museums, provides an overview of the complex fabric of the museum field. Many professional museum associations update information on their constituent bodies annually. However, there has been no comprehensive national study since the late 1980s, and one is desperately needed.

The importance of American museums to the educational and cultural life of the country's communities is documented in a number of ways. *Museums Count* recorded that in 1989 "only 4 percent [of America's museums] were founded before 1900. Three quarters have been founded since 1950 and 40 percent since 1970, testifying to the surge of public interest in museums and the rapidly expanding corps of museum professionals and specialists."[10] The AAM's Technical Information Service estimates that between 1998 and 2000, approximately $4.3 billion will be spent on improving the infrastructures of museums; more than 150 museums will be built or expanded during this period.[11] Some 26 percent of the new museums will focus on a specialized topic, including social issues and ethnic subjects. Some 34 percent are expected to be expansions of art museums.

Another important trend in museums relates to the number that are merging and also to the number of government-funded museums that are privatizing. These changes are heavily influenced by economic necessity. Mergers include the Marysville, Washington, Historical Society and the Pioneer Association in Marysville, which have merged their collections and boards and are now preparing plans for a new museum. The Corning Glass Center and the Corning Museum of Glass in New York have combined to create a new nonprofit organization that will be supported by the Corning Glass Company. The Children's Museum of Cincinnati, Ohio, and the Cincinnati Museum Center have chosen to merge. The Museum Center already houses the Cincinnati History Museum, the Museum of Natural History and Science, and an Omnimax theater. There are numerous other examples of children's museums merging with science centers and natural history museums, hoping to consolidate costs and to attract new audiences.[12]

As cities seek to reduce their expenditures and free up their limited incomes for the increasing demands of other public services, privatization seems to be another popular solution. The Founders Society of the Detroit Institute of Arts, under a new agreement (1998) with the city of Detroit, will be responsible for all the operations of the Institute. The joint boards will be dissolved and a new nonprofit corporation will be formed by the Founders Society. A three-year plan to reduce city support to the Heritage Board of the Valdez Museum in Alaska, formerly a city department, will provide time for the museum to transform itself into a public/private partnership with a membership association. The new trends of mergers and reorganizations are focused on improving financial stability and sustainability for the museum's future.

AMERICAN MUSEUMS—A BOOM

Headlines in newspapers as conspicuous as the *New York Times* and the *Wall Street Journal* note the growing influence of America's museums. Reporters inform readers that more people go to museums than to sports events. Museums have recorded an increase of almost two hundred million visitors in ten years—678 million in 1989 and an estimated 865 million in 1997–1998.[13] The *New York Times*, believing that we are in a "golden age" of the American museum, cites "a growing list of new or expanding institutions filled to capacity with eager visitors."[14] It is estimated that more than three hundred museums will be built or expanded by the year 2000, including the Science Museum of Minnesota, the Arkansas Art Center, the Museum of Fine Arts in Houston, and the Bay Area Discovery Museum in San Francisco. The celebrated openings of new museums, including the J. Paul Getty Museum and the California Science Center in Los Angeles, the Minnesota Historical

Society History Center in St. Paul, and the Museum of Jewish Heritage in New York City, have received much notice.

Architects and designers for today's museums provide plans dramatically different from those of their predecessors. Their desire for their buildings to add to the quality of life in their communities, to enhance the stature of the city and the community, have become all-important. Accommodating the diverse needs of visitors creates demands for new public facilities, including restaurants, bookstores, theaters, and the like. Internationally acclaimed architects have affirmed their focus on building museums as places of knowledge and beauty. Their concern is to create important landmarks that will contribute to civic pride and provide economic benefits to the community, the city, the region.

A decade ago, art museums were serving a relatively small segment of the American population, with science museums, aquariums, and zoos attracting the largest number of visitors.[15] Much has changed since then. The *Monet in the 20th Century* exhibition at the Museum of Fine Arts in Boston drew an attendance of over 565,000, an unprecedented number. Other major exhibitions attracting close to half a million visitors included Edgar Degas and Vincent Van Gogh shows over a three-month period. Twenty-one exhibitions attracted over two hundred thousand visitors in Brooklyn, Minneapolis, Philadelphia, St. Louis, and San Francisco. While other American cultural institutions, including symphonies, for example, witnessed declining attendance, museums have been successful, attracting large numbers of people of all backgrounds and educational levels.[16]

Fueled by the economic boom of the 1990s, museums have responded to the social, economic, and political needs of their specific environments. Continuing demographic changes and growth in the population necessarily affect the context in which museums operate. Demographic shifts, including those of age, ethnicity, and income levels, must influence both attendance and support. Changes in how people work and how they choose to spend their leisure time must affect museums in their staffing and programs. Museums have developed marketing policies to attract new audiences, to increase the access to their educational resources both at the museums themselves and through the World Wide Web. While support from individuals has been strong during this period, there has been a decline in support from governmental sources, and this fact needs to be noted.

MUSEUMS AS CENTERS OF LEARNING

The common characteristic among all museums is their role as educational institutions. While not all museums acquire, conserve, or study objects, all museums are public spaces devoted to engaging the public in learning, in disseminating knowledge. For example, while the collections and exhibitions may vary greatly, the focus on education is common to institutions as different as Mystic Seaport in Connecticut, with its exploration of America's maritime history and contemporary relationship to the sea, and the Please Touch Museum in Philadelphia, with its wealth of children's toys.

Expanded acceptance of the educational roles of museums, along with an embracing of the changing audiences that museums are serving, was articulated early in the 1990s with the publication of *Excellence and Equity: Education and the Public Dimension of Museums*. This landmark policy statement, prepared by and with the museum community, articulates the changing role of museums, focusing on their expanded role as educational institutions intended to appeal to diverse audiences, to present and interpret imaginatively their diverse collections. *Excellence and Equity* was the first major report on the educational role of museums published by the AAM. "The report links two concepts—excellence and equity. By giving these concepts equal value, this report invites museums to take pride in their tradition as stewards of excellence and to embrace the cultural diversity of our nation as they foster their tremendous educational potential."[17] *Excellence and Equity* presents an expanded definition of the museum's educational role, meant to engage the entire museum—boards, curators, educators, and other staff and volunteers. The impact of the report has been substantial; the AAM's accreditation standards have been revised to incorporate and hold museums accountable for the concepts articulated in it. Increased funding from foundations and federal agencies has been directed at those museums prepared to support new program initiatives. Major funding from foundations like the Pew Charitable Trusts and the Lila Wallace and DeWitt Wallace Foundations, as well as countless community foundations, has fueled an expansion of education programs.

Museums are increasing their capacity to provide both education and entertainment. After a period when their institutions appeared to be struggling for survival, museum professionals began to address seriously the problem of why they were losing their audiences to theme parks and the Internet. They looked at ways to revitalize their image. Today, museums are redefining themselves as learning/experience environments, studying the methods and policies of their competitors, working with new types of consultants, searching for information about their consumers—what they want, how they learn, where they come from, how much time and money they are prepared to spend. The answers to these questions have revealed that museum visitors are educated; they attend theme parks, own computers, and travel. The average age and income of museum visitors is declining; this is a satisfactory trend for it suggests that more people from more diverse backgrounds are coming to museums. The audience, seeking to discover and experience something new, unique, and educational, values the content of museum collections and exhibitions. Compelling stories and opportunities that manage to engage all the senses are the experiences that succeed in attracting new and returning visitors. The paradigm for both exhibition and education is shifting from a textual to a visual literacy form, to an approach that makes lecturing visitors less important than having conversations with them.

Involvement in learning is, of course, a lifelong process involving a rich matrix of experience, including formal education in schools and universities as well as informal learning. The learning that occurs outside schools—in the home, in travel, and in libraries and museums—supports this continuing educational experience. As their services to the public have increased, museums have involved their entire staffs in understanding and contributing to the education of their publics. The growth in the resources allocated to educational and public-service functions has been conspicuous. Museums are pushing the limits of both their hardware and their software to enhance visitors' experiences in their multisensory exhibitions. Advanced audio technologies allow for the transmission of multiple soundtracks tailored to visitors of different ages, interests, and languages. Museums are creating immersion environments, recreating real-life settings to allow visitors to participate in real-life adventures.

FAMILIES AND MUSEUMS

Market research has revealed that all types of museums are identified as places where families enjoy being together and come to learn. Eight out of ten museums now have programs for nonschool audiences.[18] Museums are increasingly directing their attention to the family audience, in part because they know that the experience of young learners will have a direct effect on their participation as museum visitors in the future. Museum environments are identified as safe places, allowing the family to discover and explore, stimulating the senses and creating memories that are shared. Museums greatly enrich the sensory and symbolic vocabulary of individuals; they empower children and adults to engage in experiences that use language, arts, and movement, giving them a new appreciation of both the natural and the cultural worlds. Museums help families to learn about themselves, connecting them to the world—past, present, and future.

Some museums with collections have invested heavily in family experiences through the development of discovery rooms, demonstration areas, theater programs, and other ways to provide access to those collections that would otherwise be unavailable. These participatory programs and exhibitions provide comfortable places where parents and children can learn together while using objects from the museum's collections. These learning activities are designed to help both young and old to ask questions and discover things together. The expanded influence of families on museums can be seen in the replacement of discovery rooms by experience-oriented complexes and new theater productions intended to engage families. Currently, the Chicago Zoological Park (Brookfield Zoo) and the San Francisco Zoological Gardens are building indoor/outdoor complexes that will include interactive exhibitions and programs to educate families as to how zoos work. The Art Institute of Chicago, the Minneapolis Institute of Arts, and the Denver Art Museum have expanded programs and spaces allocated for families throughout the museum galleries. They have also provided training programs for staff and launched marketing initiatives to attract families.

The Everett Children's Adventure Garden at the New York Botanical Garden fosters an attitude of wonder; it helps create an understanding of nature among children and adults, supporting the science areas of the school curriculum. The garden provides a retreat for families eager to spend time together while addressing the specific curricula needs of their children from kindergarten through the sixth grade. The twelve-acre Children's Garden utilizes the landscape to teach the biology of gardens and wetlands. The garden, specifically designed with decompression features—where children can run through the meadow maze, climb on the boulder maze, and explore the hedge maze—directs children's focus to the landscape around them. They learn about plant biology, plant anatomy, pollination, seed dispersal, and the like. The success of the Adventure Garden has resulted in plans to improve other areas of the Botanical Garden for increased visitation by family groups.

SUPPORT FOR SCHOOLS

Each year, millions of students tumble out of their yellow school buses and into the halls, galleries, and gardens of museums around the country. Eighty-eight percent of the museums that responded to the 1998 Institute of Museums and Library Services (IMLS) survey reported that they provided K-12 school programs. The survey notes that aquariums, zoos, and botanical gardens as well as art, history, natural history, and children's museums around the country spend over $193 million on school programs. The most frequently identified museum program is that of the field trip, with staff-guided programs offered by 88 percent of the institutions and volunteer-guided programs of-

fered by 76 percent. Most museums offer multiple-visit programs, with previsit lessons and materials linking the museum
visit with the curriculum studied in the classroom. Museums
recorded in the IMLS survey suggest that they coordinated
with the school curriculum in subjects as different as math,
science, art, and history.[19]

In recent years, there have been several important additions
to the traditional list of museum school programs. The focus on
early learners (infants through kindergarten), the creation of
charter schools, and the increased emphasis on writing and
teacher training have all affected museums' educational programs. Museums are increasingly seen to be partners with
schools and other community institutions that are seeking solutions to reform the quality of American education. The Smithsonian
Early Enrichment Center (SEEC), a privately incorporated,
nonprofit developmental and education program for young
children, is located at the Smithsonian Institution. There are
facilities for preschool children at the National Museum of
American History and the National Museum of Natural History, and an infant and toddler center at the Arts and Industry
Building. SEEC, established to be a model of museum-based
education for preschool children, is training museum professionals and early childhood educators in the use of its curriculum; it is licensing its program to universities and early childhood education centers around the country.

The first charter school in a museum was opened in 1991 in
Minnesota. Eight years later, there are over nine hundred charter schools in twenty-four states, including the District of Columbia. While each state has developed its own laws, charter
schools are generally free of most of the state educational
regulations and restrictions. The charter-granting authorities
have accepted museums in Arizona, California, Minnesota,
Michigan, and New York. One example of the museum-based
charter school is Henry Ford Academy, a public high school
located on the premises of Henry Ford Museum & Greenfield
Village in Dearborn, Michigan. The charter school is founded
on a collaboration between the museum, the Ford Motor Company, and the Wayne County Regional Educational Services.
The first class will graduate in 2001, having had access to the

resources of the museum's collections, including authentic objects, stories, and traditions of American innovation and ingenuity.[20]

The Autry Museum of Western Heritage worked with the Los Angeles Unified School District on a collaborative program to develop a new curriculum based on the multicultural character of western communities, making use of the museum's resources. Teachers in rural Minnesota are working in partnership with the Minneapolis Institute of Arts to create a Visual Thinking Strategies Curriculum that will support the museum's commitment to provide access to a framework for learning the arts. There are countless examples of outstanding school-museum partnerships, including the New England Aquarium's project with Boston-area schools. This liaison is designed to teach youngsters about the science of water using a variety of capacity-building strategies, targeted to children who do not have direct access to the Aquarium. There are other museums that specialize in the development of curriculum materials, including the Lawrence Hall of Science at the University of California, Berkeley, with its nationally acclaimed curriculum and teacher-education programs.

CONSERVATION AND PRESERVATION AS THE FOCUS OF LEARNING

Concern about the survival of the planet has brought increased attention to the need for understanding and appreciation of the interconnectedness of species and the ecosystem. The story of diminishing resources and expanding populations and their effect on our planet is a compelling one, critical for museums that wish to explain the phenomena based on the research made possible through their collections, which often include examples of vanishing cultures and species. This is a profound shift from Peale's display of objects of natural history in order to excite wonder and curiosity to exhibits that focus on science and are concerned with the preservation of species and life on earth. Although the stewardship of the natural world was an integral part of the founding missions for natural history and anthropology museums, aquariums, zoos, and botanical gardens, there is today a heightened awareness of the importance of this mission.

One of the major trends of the past twenty years has been the expanded role of education and learning in museums that care for living collections—zoos, aquariums, botanical gardens, and natural history museums. The critical ecological crisis of the planet, and the growing support for a careful stewardship of our natural and cultural heritage, have focused more attention on teaching about conservation and preservation. The primary messages emphasize the critical role biodiversity plays in sustaining life. As the human population grows, over thirty thousand species of plants and animals are lost each year. The loss of rain forests and the death of the coral reefs, together with other such changes, result in the expansion of deserts, the absence of safe drinking water, economic decline, and sometimes mass starvation. The need to protect and preserve fragile world resources, locally, nationally, and internationally, can be made more graphic through programs and exhibitions that demonstrate the need for a thoughtful preservation of the interdependence of life.

Ellen Futter, president of the American Museum of Natural History in New York, writes:

> Exhaustive documentation demonstrates that nearly every ecosystem—every network of biological species in a natural setting—is under threat. Many of the habitats are virtually lost. One need only consider the sobering statistics for the loss of 21 percent of all forests and woodlands in the last century or the decimation of over 2,000 species of resident birds in the Pacific Islands over the last millennium to realize that we have already moved to the compromised strategy of saving what is left for future generations. Equally disturbing is the fact that these ecosystems and their component species play roles in recycling nutrients, balancing energy, and maintaining a global environment in ways that are far from completely understood.[21]

Natural history museums, as well as botanical gardens, zoos, and aquariums, have both the resources and the commitment to bring to their publics an awareness of the importance of biodiversity. Attendance in these museums is higher than many others, and their demographic visitor profile suggests that economic and social class barriers as well as those of education are relatively low. Embracing the widest possible audience, committed to learning and understanding the importance of the natural world, these institutions are today at the forefront of an effort to sustain a habitable universe.

The American Museum of Natural History, having established a Center for Biodiversity and Conservation, encourages scientists to integrate into their research programs the study of habitats, taxonomic surveys, and other such related subjects. The museum's special exhibitions on global warming and on endangered species have toured nationally. In 1998, the Hall of Biodiversity opened with an "extraordinary array of animals, plants and other organisms in a diorama that allows visitors to step behind glass and experience a constantly changing African rain forest habitat alive with sights, sounds, smells. . . ."[22] The Hall of Biodiversity uses the World Wide Web to link field research with schools, using electronic bulletin boards to provide updates on scientific developments, seeking to foster an increased awareness of the urgent and fragile issues of biodiversity.

The Field Museum of Natural History in Chicago has established two centers to unite its interests in collections, education, exhibits, and research. This is an integral part of the outreach functions of the museum. The Center for Evolutionary and Environmental Biology, like the Center for Cultural Understanding and Change, is a cross-functional center designed to coordinate and focus the museum's educational and research efforts while increasing access to its collections. Rather than focusing on a specific culture or geographic region, the museum's permanent exhibition, *Living Together*, is "based on a simple idea that is central to contemporary anthropology: that all cultures have common concerns but respond to them differently in the context of their different histories and environments."[23] Museums with living collections, such as zoos, botanical gardens, and aquariums, are working together to teach about the need to protect and preserve species and the impact that this will have on our planet's future.

MUSEUMS AS FORUMS

America's communities are changing dramatically, and as a result museums are increasingly becoming public forums, gathering places for the exchange of ideas, creators of shared memories. As museums accommodate audiences that are becoming more diverse ethnically and economically, as physical abilities and education levels are increasingly disparate, new features are being added to the museum's offerings.

The architecture of museums is being altered to make museums more welcoming to visitors. Two museums that have undergone major physical transformations are the Exploratorium and the Minneapolis Institute of Arts. At the Exploratorium, the cavernous, dark environment, which had a quality like that of Merlin's cave, has been opened up with new skylights and doors that allow natural light to come in. The regrouping of exhibitions creates a more coherent order for visitors, and the redesign of the museum admissions area includes improved visitor services, with interactive exhibits helping to orient visitors. The Minneapolis Institute of Arts' $150 million revitalization project added thirty-three new galleries, reinstalling the collections, and changed the physical design of the entrance to serve as a "main street," providing a sense of warmth and liveliness. The desire to expand offerings to families provided the rationale for a family center, where adults and children might rest, eat, drink, and enjoy a quiet moment. Other amenities include community rooms with books and computers made available for interactive learning.

The issue of safety in museums is a matter of no small consequence. Safety in art museums is at once visually apparent with the security guards, surveillance cameras, and other elaborate security systems that protect the collections. By contrast, the Bay Area Discovery Museum has no guards and no surveillance cameras, nor does it have an extensive security system. Parents perceive the museum's eight-acre campus as a safe gathering place for their children. The provision of safe places for children is especially important today. Parents and children, having experienced a loss of wild spaces—having moved from creeks to parks to front yards to neighborhood streets—are naturally concerned about safety. Museums are today providing communities with programs for young people that give them a safe haven, supporting their learning through discussion with trained staff members. One thinks, for example, of the Toledo Museum of Art's afterschool programs, the Providence Children's Museum afterschool care program, and the programs for teenagers at the Brooklyn Children's Museum.

The explosion of the World Wide Web has added yet another dimension to the role of museums as forums. Museums are becoming "virtual museums" with beautifully produced pages that summarize their offerings, take you on a virtual tour of their galleries, and provide access to the collections and exhibitions with images and audio. The Museum of Modern Art in New York reports that in 1997 1.2 million individuals used their web site while 1.65 visitors actually visited the museum.[24] *Live@the Exploratorium* Webcasts are produced in a new studio and cover live science events worldwide, linking scientists and experts with audiences at the Exploratorium as well as in classrooms and at home. A total solar eclipse traveled over the Caribbean island of Aruba and was witnessed by nearly one thousand Exploratorium visitors and more than three million Internet visitors worldwide. The Exploratorium, by expanding its popular and award-winning web site, provides an interactive, on-line look at scientific phenomena. The Exploratorium's *Memory* exhibition launched a discussion on the Web about the atomic bomb that persists today, a year after the exhibition closed.

Museums have served for decades as places where the community can gather to discuss and resolve issues. Yet there is much that is new. The Brooklyn Children's Museum, for example, served as a forum where Hasidim and African-Americans were able to come together to resolve their differences during the Crown Heights crisis of the early 1990s. A very different example is provided by the Isabella Stewart Gardner Museum in Boston, which is legally prevented from adding to its collection or changing the location of the objects within its walls. The "Eye of the Beholder" initiative encourages the museum to work with schools; its artist-in-residence programs, lectures, musical performances, audio tours, and web sites have lectures, musical performances, audio tours, and web sites have created lively new roles for the museum. Attendance has grown to such levels that questions of how to maintain the collection in the house without creating access barriers are being addressed by members of the staff. It is significant that the Gardner has achieved its goal of becoming an urban meeting place for community learning.

MUSEUMS AS CENTERS OF CIVIC PRIDE AND ECONOMIC
DEVELOPMENT

The popularity of American museums has given communities a new appreciation of how they can achieve recognition and enjoy influence. The motives for creating or expanding museums vary greatly; gifts by private individuals and investment of tax dollars by city governments are increasingly common. As cities experience the erosion of their industrial bases and the continuing residential flight to the suburbs, urban centers look to museums to bring visitors to the downtown areas. Originally, museums were anchors for the downtown cultural centers—with architecturally distinguished buildings able to attract audiences. Today, museums are increasingly serving as catalysts for metropolitan renewal projects.

San Francisco, Baltimore, Kansas, Orlando, and Atlanta have all embarked on aggressive projects designed to revitalize sections of their downtowns, encouraging redevelopment and increasing cultural tourism. Kansas City opened a Jazz Museum and a Negro Leagues Baseball Museum; Cleveland has the Rock and Roll Hall of Fame and a new science center along the river front; the Seattle Art Museum and San Francisco Museum of Modern Art, along with the cluster of museums located at the Yerba Buena Center in San Francisco, are new developments. In Seattle, the placement of the art museum helped attract a new symphony hall, located across the street, with new businesses burgeoning, including art galleries and restaurants. In San Francisco, more than seven cultural institutions have relocated around the Yerba Buena Center; in most cases, the new or renovated buildings have been designed by internationally prominent architects. The goal of these projects is to attract people to downtown areas, to prolong their stay, contributing to the region's economy.

Port Discovery, the Children's Museum in Baltimore, is another example of a new museum in a city that is depending on its museum to reenergize the downtown district. A long-vacant fish market transformed into a $32 million children's museum and library for family entertainment and learning, Port Discovery assembled a creative design team that included individuals from the Disney organization. With financial support from the city, the county, and the state as well as investments from corporations and private donors, the museum created Kidsworks, a giant urban playground of three stories in a jungle-gym-like maze; a television station; and new access to the Enoch Pratt Free Library. Port Discovery sees itself as a gateway to such object-oriented institutions as the Walters Art Gallery, the Baltimore Museum of Art, the Maryland Historical Society, and the National Aquarium.

The Tech Museum of Innovation in San Jose focuses on innovation and invention, with strong support of and homage to industries in the community; it enjoys extensive funding from the Redevelopment Agency of the city of San Jose. The Redevelopment Agency has also been a supporter of other downtown projects, including the Children's Discovery Museum and the San Jose Museum of Art's collaboration with the Whitney Museum of American Art in New York. The $96 million Tech Museum of Innovation has been driven not by its collections but by featuring the innovations and new technologies that have created this community.

CONSIDERING THE FUTURE

The future that museums face is indubitably complex. Two defining issues—access and sustainability—are crucial, as is the matter of accountability. They direct attention to the costs, governance, and management of what is today a vast proliferation of the number of American museums, not to speak of their steady expansion.

Access

Today's definitions of community require some understanding of both the land-based and the virtual, the local and the global. The life of museums is intimately connected to the life of communities that are evolving in quite new ways. Individuals belong to a number of quite different communities defined by geography, religion, ethnicity, occupation, leisure interests, competencies, and disabilities. Community can also be defined by modes of participation and engagement—through local gatherings in a specific physical space or through the electronic media of the World Wide Web. Boundaries that existed in the past are now membranes—we are not required to go to museums to see certain objects, hear lectures, conduct research, or participate in discussion.

The AAM's *Excellence and Equity* encouraged museums to become integral parts of their communities, expanding their educational, social, and cultural roles. In advocating institutional partnerships and the adoption of new technologies, the document acknowledges the importance of the relationship between museums and their communities. Federal agencies and private foundations have been active in their additional support of programs that bring together resources, provoke new thinking, and call for new levels of committed partnership.

The value of partnerships designed to increase access to the resources of museums and to raise their visibility is demonstrated through the successful work of the Brooklyn Expedition, an educational web site created jointly by the Brooklyn Children's Museum, the Brooklyn Museum of Art, and the Brooklyn Public Library. The site combines the on-line resources of the three institutions, organized by theme. Its problems were many—networking the museums and the public libraries and teaching their staffs how to communicate through electronic media were arduous tasks—but the benefits were enormous. The ways we use new technologies will necessarily redefine museums in the coming century.

Sustainability

Museums require effective operating plans to allow them to be financially sustainable. Because museums have increased in number and size, the need for increased funding becomes more imperative. Operating costs are rising at a time when government support has declined. For-profit organizations, seeking to capture larger segments of the market, particularly those families that find their attractions entertaining, provide educational experiences and appeal that cannot be discounted. "Edutainment" centers are expanding, with new facilities constantly created by major corporations like Disney and Sony. There is also increased competition among museums within their communities and regions, as each seeks to attract larger but often similar audiences. "Experience economy," a recent theory developed by B. Joseph Pine, James H. Gilmore, and B. Joseph Pine II, as well as other current marketing and management theories, has had a dramatic impact on the ways museums develop relationships with their visitors.

Financially, many museums are in a precarious position, with fewer than 60 percent having endowments sufficient to sustain their operations.[25] Private-sector support continues to be the major sustaining base for many of America's museums. Art museums and living collection institutions have the largest endowments,[26] but the declining funds from government—national and local—have compelled museums to search for funding in new ways, including individual giving.

Building a new facility is only the first problem. There is intense pressure to bring in new revenues, and museums are perpetually seeking new sources of income. Merchandising of branded products, such as hats and shirts with logos, or umbrellas with reproductions of the collection, are offered in museum stores located both on- and off-site, but also through catalogs and increasingly on web sites. Museums extending their hours to maximize attendance, sponsoring trips abroad, and receiving support from corporations for their exhibits—such as the Orkin-sponsored *Insect Zoo* exhibition at the Smithsonian's National Museum of Natural History—have become common practice.

The new Cantor Center of the Visual Arts at Stanford University added to a century-old building an auditorium, a bookstore, a café—whimsically called the Edible Arts—and the museum's first conservation lab. The new and renovated buildings were designed with attention to the installation and presentation of the collections, in light of a careful review of visitors' needs, and with an eye toward discovering ways that the museum could make money to support the increased costs of operation and to achieve its art education goals. The Chicago Children's Museum and the Children's Museum of Boston have developed business relationships with local airports. The Chicago Children's Museum created a small interactive exhibition for young children at O'Hare Airport; the Children's Museum of Boston set up KIDSPORT, a satellite exhibition on travel, together with a gift store, at Logan Airport.

There are, very naturally, concerns that the non-profit sector, including museums, will be negatively affected by the pressures of self-sustainability, that there will be an inevitable increase in commercialization. Rising prices and the increased promotion of branded products, together with other business activities, may bring attention to tax issues—such as the Unrelated Business Income Tax—that affect the nonprofit status of museums. The consequences of all such commercialization raise questions of local tax exemption, but also point to the need for private and government support to implement what are thought to be essential museum missions and goals.

Accountability

Museum trustees and staffs increasingly use business management practices to make effective use of their resources. The development of business plans, with strategic objectives, marketing plans, capital investments, and performance goals determined by customer needs, is now common. The increased professionalization and businesslike practices of museums call for insightful management, with thoughtful and dynamic use of professionals and volunteers. Internal changes, required to provide museums with well-trained staff and boards, with new management structures and planning processes, address the desire of museums to offer increased access to those who wish to use their resources.

Museum professionals, involved in research and the use of management practices and theories to support their need to change and adapt, are increasingly calling on professional consulting firms such as Arthur Andersen and McKinsey & Company and on specialized museum firms to assist them with their research and planning. Trustees, mindful of the need to analyze the operations of their institutions with care, recognize that new expertise is required of both staff and board to assist with market analysis, advertising campaigns, technology upgrades, building maintenance, and the investment of the museums' resources. In general, over one-half of many museums' operating budgets is dedicated to personnel costs, and museums are greatly affected by the demands of managing very diverse staffs and volunteers. Human resource concerns—recruitment, compensation, and training—are increasingly important as museums seek to retain qualified and effective staffs. Perhaps one of the most significant needs facing all museums is for an experienced and well-trained work force. Museum curators and educators today must not only demonstrate expertise in areas of collection or in the subject matter they are responsible for but are expected also to have interpersonal and management skills. Museums, hiring staff with different skills to meet the requirements of their operations, which include marketing, evaluation, visitor services, and new technologies, are obliged to maintain a qualified work force, and this calls for large investment in professional training.

Museums, having such importance for the economic, civic, and educational quality of community life, are engaged in quite new ways with the communities they serve. If the boards of directors and advisory committees that help guide museum policies and programs understand that the requirements for finding funds to support museums have changed, they know also that it is essential to consult the various interests of their communities. The marketing programs developed by museums around the country have increased—both the funding allocated to support the work of reaching out into the community and the presenting of museums to audiences through advertisements and other news media in foreign languages, including Spanish, Cantonese, and Japanese. Changes are certain to continue as museums respond to the needs of their expanded audiences and their changing communities.

CONCLUSION

Museums, despite all the frenetic activity, still offer a place for contemplation and reflection. There are museums, or spaces within many of them, designed for small numbers rather than crowds—the elegant halls of the Frick Collection in New York, the gentle lines and quiet ponds in the Japanese Garden at the Missouri Botanical Garden in St. Louis, the small building nestled on the sugar plantation at Grove Farm in Kauai, and the meditative atmosphere of the Menil Collection in Houston, produced by its diffused lighting. Museums are able to provide a place to rest from an increasingly hectic and media-driven world. While there are many problems facing museums now and in the future, we should focus not on the difficulties but on the incredible opportunities that will engage museums as entirely new audiences gain access to the information and ideas housed in their collections and exhibitions. Museums are working together to share services, expertise, and collections to increase their abilities to communicate with and actively engage the public.

ENDNOTES

[1] National Endowment for the Arts, *1997 Survey of Public Participation in the Arts* (Washington, D.C.: National Endowment for the Arts, 1998).

[2] American Association of Museums, *A Higher Standard: The Museum Accreditation Handbook* (Washington, D.C.: American Association of Museums, 1997), 19–20.

[3] Karl Meyer, *The Art Museum: Power, Money, Ethics: A Twentieth Century Fund Report* (New York: William Morrow and Co., 1979), 24.

[4] Edward P. Alexander, *Museums in Motion: An Introduction to the History and Functions of Museums* (Nashville: American Association of State and Local History, 1979), 11.

[5] Steven Conn, *Museums and American Intellectual Life, 1876–1926* (Chicago: University of Chicago Press, 1998), 8.

[6] Ibid., 8–9.

[7] Alexander, *Museums in Motion*, 11.

[8] Conn, *Museums and American Intellectual Life*, 29.

[9] Meyer, *The Art Museum*, 31–32.

[10]American Association of Museums, *Museums Count*, ed. Ann Hofstra Grogg (Washington, D.C.: American Association of Museums, 1994), 33.

[11]Roxana Adams, "Research Report on Museum Development and Expansion," American Association of Museums Technical Information Service, 1998, 1.

[12]Ibid., 5–6.

[13]"The Boom—and What to Do About It," *Museum News* (November/December 1998): 59.

[14]Ibid., 35.

[15]Judith H. Dobrzynski, "Art Museum Attendance Keeps Rising in the U.S.," *New York Times,* 1 February 1999, B1–3.

[16]Ibid.

[17]American Association of Museums, *Excellence and Equity: Education and the Public Dimension of Museums*, ed. Ellen Cochran Hirzy (Washington, D.C.: American Association of Museums, 1992), 3.

[18]American Association of Museums, *Museum Financial Information 1997: A Report of the National Survey Results* (Washington, D.C.: American Association of Museums, 1998), 27–28.

[19]Ellen Cochran Hirzy, *True Needs, True Partners: Museums Serving Schools 1998 Survey Highlights* (Washington, D.C.: Institute of Museum and Library Services, 1998), 4–5.

[20]Wendy Pittman and William S. Pretzer, "Museums and the Charter School Movement," *Museum News* (September/October 1998): 41–42.

[21]Ellen V. Futter, in "Toward a Natural History Museum for the 21st Century," *Museum News* (November/December 1997): 40.

[22]Ibid., 42

[23]Peter R. Crane, in "Toward a Natural History Museum for the 21st Century," *Museum News* (November/December 1997): 45.

[24]Steven Madoff, "Where the Venues are Virtually Infinite," *New York Times*, 10 January 1999, 41.

[25]American Association of Museums, *Museum Financial Information Survey 1997: A Report of the National Survey Results.*

[26]Ibid., 37.

The function of a museum is the encouragement of the enjoyment of art and through this the indirect encouragement of the creative artist. Visual art is basically a sensory experience, one of relationships of form, of colors, and of associations, physical, unconscious, or representational. Therefore, the first step in a museum's educational process is the confrontation of the spectator with the actual work of art, so that the artist can speak directly to the spectator. The immediate sensory experience of a work of art is the only direct approach to the artist's communication. Mass media cannot provide this experience, but the museum can and should. On this foundation of a direct sensory acquaintance, the experience of a work of art may be soundly enriched by its peripheral associations. It is the responsibility of the museum to stimulate the indolent public to approach art directly through aesthetic experience, pleasurable and enjoyable, and to incite the visitor to make the effort, always more or less arduous, which is necessary for him to enter into communication with the artist through the artist's personal expression. For it is this interaction between the observer and the creative artist that makes it possible to maintain or raise standards of judgment and appreciation.

James Johnson Sweeney

From "The Artist and the Museum
in a Mass Society"
Dædalus 89 (2) (Spring 1960)

Neil Harris

The Divided House of the
American Art Museum

EASURED BY ALMOST ANY quantitative criterion, the American art museum stands at a historic peak of institutional power and prominence. Rising attendance figures, growing collections, building expansions, renovations, new foundations, busy home pages, interactive display systems, enlarged memberships, enormous endowment campaigns, splendid gifts, and continuous press coverage all testify to a handsomely enhanced status within American cultural, social, and economic life. "Fueled by a powerful national economy and aided by management policies put into effect over the past decade, museum growth appears, by some indices, to be a verifiable 'boom,'" declares a recent article in *Museum News.* "There's an explosion," agrees one Philadelphia museum director, who is quoted in the same article.[1] Business leaders, politicians, and newspaper editorials alike honor the museum as a force in the health of local economies and as a source for social integration.[2] Merchandisers acknowledge the energy of museum product management and promotion, particularly the tactics associated with special exhibitions.[3] Scholars have become frequent and energetic contributors to an eruption of symposia, lecture series, texts, and catalogs sponsored by museums and heavily subsidized by them. Foundations and corporate sponsors systematically underwrite ambitious exhibition programs. And activists praise museums as exemplars of the special American system of cultural philanthropy, blending tax-subsidized private giving with shifting levels of public support, which serve

Neil Harris is Preston and Sterling Morton Professor of History at the University of Chicago.

variously to support existing needs or energize new departures. Even current controversies, exciting so much media attention, demonstrate the newsworthy status of American museums.

Such absorption and interest are, in their expanse and intensity, relatively new. While the self-conscious professionalism and broad cultural ambitions of the American museum community may be more than a century old by now, and while critics and commentators, here and abroad, have long acknowledged the special user-friendly style of American museums, their rise to distinction, if not celebrity, has been a product of the last three or four decades.[4]

So late an ascent has not been for want of trying. For much of this century museum staffs have tried to secure public attention for their institutions; public-relations programs, some of them scoring spectacular successes, go back many years. But for a variety of reasons, the social functions museums perform, their significance in the larger life of the community, and the interest taken in their activities are perceived to have moved up to another level.

With gains, of course, come costs. And critiques. Criticism of museums, once more, is not new. The size, wealth, internal arrangements, and architecture of museums, as well as the inherent decontextualization of museum exhibits, had attracted hostility in the nineteenth century and certainly in the early twentieth century. The gargantuan temples of the early twentieth century were labeled by some critics "dignified disasters"; their organization of exhibits resembled nothing more than a "Minotaur's labyrinth," ran one, not atypical, complaint; museum policies were condemned as socially aloof and indifferent.[5] Some educators fumed about museum failures to acknowledge contemporary needs and interests, while others condemned large-scale collecting as the poisoned fruit of capitalism.

But such charges, however numerous, were embedded within a broadly positive set of endorsements. The museum, in theory at least, seemed to epitomize the best of civilization. Reflecting high standards of scholarship or connoisseurship, selfless giving, and a democratic interest in self-improvement, it apparently transcended political and social divisiveness. The criticism of the last few decades has been far more fundamental.

Accompanying the dizzying rise of museums in public awareness have been a series of challenges, some mounted by scholars, some by museum administrators and curators, some by
members of the public, and some by competitors. Collecting
policies, exhibition planning, governance, financing, institutional arrangements, hours of opening, fee charging, commercial exploitation, interpretive stances, even cultural legitimacy
itself have stimulated assaults. They have not necessarily been
consistent. Museums have been labeled racist, revisionist, hegemonic, elitist, politically correct, mercenary, greedy, and self-
serving. Responding to their growing sets of critics, many
American museums sound a defensive note rather than basking
in their growing influence. This apparent paradox—triumphant
public achievements coexisting with sternly issued warnings—
deserves explanation. When and how did American museums
come to change? How have they not changed? And why has so
much controversy erupted over their professional mission and
practices? Links between the two trends have grown closer in
the last thirty years, the period of this survey.

Revealed in a composite snapshot of the 1950s, American
museums, art museums particularly, my special focus here,
strongly resembled their ancestors of several generations earlier, if not in size, number, and wealth, then at least in management style, governance, financial support, philosophy, and general reputation. Self-perpetuating boards of trustees, representing major business, professional, political, and collecting interests, leavened often by social pedigree, supervised programs
that were financed largely through endowment, contributions,
and, in a few places, by massive memberships or local taxes. As
in most other areas of American institutional life, the influential
figures tended to be white males of Northern European descent,
and the same thing was true of institutional staff, with some
exceptions forced by a need for specialized skills. Active educational activities with professionally trained staff linked to public school systems characterized most metropolitan areas.
Museum buildings tended to be traditional in appearance, a
number of them already, in the 1950s, receiving substantial
additions to house growing collections of objects. In keeping
with democratic ideology and most charters of incorporation,

museums tended to emphasize the value of large attendance, clear and comprehensive labeling, docent and lecture programs, and other devices meant to encourage broad public visitation. Collection development rested largely, although not entirely, on the opportunities presented by local connoisseurs and collectors, along with the criteria and desiderata established by professional staff and administrators. Few institutions possessed funds sufficient for them to shape their holdings. In art, at least, comprehensive anthological collections were deemed the most appropriate way of establishing distinction. Promotion and publicity were already part of larger operations but obeyed generally agreed upon limits of propriety. Newspapers, radio, and the new medium of television were exploited in moderation, but there were brochures, catalogs, postcards, handouts, and some souvenirs available, more frequently for visiting exhibitions and special occasions than for permanent collections.

Generally speaking, American museums, while understood to be slower-paced, more formal, quieter, even deader sectors of social action than most other areas of contemporary life, were treated respectfully by the local press. Visitors from abroad testified to the good reputation enjoyed by American museums for their accessibility, coherence, aggressive educational programs, labeling, and cultivation of private gifts. Museum history and analysis were largely matters of professional interest; the American Association of Museums had a tradition of commissioning special surveys, while individual museums, as part of larger programs of self-promotion, supported authorized and largely uncritical histories of their operation. While not especially smug or complacent, given the continuing need to raise private funds for ordinary operations, and humbled to some extent by the competition of mass entertainment, museum staffs up through the 1950s might be said to have operated within an atmosphere of self-satisfaction. To be sure, contemporaneous observers defined certain problems, among them issues of boundary keeping, a certain passivity in stimulating new activities, and a general air of fatigue, which apparently got in the way of attracting broader audiences. As suggested earlier, such critiques had been a part of museum discourse by then for more than half a century, voiced by trustees, administrators, and curators as well as by journalists and lay people. Such qualifications not only obtained some attention, they occasionally stimulated actual reforms. Repudiation of the immediate museum past as dusty, remote, lifeless, and unimaginative became an expressive ritual for each generation of museum professionals since the late nineteenth century. One German art historian described the art museum in 1890 as a place "where every separate object kills every other and all of them together the visitor."[6] Twenty years later, Mary Hartt was telling readers of *Outlook* magazine that docentry had recently "transformed the museum from a grim fastness for the safeguarding of the treasures of art into a people's palace of delights," converting the staff from "a body of narrow-ranged specialists . . . into a company of eager proslyters [*sic*]. . . ."[7] The day is passing, Benjamin Ives Gilman of the Museum of Fine Arts, Boston, wrote one year later, when "the accumulations of museums will be accepted as a measure of their success. They will be asked what they are doing to make their accumulations tell on the community."[8] Still before World War I, a Metropolitan Museum of Art lecturer declared that while nineteenth-century museums existed "simply to provide an esoteric and aesthetic mausoleum of pictures, open on certain days of the week to a few people," now "the museums desire to reach the largest number of people and do the greatest amount of good."[9] Twenty years later, during the depression, museum specialists were still announcing the birth of new, more socially conscious institutions. The Art Institute of Chicago, Elizabeth Luther Cary reported to readers of the *New York Times*, was "deliberately sacrificing opportunities of acquiring art for what it considers the more important opportunity of inspiring art and the appreciation of art."[10] In 1935 Grant Code of the Brooklyn Museum pointed proudly to a recent shift of attention "from the museum object to the museum visitor."[11] Reform, then, is a long-standing tradition within American museums. Experiments in media programming, in branch museums, in longer and more convenient opening hours, in hosting of musical and social events, and in sponsorship of cooperative community activities formed a corps of active responses. The much maligned Metropolitan Museum of Art was showing portions of its collections in neighborhood venues throughout the city—mainly high schools and libraries—to some 474,000 visitors in 1937.[12]

But despite the rhetoric, the exceptions, and the promises, despite the continuing sense of new beginnings, despite occasional lapses into populist activity at moments of crisis, this sense of adventurous marketing was not sustained. On the whole, American museums, and art museums especially, up through the early 1960s might be said to have constituted a self-enclosed world, clearly defined by hierarchies of prestige and privilege, visited by largely traditional audiences, and promulgating an ideal of self-restraint in their display of art, history, science, and culture.

Have they changed? From the standpoint of governance and maybe even of staffing, perhaps not all that much, despite the recent boom and growth in size. But in many other ways they have changed quite a lot. American museums today, building on the last several decades, claim new and unprecedented levels of support as well as increased attendance and a great number of user-friendly programs. They are active suitors of new audiences, they partner with a variety of civic and cultural organizations, they welcome gifts and exhibitions of classes of objects they once dismissed as irrelevant or unimportant, they tackle themes that are socially relevant and court controversy, and they promote and merchandise themselves with impressive aggressiveness. They seem unashamed of their mimicry of business corporations and willing to experiment with aggressive systems of outreach. Who or what has been responsible for these shifts? And what difference have they made to the museum as a social institution?

It is difficult to know precisely when to date the reinvention of the American museum or where to locate its shift toward active audience development. But signs of awareness can be found even in the 1950s and early 1960s that the stable serenity of the museum world could not go on forever.

One source for all this was economic. Museum budgets, especially those of nonprofit museums, have always been highly vulnerable to inflationary pressures and to rises in energy and labor costs. During the Eisenhower years, inflation remained relatively low and stock-market yields high, enabling traditional methods of financing museum operations to stay largely intact. Only two of the years between 1949 and 1959 saw a negative return from stocks, and in five of those years, the real returns averaged more than 20 percent annually. Wealthy board members and individual patrons could still make up the difference between income and outgo on an annual basis, although calls for help might become increasingly frantic. To take one example, the operating costs of the Museum of Fine Arts, Boston, increased over the ten-year period from 1948 to 1958 by 56 percent, but the museum's operating income moved up 68 percent. There were deficits, to be sure, and they were worrisome, but they were beginning to decline and the problem did not seem insurmountable. In New York, Philadelphia, Chicago, and Cleveland, where, unlike Boston, there were significant public subsidies to museum operation, the story was not fundamentally different: controlled growth with heavy reliance upon endowment income and annual contributions. The New–York Historical Society, an institution that would experience severe financial difficulties in the 1980s and 1990s, in 1956 obtained 94 percent of its total income from a return on investments, and, like quite a few other museums and libraries, could confidently think about expansion of its mission.[13]

By the mid 1960s and early 1970s, signs of real trouble had emerged. Fueled in part by the Vietnam War and in part by national economic policies, inflation had begun to erode the power of endowments. With returns on equities reflecting a sluggish stock market, the term "stagflation" became popular as a way of capturing the strange if depressing conjunction of two unhappy economic trends.

Increasing costs, however, were caused only partially by a general inflation. They reflected, as well, the pressures put on building maintenance and energy costs by enlarged attendance, the need to modernize obviously outdated facilities, and the skyrocketing prices demanded for acquisitions. The inflation of the 1970s led many individuals to invest in arts and antiques, among other objects, as a form of hedging. While this eventually would intensify the appeal of the art museum to the general public as a repository for fabulously valuable objects, it also produced unprecedented constraints on institutional purchasing. Museum officials lost no opportunity to point out the discrepancies produced; drowning in popularity became a popular refrain.

Financial pressures spawned a number of effects. One was a turn to government, at every level—local, state, and federal— for increased support. The establishment of the two National Endowments in the mid 1960s and the activities of various state arts and humanities councils constituted not only a source of immediate revenue but a larger promissory note. These were followed by the creation of the Institute of Museum and Library Services a decade later. The expansion of governmental support rested on many things, but the rhetoric of cultural competition, inspired by Cold War rivalries, constituted one of the more significant factors. Throughout the Eisenhower, Kennedy, Johnson, and Nixon administrations there existed a willingness to tolerate subsidy of the arts and humanities in order to counter the charges of soulless materialism being advanced by America's adversaries. State Department art and lecture tours, White House conferences, international fellowship programs, student loans, visiting professorships, and ultimately the two National Endowments and the Institute of Museum and Library Services formed part of the response. Although they were far behind universities in obtaining rewards from these programs, museums benefited directly and indirectly from these activities, as they did from the federal indemnification program, a device that made the federal government the principal insurer for great (and expensive) international exhibitions. Public funding thus permitted museums to host unprecedented blockbuster exhibitions, to expand education programs, to invite scholars to participate in publications and exhibition planning, to modernize management and facilities, and generally to expand programs of many kinds.

But museum financial pressures were affected only marginally by public subsidies. More fundamental was the need to create larger constituencies of supporters and to increase revenues through increased attendance and the sale of goods and services. American museums had never been totally averse to commercial opportunism; in early years institutions as distinguished as the Art Institute of Chicago counted on renting out part of their facilities to other organizations, and indeed the Art Institute could not have constructed its monumental Michigan Avenue building without the cooperative support of Columbian Exposition authorities who used it for congresses, lectures, and seminars before the museum's formal opening. Postcards, souvenirs, and other promotional materials had been available in gift shops before World War II. In the 1930s organizations like Colonial Williamsburg had begun to license manufacturers to produce reproductions of their holdings in return for royalty fees. And, responding to financial challenges in the 1950s, some museums, to step up their membership levels, developed creative recruitment strategies. Some even began to redesign their annual reports, peppering them with photographs and eye-catching graphics in imitation of the corporate model.

But these commercial activities were mere dalliances compared to what happened in the 1960s and 1970s. As museums coped with larger crowds and as the consumer market grew in scale and ambition, there came a realization that the shop could become a major source of profit. Books, catalogs, articles of clothing, reproduced antiques, sometimes actual antiques, craft objects, greeting cards, jewelry, clothing accessories, and novelties of all kinds (many, but not all, based on museum collections, but not necessarily on the host museum's collection) filled the shelves of these stores and, in time, the pages of mail-order catalogs.[14] The museum visit became part of a larger buying experience. In fact, many museum stores were strategically located so that visitors could patronize them without actually entering the museum. So active would museum stores become over the next few decades that their tax-exempt status in satellite sites became the subject of special inquiries.

That museums could become shopping destinations, dependent upon patronage, not only in stores but in restaurants and cafeterias as well, meant they would need to develop exhibition strategies to support the visitor numbers these services required for effectiveness. The string of blockbusters in the 1970s and 1980s included shows featuring the art of ancient Egypt, Vatican collections, gold from the Caucasus, and Impressionist masters. These became news stories and media events because of the unprecedented crowds they attracted. Blockbusters brought in new members (at least for a time) and new visitors, and some of them soon attracted corporate sponsorship as well. In their quest for support, museums had begun to court large corporations and their foundations, which found exhibition patronage to be a powerful instrument of beneficent publicity. Some museum officials worried that blockbusters eclipsed the museum's more ordinary functions (and permanent collections), overemphasized the value of large numbers, consumed far too much revenue and staff time, degraded the viewing experience with uncomfortable and inappropriate crowding, and set institutions on boom-or-bust cycles. But the publicity, the income, and the sense of serving a public far larger than the museum's customary constituencies proved too enticing to be resisted most of the time. Museum facades began to resemble movie theater marquees, more and more of them now sporting banners that proclaimed current temporary exhibitions. Because of their limited durations, such exhibitions ensured, as certainly as theaters did with their changing programs, returning patrons eager to see the next show.

Once more, the phenomenon of frequently changing exhibitions and spectacular blockbusters was not invented in this period. American museums had cultivated the visiting show earlier in the century when their own collections were not always up to sustained scrutiny. And during the 1920s and 1930s specific shows—the Museum of Modern Art's traveling Van Gogh show, the Guelph Treasures at the Cleveland Museum, the *Century of Progress* exhibition at Chicago's Art Institute—had attracted enormous crowds. But these events, exceptional in the 1920s and 1930s, and a bit more common in the 1950s and 1960s, became routinized in the 1970s, absorbed into the ordinary calendar of events, and treated by urban audiences as a normal part of the cultural agenda.

By the 1990s some museum shows had achieved the complex planning levels of major trade fairs, with tie-ins to hotels, restaurants, railroads, and airplane systems; they yielded impressive benefits to local businesses and municipal tax revenues. They were also graphic evidence of the museum's involvement with the larger life of the community. It was difficult to charge museums with standoffishness and withdrawal when hundreds of thousands of visitors would make their way, in just a few weeks, to particular cities simply because of their interest in a museum exhibition. In some cities, museums seemed more significant than professional sports franchises, or at least more lucrative. The income generated by very popular shows served to subsidize, of course, more scholarly, specialized, or recondite exhibitions that otherwise would have been difficult to support. Curators and museum directors, responding to critiques of their new consumer-friendly policies, pointed this fact out on many occasions, without always convincing doubters that the larger policy made sense.

What could not be denied, however, were the gains of energy, drama, excitement, newsworthiness, prestige, and membership (not always a permanent gain) that blockbuster shows added to their host museums. And this, in turn, strengthened the credentials of museums as they applied to governments for further support. In a curious and even ironic way, consumerist orientation seconded the public-service rhetoric that had so long been part of the museum vocabulary. And many of these developments were simply responses to the financial stringencies born out of the weakened power of endowments.

But simultaneous with financial motivations for programmatic expansion and public cultivation were ideological imperatives born from a mood of public protest and carried forward by a broader sense of social equity. Here emphasis was placed not simply on numbers, as it had been decades earlier, but on demographic representation. A pervasive sense existed that museum governance, attendance, collecting, and exhibition policies reflected racial, gender, religious, and class dominance. Critics argued that traditional boundaries no longer suited an increasingly self-conscious multicultural society. Swirling around museum discussions was, of course, a much larger movement that would, in time, be translated into debates about affirmative action, equal opportunity, hiring practices, ghettoization, and gender and racial stereotyping, among other things. A compound of the struggle for racial justice, the protests against the Vietnam War, a revolt by youth against the authority of parents and teachers, the new era proclaimed itself most dramatically in the museum universe in January of 1969, just thirty years ago, with the intensely polarizing exhibition hosted by the Metropolitan Museum of Art in New York, *Harlem on My Mind*. Decades later, the echoes of the angry words it provoked still resonate. Like the famous Armory show half a century earlier, *Harlem on My Mind* was as important for its revelation of existing assumptions and expectations as for its actual exhibits. A multimedia documentary history of African-American life in Harlem, studded with extraordinary photographs, the show and its catalog raised many questions: about appropriate exhibition subjects, about curatorial staffing and editing, about audience makeup, about originality and scholarly accuracy, and, above all, about the relationship between the inside and outside of the museum. These questions would ferment for decades to come.[15]

Again, it was not that such issues had never been raised before the 1960s. But what *Harlem on My Mind* did was dramatize a sense of injury and exclusion felt by whole groups of people: exclusions of caste, class, viewpoint, status, value, ethnicity, activity, or affiliation. The museum's historic claims to transcendent representation, its sense of standing above the fray of contending opinions, already called into question by reformers, professionals, and practicing artists for several generations, were now subjected to angry rebuke by other constituencies. The specifics of the New York show, the angry debates about distortion, responsibility, demagoguery, plagiarism, exploitation, and pandering, are, once more, less significant than the way the exhibition proclaimed itself to be an obvious watershed, announcing the arrival of a new era and claiming to challenge museum practices that it declared far too comfortable and self-congratulatory. With its photographs of Harlem, its deliberately provocative catalog, and its new groups of museum-goers, the show posed three different challenges to the museum: first, dramatically to redefine its urban audience; second, to tackle controversial contemporary social issues; and third, to incorporate formats, objects, and artists who, until then at least, did not appear to belong in an art museum.

These issues were dramatized by a confluence of circumstances, some of them contingent, that pinpointed the crisis in the country's city of art and in its greatest museum. That this museum was being directed by a young, newly appointed, self-celebrating, and rhetorically ambitious prophet, prepared to cleanse the temple and restore it to the purposes he believed it once was meant to serve, made the moment all the more painful, problematic, or triumphant, depending on one's view. Just months before the exhibition opened, Thomas Hoving, speaking at a meeting of the American Association of Museums, reported that, in response to the set of crises the nation was experiencing, the Metropolitan had awakened in itself "a keener conscience and social responsibility," reexamining community relations and public services, shaking up its organization, and reaching out to new audiences. "Instead of sitting back and accepting the arrows of their discontent, we're trying to bring them into the shop...."[16] Hoving spoke respectfully of an earlier point in the Met's history, when trustees had apparently welcomed involvement with the social order. Museums had to recover that heritage. The "crusading museum is a reflection of the political ethos of today," he declared elsewhere. "It is part of the same thing as the attack on poverty, the urban extension of services for all sorts of people."[17]

The storm of controversy surrounding *Harlem on My Mind* was even more significant because its host, the Metropolitan, was just passing the century mark, planning a heady round of exhibitions, publications, receptions, and fund-raising efforts designed to celebrate its past and launch an extraordinary expansion into the surrounding groves and meadows of Central Park. Centennials are made for introspection and reassessment; it was the Met's fate to hold its birthday party for guests who were uncertain whether they were attending a celebratory banquet or a ritual of atonement.

The Met, of course, was not alone. Urban museums across the country encountered a whole series of protests. Like many other professional meetings, the annual convention of the American Association of Museums was disrupted by demonstrations aimed at challenging policies declared repressive and inequitable. Museum trustees faced embarrassments ranging from picket lines to the release of cockroaches. Art magazines ran symposia on the status of museums and hosted intense debates about the harmful impact or irrelevance of museum-going. For the "vast majority of people throughout the world," wrote Linda Nochlin in 1971, concluding an essay on museums and radicalism, "struggling against poverty, decimated by war and hunger or crushed by demeaning life-styles, neither art nor culture nor the museums themselves have ever really been alive."[18] The "Museum age," declared Brian O'Doherty in 1971, "is over."[19]

Despite this tone of formality, proposals for redemption emerged. They included the expansion of art categories to include kitsch and graffiti rooms, the creation of vest-pocket museums, the addition of community representatives to boards of trustees, pageant productions to make the megamuseums more inviting and less intimidating, drastic decentralization, downsizing, and branch facilities.[20] While traditional charges of jumboism, clutter, and irrelevance were not entirely quieted, as this list suggests, they were overshadowed by newer attacks on museum power-politics, public-relations efforts, and cultural colonialism.

During the thirty years that followed, despite a string of great triumphs, American museums have put into effect few of the fundamental reforms proposed. Museum governance has not changed significantly, decentralization has not become characteristic, branches are few in number, and staffing criteria have not been dramatically modified. But in planning exhibitions, developing collections, targeting new audiences, and, finally, confronting significant contemporary issues, museums did begin to change. Some of these responses, again, were linked to financial stringencies. Courting popularity, after all, made commercial sense. Others were functions of increased public funding. Government grants often emphasized diversity. But the aggressive pursuit of minority visitation reflected new knowledge and a new will.

To speak about knowledge first, it is difficult to realize the crudity of earlier conventional wisdom about museum attendance. Before the 1970s few museums possessed significant information about just who their audiences were and why they came to visit. Most were simply not interested, or assumed that common-sense assumptions were a sufficient basis for policy making. There were, to be sure, periodic surveys undertaken, and in the 1920s several psychologists made some pioneering efforts to investigate gaze time and gallery memory. But in those years the primary thrust of research into consumer preferences was reserved for profit-making enterprises and factored into the costs of marketing such goods and services. Moreover, during these same years, probably right through the 1950s, there was a reluctance by museum professionals to link their institutions to others concerned with market share. The very basis of museum identity was shaped by a sense of exceptionalism so far as the larger political economy was concerned, in indifference to or even in opposition to mere popularity. What the growth of public subsidies did was increase the pressure on museums to demonstrate their relationship to broader audiences and ultimately force a series of more sophisticated audience surveys. Incomplete, spasmodic, and uneven as they were in the 1970s and 1980s, the surveys began to break visitation down by age, race, income level, residence, and other indices. Although many museums were (and indeed some remain) slow learners about their visitors, some progress developed. Specialists in audience analysis appeared, sociologists and statisticians among them, capable of analyzing the racial, social, and economic makeup of museum constituencies (as well as the patrons for other nonprofit cultural organizations). Employed by government agencies as well, these experts pinpointed underserved sectors, although they could not necessarily devise strategies that would change the mix or increase the pool. But armed with the information, and aided by foundation support and merchandising advisers, some American museums began to do just this, attempting to shift the profile of their visitor populations in the interests of making it more representative of the general population. Self-evaluation was becoming a standard part of ongoing institutional activities.

And the quest for more knowledge was driven by something beyond mere technical needs. The growth of focus interviewing, a series of supervised, sometimes lengthy, and often expensively monitored encounters with museum-goers, demonstrated this during the 1980s and 1990s. These conversational efforts, in several cases funded by the Getty Trust, attempted to discover which museum features attracted or repelled visitors, what kinds of displays they found particularly appealing or especially unappealing, what their assumptions, expectations, and actual gallery experiences were like, and which kinds of promotion and publicity seemed to work better than others. Major museums undertaking such projects could repair policies that were not always working, but these repairs were often expensive when sustained, and grants to support inquiries did not invariably subsidize improvements. But the turn to focus interviews, among a series of other techniques, demonstrated a hunger to learn more about the museum as visitors actually experienced it. This went beyond mere responses to financial need or governmental and foundation mandate. It reflected an awareness that interactions between themselves and objects remained complex, mysterious, and profoundly significant to twentieth-century people, and that somehow, as instruments of pleasure, sources of personal and collective validation, and mediators with history and science, museums helped to define these relationships.

The absorption with self-improvement that has characterized American museums with such special intensity these last three decades may also have owed something to the fact that the international museum community was simultaneously being energized by extraordinary new levels of support. Where once the educational, architectural, and curatorial innovations of American museums had created a clear standard of world performance, now all over Europe, Canada, and in parts of Asia, boldly assertive museums, often armed with generous public support and significant private collections as well, opened to the public with elaborate programs of education and publicity. Montreal, Ottawa, Rotterdam, Stuttgart, London, Paris, Barcelona, Madrid, Helsinki, Stockholm, Turin, Tokyo, and Bilbao were among the many cities outside the United States to sport cultural complexes that were sometimes astonishing in their boldness. Older institutions such as the Louvre have not hesitated to adapt to and then move well beyond the marriage between commodity merchandising and art display that American museums promoted. Indeed, most American museums may seem somewhat dowdy and conservative by comparison, their alliances with commercial and political interests who are willing to subsidize operations and exhibitions more tentative than in Europe and Canada. A walk around the shopping center that girdles the entrance to the Louvre is enough to establish this point. American architects, museum professionals, and tourists have contributed mightily to the vigor of this overseas museum empire, but its somewhat competitive vitality may well have stimulated some American museums to even greater activity.

If the growing social and economic significance of museums was trans-Atlantic in character, so too was the expanding critique of their practices and influence. In Europe the contributions of Pierre Bourdieu, Michel Foucault, and Jacques Derrida, quickly translated into English, helped transform contemporary theories of subjectivity, representation, and otherness. Critiques of post-Enlightenment history, supplemented by contemporary investigations into audience composition, essentially eviscerated a whole range of reformist institutions that had long laid claim to progressive admiration: hospitals, reformatories, public-school systems, universities, libraries, and museums. These institutions, and others like them, turned out not to be trophies of benevolence but disciplinary devices in an extended class war, with spectacle and gaze as part of the new economy. Explaining the growth of the hospital, Foucault said that it "became viable for private initiative from the moment that sickness, which had come to seek a cure, was turned into a spectacle. Helping ended up by paying, thanks to the virtues of the clinical gaze."[21] With pain itself a spectacle, looking and showing in order to know and to teach became violence upon sick minds and bodies that more immediately demanded comfort rather than display. If the language of spectacle, gazing, and display could be applied to illness and incarceration, how much more easily could it be applied to art? And how quickly one could turn from Jeremy Bentham's panopticon to enveloping, sacralizing institutions like museums. Even when museums were differentiated from these other sites, they nonetheless enjoyed extraordinary powers. Tony Bennett, an Australian student of museum history, posited an "exhibitionary complex" that contrasted with the asylum, the clinic, and the prison—the cluster Foucault had examined. This approach concerned itself not merely with a governable, disciplined populace, but one that assented to its status. Museums "sought rhetorically to incorporate the people within the processes of the state. If the museum and the penitentiary thus represented the Janus face of power, there was none the less—at least symbolically—an economy of effort between them. . . . Where instruction and rhetoric failed, punishment began."[22]

Aside from specifically privileging certain classes of objects and dignifying their owners—longtime criticisms—during the late twentieth century museums have been fingered as significant social narrators, codifying modernity, organizing history, subduing nature, and ultimately disciplining their visitors. The great national and civic museums of art were organized, argues Donald Preziosi in one representative analysis, "so as to stage the dramaturgies of modern nation-states." The museum itself had become an institution "of astonishingly potent and subtle illusion . . . one of the most powerful factories for the production of modernity." While the late-twentieth-century museum was bringing together many varied aspects of human creativity, it "remains as the very emblem of desires set into motion by the enterprise of the Enlightenment," one of the "premier theoretical machineries for the production of the present."[23] The museum, condemned decades earlier for its irrelevance and distance from contemporary life, was now discovered to be a theater for the performance of hegemonic rites, a central instrument for promoters of modern values and systems of discipline.

Such appraisals have swelled in number. One recent reviewer of texts on museums and collecting refers to a "museophobic discourse."[24] Two historians wrote in 1994 that over the past twenty years, "a broad range of critical analyses have converged on the museum, unmasking the structures, rituals, and procedures by which the relations between objects, bodies of knowledge, and processes of ideological persuasion are enacted."[25] Nothing the museum did was unconnected to its instrumental functions: its systems of classification and display, its site and architectural plan, its choice of special exhibitions, its permanent collections, its educational programs, its catalogs and stores, its bestowal of honor and prestige. Drawing on and occasionally merging Marxism, semiotics, structuralism, and post-structuralism, a cluster of scholarly critics produced a series of treatises offering prominence to earlier commentators like Walter Benjamin, T. W. Adorno, Georg Lukacs, Georg Simmel, and Antonio Gramsci, among others. It is difficult to summarize the complexity and hard to overemphasize the intellectual influence of these analyses, which helped stimulate a vigorous international literature on the history and sociology of collecting, display, classification, and museums. Museums themselves, exemplifying the levels of co-optation that were part of the accusations, invited some of their critics to serve as exhibition curators and began to incorporate, within exhibition labels and catalogs, questions about their functions as bringers of authority and codifiers of order. Being sensitive to the new museum scholarship and incorporating representatives of the new sensibility into their staffs, directors and curators occasionally agreed to deconstruct the sources of their expertise and emphasize the fallible character of interpretation.

But the new museology, with its revisionary views of museum history and function, probably affected museums less than did a series of dilemmas, swelling in number and complexity as the millennium approached. Each of them merits extended analysis, but for present purposes a short list may suffice. Some, of course, have already been addressed, and they did not always possess the value of consistency. On the one hand, charges of elitism, of catering to wealthy, well-educated audiences with attractions subsidized by public money, continued to attract the attention of critics and newspaper editorialists, determined to put a halt to federal funding. On the other, often coming from the same mouths, were complaints about crass commercialism, philistine exploitation of artistic masterpieces, vulgarity, Disney-like imitations, technological hype, and concentration upon the bottom line. Museum directors could legitimately claim bewilderment at being told, simultaneously, to avoid the public trough and stand on their own two feet, but not to resemble too closely the commercial world that, after all, had to show a profit. Although there were some limited victories in these skirmishes— the two National Endowments and the Institute of Museum and Library Services continue to exist—American museums, like other cultural institutions, failed to make much of a dent in the larger discussion of public subsidies.

But ballyhoo and elitism are far from exhausting the list of current challenges. Controversial shows—on art, history, and science alike—have, while testifying to museum willingness to confront social relevance, also stimulated attacks and efforts to distinguish the museum from the school or university, as a site not for contesting and debating truth but one that more appropriately celebrates consensual values. While not a universal view by any means, the notion that exhibitions are more difficult to argue with than lectures or written texts is a popular one. If museum displays are by nature more authoritarian than the printed page, and if their visitation is more heterogeneous and more vulnerable than the classroom, some critics see all the more reason for them to rise above the vortex of scholarly interpretation and stick to clearly established facts, whatever their limitation.[26]

Still others challenge museums on issues of ownership and possession. Newspaper exposés paint respected institutions as complicit abettors of a series of crimes: theft, smuggling, and expropriation of property among them. Whether accused of the purchase or acceptance of classical antiquities with dubious provenance, the display of treasures smuggled out of Latin America or Southeast Asia, or the presentation of art expropriated from its rightful owners by Nazi officials, museums are forced to defend both their policies and their integrity and to investigate more effectively the provenance of everything they own or exhibit.

There are some who take a different line, attacking museums for taking the path of least resistance in their quest for attention, abjectly obeying the elaborate surveys and planning strategies that are designed to increase attendance, funding, and popularity. Instead of setting standards, they assert, museums are responding to them, dumbing down exhibits and labels, relying upon elaborate (and expensive) orientation films, audio tours, and interactive terminals—anything to avoid concentrating upon the fundamental if difficult experience of confronting objects on their own. The expanded educational staffs, the elaborate school and family programs, the broad range of social activities intended to market the museum to new audiences, all have aroused the scorn of purists who accuse museums of becoming therapy centers or adopting the techniques of Disney, Nike, and Universal Studios.[27]

Actually, of course, these are among the museum's competitors for patronage and attention, particularly among the young. Even while museums have gained so impressively in size, numbers, and influence during the past three decades, their growth has been dwarfed by the explosive advance of entertainment, destination marketing, theme parks, professional sports, and other recreational outlets. The fact that the boundaries separating museums from commerce, hospitality, and entertainment institutions are more porous today merely reflects the pervasive presence of these powerful forces that do indeed shape expectations for exhibitry.

There are grounds for wondering, then, just how significant a cultural and social force museums have become. The rhetoric of both their promoters and their critics suggests levels of influence and power that they may not possess. The exaggerated tirades of an earlier day, created by those who persistently labeled museums morgues, mausoleums, charnel houses, and institutions dead to the world around them, are complemented by contemporary assignments of responsibility for sustaining the class structure, spreading racism, and protecting the canonized narratives of Western civilization. Only the university rivals the museum among contemporary institutions in its simultaneous position of prestige and vulnerability to criticism. But the university, unlike the museum, gives credentials to its consumers and shapes their careers as well as their values.

What are we to make, then, of the position of museums in modern American life? Do they shape anyone's values, validate anyone's identity, impose any lasting sort of order? Their significance is clear for scholars, students, connoisseurs, and enthusiasts. But for most ordinary visitors, has the American museum shed its traditional functions of yielding pleasure, diversion, and status? Does it continue to store and highlight broadly valued objects? How are we to measure the impact of the museum experience, or even to talk about so diverse a universe of institutions in any categorical way? Something has happened, these last thirty years particularly, but just what that is remains unclear. Finding that out will continue to defy our patience, our energy, and, above all, our ingenuity.

ENDNOTES

[1] As quoted in Jane Lusaka and John Strand, "The Boom—And What To Do About It," *Museum News* 77 (November/December 1998): 57. The article brings together some of the statistical support for the notion of a "Golden Age" of museums.

[2] See, for example, the series of articles published in a special section of the *New York Times* ("Museums," *New York Times,* 21 April 1999) for evidence of the art museum's transforming urban influence.

[3] Among a raft of recent analyses see Julie Connelly, "The Impressionists Sure Move the Merchandise," *New York Times*, 21 April 1999, D2.

[4] This is not to argue, of course, that serious intellectual ambitions and activities are new to the American museum. For one recent study arguing the case for the centrality of museums in the epistemology of nineteenth- and twentieth-century America, see Steven Conn, *Museums and American Intellectual Life, 1876–1926* (Chicago: University of Chicago Press, 1998). For admiring European comments on American museums see, for example, the observations of Sir Henry Miers quoted in the *New York Times*, 27 May 1928, 6.

[5] For such critiques, some from inside the art-museum community, see Henry W. Kent, "Museums of Art," *Architectural Forum* 47 (December 1927): 584; Fiske Kimball, "Museum Values," *American Magazine of Art* 19 (September 1928): 480; and Forest H. Cooke, "Culture and Fatigue: Some Reflections on Museums," *Century* 111 (January 1926): 291–296.

[6] This was Julius Langbehm in *Rembrandt als Erzieher*, as quoted in Benjamin Ives Gilman, *Museum Ideals of Purpose and Method* (Cambridge: Riverside Press and Boston Museum of Fine Arts, 1918).

[7] Mary Bronson Hartt, "Docentry: A New Profession," *Outlook* 94 (January-April 1910): 708.

[8] Benjamin Ives Gilman, "Docent Service at the Boston Art Museum," *Nation* 91 (1 September 1910): 197.

[9] These were the comments of Kenyon Cox in Stockton Axson, Kenyon Cox, G. Stanley Hall, and Oliver S. Tonks, eds., *Art Museums and Schools: Four Lectures Delivered at the Metropolitan Museum of Art* (New York: Scribner's, 1913), 70.

[10] Elizabeth Luther Cary, "Modern Attitudes of Our Museums," *New York Times,* 17 December 1933, ix, 12.

[11] Grant Code, *Brooklyn Museum Quarterly* 22 (April 1935): 65.

[12] See Richard F. Bach, "Neighborhood Exhibitions of the Metropolitan Museum of Art," *Museum News* 16 (1 September 1938): 7.

[13]For more on the financial history of the New–York Historical Society see Kevin M. Guthrie, *The New–York Historical Society: Lessons From One Nonprofit's Long Struggle for Survival* (San Francisco: Jossey-Bass, 1996), particularly chap. 4.

[14]For an amusing and often ironic examination of the museum store and its authority see the essays, illustrations, and glossary in Gottfried Fliedl, Ulrich Giersch, Martin Sturm, and Rainer Zendron, eds., *Wa(h)re Kunst: Der Museumshop als Wunderkammer. Theoretische Objete, Fakes und Souvenirs, Werkbund-Archiv*, Bd. 26 (1997).

[15]For retrospective observations by the curator, see Allon Schoener, ed., *Harlem On My Mind: Cultural Capital of Black America, 1900–1968* (New York: New Press, 1995), introduction to new ed. This is a reprinting of the original catalog published in 1968 by Random House.

[16]Thomas P. F. Hoving, "Branch Out!" *Museum News* 47 (September 1968): 19.

[17]Russell Lynes, "The Pilot of the Treasure House—Mr. Hoving at the Met," *Art in America* 55 (July-August 1967): 24.

[18]Linda Nochlin, "Museums and Radicals: A History of Emergencies," *Art in America* 59 (July-August 1971): 38. This issue of *Art in America* was a special museum issue, bringing together critiques and jeremiads reflecting the mood of the day.

[19]Brian O'Doherty, "Introduction," *Art in America* 59 (July-August 1971): 75.

[20]For some of these suggestions, and for evidence, by scholars and critics, of considerable indignation at what were perceived to be self-aggrandizing public-relations steps undertaken by the ambitious Metropolitan Museum of Art, see "The Metropolitan Museum, 1870–1970–2000," *Artnews* 68 (January 1970): 27–45, 58–60b. The fourteen contributors included Barnett Newman, Linda Nochlin, Harold Rosenberg, Meyer Schapiro, and Rudolf Wittkower.

[21]Michel Foucault, *The Birth of the Clinic: An Archaeology of Medical Perception* (New York: Vintage Books, 1975), 85. This book was originally published in France in 1963, and in English translation in 1973.

[22]Tony Bennett, "The Exhibitionary Complex," *Thinking about Exhibitions*, ed. Reesa Greenberg, Bruce W. Ferguson, and Sandy Nairne (London and New York: Routledge & Kegan Paul, 1996), 109.

[23]Donald Preziosi, "Art History, Museology, and the Staging of Modernity," in Maurice Tuchman, *Parallel Visions: Modern Artists and Outsider Art* (Princeton: Princeton University Press, 1992), 299–300.

[24]Ivan Gaskell, *Art Bulletin* 77 (December 1995): 675.

[25]Daniel J. Sherman and Irit Rogoff, eds., *Museum Culture: Histories, Discourses, Spectacles* (Minneapolis: University of Minnesota Press, 1994), ix-x.

[26]For an extended critique of one contemporary museum's effort to deliver and package the facts, see Richard Handler and Eric Gable, *The New History in an Old Museum: Creating the Past at Colonial Williamsburg* (Durham and London: Duke University Press, 1997).

[27]The "biggest problem facing art museums today" is the "emerging 'consensus' among politicians, community activities, funding sources, and engaged academics that the art museum is first and foremost a social institution, an active educational center with a mandate to encourage therapeutic social perspectives for learning about and appreciating the visual arts." James Cuno, "Money, Power and the History of Art," *Art Bulletin* 79 (March 1997): 7.

Chon A. Noriega

On Museum Row: Aesthetics and the Politics of Exhibition

I AM DRIVING DOWN THE HIGHWAY when the sign appears: "Museum Row Next Exit." The exit itself further informs me that museum row is on the "miracle mile," suggesting the combined forces of cultural heritage, urban renewal, and tourism. And so I arrive at the museum for a panel discussion that I had a nominal role in putting together, which is to say, my name is well-placed in the program but the event itself is in no way an expression of my own intentions, whether as a scholar or as a curator. Such things happen quite often on museum row. But rather than indict the museum for not honoring my intentions, I would like to sketch the generic features by which such an event comes together. While somewhat different from those for exhibitions proper, they nonetheless reveal the institutional context within which notions of aesthetic, scientific, and historical value are determined prior to public exhibition. My brief sketch is a composite of several incidents.

The phone call comes several weeks before the panel discussion. The director explains the various rationales for the event: outreach to the "community" as part of a current exhibition; a programming requirement by the foundations that are footing the bill; and a public-relations gesture toward grant makers, artists, civic leaders, and the "community." In a nod to the redemptive power of art, these rationales will be explored through a discussion of new approaches being created by art-

Chon A. Noriega is associate professor of film and television at the University of California, Los Angeles.

ists in the face of some relevant crisis—in this case, the decrease of federal support coupled with a visual culture increasingly defined by global corporate media.

But above all else, I am told, the panel should not be "academic." This last point has been a recurrent and annoying admonition from both foundations and museums since the early 1990s. In effect, what I am being told is that the panel will serve various social functions and that academics are anathema within that public sphere. Such a positioning requires more sociological consideration than I can provide here, since it speaks to the particular way in which the university has been both isolated from public discourse and made more dependent on private interests. For my part, I am called because I participate in museum and foundation activities, not as an academic per se, but as a curator, advisor, and writer actively involved in the arts. But rather than see myself as an exception, I believe that my own work proves that academia, the museum, and foundations share a common ground as social institutions. What I know as a scholar follows me into these other arenas, just as what I know as a curator and advisor follows me back to the university. In any case, the panel will not be "academic."

The phone call itself evidences an incredible skill on the part of the administrator, that of a calculated and strategic ambivalence: I am never quite sure if I am organizing the event or merely providing some advice. I do know that "community" is a code word for either a single minority group or all minority groups, depending on the context. The other functions to be served by this event pull in another direction, namely, to satisfy the institutions that provide funding and political support and that also share a professional culture within which the museum operates. The "community" is merely a content within this context, meaning that the institutional arena has its own internal demands and requirements distinct from whatever or for whomever it may advocate at a given moment.

Taking all of these considerations into account, I suggest something bold, provocative, engaging, and thereby constructive. As a scholar who also curates exhibitions, I believe in dialogue, which means understanding your audience, voicing a clear and coherent position, and then being prepared to listen to and engage the responses. Toward that end, I suggest three artists whose work combines community-based practices with a critique of institutional spaces. These artists also appropriate aspects of media culture, but do so within an alternative arts sector far removed from the machinations of the art market, let alone global corporate media.

The director, on the other hand, wants "balance" within the process and in the event itself. In fact, for such an administrator, the process *is* the event, since it is here that the institutional network that sustains the museum comes into play. Thus, the director notes in an awkward and self-conscious way that the artists I have suggested are all women of color, as if that is the limit of what they can represent, but continues to proceed apace. After all, process is everything. The three names are run past the funders, the other organizations involved, staff members, and trustees before the director returns to me with the result of these many conversations: three other artists have been selected, each for valid reasons having to do with the original rationales. But the panel itself lacks an overarching conceptual coherence. The panel is diverse, but each artist is reduced to a demographic niche, very much reflecting the interests of the various players involved in the decision-making process. My suggestion would *not* have avoided this problem, but it did address an underlying assumption manifested by the final panel: minorities never get to represent more than their marginality.

The interesting thing about this process is that I am not taken out of the loop; rather, I am put into the loop, and it is the needs of the loop itself that determine the final outcome. Indeed, public presentations are as much the product of dialogue as they are the catalyst for dialogue. Thus, while exhibition curators have more autonomy than in the above example—their selections being implicitly protected by freedom of expression—such autonomy is by no means absolute. If anything, there are a few more players added to the loop, most often planning groups and advisory committees, which function on a more formal basis. These groups satisfy humanities-based funding sources as well as project a democratic aura: whether for expertise or representativeness, the right people were consulted before the curator made the final decisions.

In this manner, curating an exhibition looks more like an instance of policy formation than an individual choice made on the basis of aesthetic considerations or rational cognition. Even if the curator operates with a sense of complete autonomy, the parameters for that autonomy have already been determined in the steps leading up to the "go-ahead" decision. Of necessity, the curator breathes the ether of political contingency. The internal politics of the museum, plus what have been deemed to be the relevant external factors (funders, the government, and social groups), constitute an arena within which the museum seeks to establish "balance" in the process and "authority" in the product. To the extent that balance and authority contradict each other, the museum necessarily walks a tightrope from one extreme to the other. To start, the museum must deal with the fact that authority is already diffused across the professional culture, state agencies, the political representation system, foundations, corporations, trustees, social groups, and the press. As a strategic matter, then, the notion of "balance" incorporates these groups within the exhibition process but subordinates them to the imperatives of expertise, order, and purpose. Even if one or another group acquires an inordinate amount of influence in the process, the end result—the exhibition—expresses the museum's own authority.

Museum scholars tend to look at this situation backwards, studying the content of exhibitions in order to abstract the museum's social authority, thereby leaving little sense of the museum as a hierarchical organization that bears an uneasy correspondence with the world in which it participates. Instead, the museum functions as a sort of "black box" out of which emerge exhibitions that orchestrate the fragments of material culture for the purposes of the nation-state, the bourgeoisie, and social control. It is not that such an approach is wrong; in many ways, it produces rather insightful histories of the cultural "meaning" of the museum. But its methods—basically, discourse and textual analysis—leave at least two major questions unanswered: Did audiences ever respond along these lines? And how do changes come to pass within the museum itself?

After all, the museum has changed. Forty years ago the decision-making loop looked a lot different. It was smaller and more homogeneous, divided between the major museums that acquired international prominence, especially after World War II, and smaller municipal museums that reflected the local elite class. Since then, the decision-making loop has become more complicated as the federal government has played a more significant role in museums, in large part due to the rise of arts and humanities funding agencies. The civil rights movement of the 1960s and 1970s as well as the neoconservative backlash of the 1980s and 1990s also resulted in legislation and political pressures that impacted the day-to-day life of museums, from employment issues to censorship struggles. But if government became more important, so, too, did other sources rooted in the private sector, including corporate and family foundations. Prior to the late 1970s, the Ford Foundation seemingly dominated the field with assets equal to one-sixth of the assets of the other twenty-five thousand U.S. foundations combined. Today, a wide range of both foundations and corporations have become major funding sources.

The past four decades have witnessed a two-part shift in museums and public culture. In the first part, rights-based movements opened up the electoral process and social institutions, culminating in the Civil Rights Act (1964) and Voting Rights Act (1965), which were followed by a state-sponsored and -regulated public sphere within which to accommodate this inclusiveness, most notably through affirmative-action programs. But this intervention actually spread much wider, from the creation of public television to an increase in support for the arts, neither of which was particularly diverse or inclusive. If civil-rights legislation resulted in universal rights and suffrage, the state played an equal role in expanding the public sphere to incorporate racial and sexual minorities now granted the rights of full citizenship. But it did so in a calculated way that maintained class and racial stratification: in effect, white middle-class artists went to the National Endowment for the Arts (NEA); minority and working-class artists went to the Comprehensive Employment and Training Act (CETA). When these distinctions broke down in the early 1980s, largely due to the dismantling of CETA and similar programs, the culture wars began.

While the legacy of these changes continues, their underlying political and economic support vanished almost overnight with the global recession in 1974. The impact of the recession cannot be overestimated, even if it has been overlooked in favor of more ideological factors originating in the 1980s. Quite simply, wholesale changes took place in that one year: rights-based movements were supplanted by cultural nationalism and identity-based politics; and diverse public-affairs programming on network television ended, replaced over time by corporate-funded and -produced finance programs and conservative talk shows on public television. The Ford Foundation lost half its assets and cut its funding accordingly, especially with respect to its more activist programs, for which it was often the sole or major supporter. This abrupt change brought an end to the media reform movement, while it required that minority civil rights and community-based organizations turn to the private sector—the very arena they had been created to challenge. Given this context in the arts, 1974 serves as perhaps the best (and most materially consequential) year with which to mark the shift from the modernist avant-garde to postmodernism.[1]

In the second part, a market-based approach to social issues emerged in the late 1970s and has been official state policy since the 1980s. Ironically, while government support decreased, its significance increased, serving as the staging ground for ideological conflicts over the public sphere. Racial and sexual minorities received the lion's share of the attention in the press and public debate, but the real change had less to do with minorities per se than with the role of the federal government in securing public institutions to serve a diverse nation. To be blunt, inclusion required either more space to accommodate the new groups knocking at the door or that whites accept the possibility that the public sphere they once claimed as their own might no longer be their exclusive domain. The former proved economically unsustainable in a Cold War economy and what is now a global economy; the latter proved politically untenable for a still largely white electorate. In the political struggle that ensued, everyone looked to the past for an answer. But if the

Left looked back to a time when these public institutions were autonomous, and the Right looked back to a time when these public institutions were homogenous, they both were looking at the same thing: the American university and museum at mid-century.

These two forms of nostalgia are intimately linked, which is why I prefer to see the past four decades as manifesting a two-part shift rather than to privilege one part over the other. Change is necessarily more complicated. Since the 1960s, the social function of the American museum correlates both to a more diverse public and to a more diverse institutional arena. With respect to the public, as Tony Bennett argues in *The Birth of the Museum*:

> There are . . . two distinctive political demands that have been generated in relation to the modern museum: the demand that there should be parity of representation for all groups and cultures within the collecting, exhibition and conservation activities of museums, and the demand that the members of all social groups should have equal practical as well as theoretical rights of access to museums.[2]

In contrast, the museum itself increasingly operates within a political and corporate environment seemingly removed from such concerns. What bears special emphasis, however, is that neither social demand identified by Bennett would have emerged without the loss of autonomy, wherein the museum came under the increased administrative control of the political representation system and the economic imperatives of the corporate marketplace. Here my policy analogy provides some insight with respect to the period before these changes. If policy articulates a commitment of resources, then, as political scientist H. K. Colebatch notes, "the most important form of commitment is inertia."[3] What Colebatch is calling attention to is the way in which policy reinforces the status quo. Prior to the 1960s, museums exhibited a similar inertia. Whatever the democratizing function of the American museum in the nineteenth and early twentieth centuries, its institutional configuration—including its policy of assimilation through edification—countermanded either parity of representation or rights of access for

minority groups. Today things are different, in large part because the resources are different.

The American museum has become more dependent on earned
income and more accountable—if that is the right word—with
respect to public funds. The result has been a drastic change in
the way museums approach their audience. Rather than edify-
ing, the museum increasingly plays to the masses in competition
with tourist sites, amusement parks, cultural centers, bookstores, and shopping malls.[4] As such, the museum exhibition has
become much more event-oriented—in roughly the same way
as motion pictures during this period—while the museum itself
now offers a wide range of revenue-generating services and
activities beyond that of the exhibition proper. In a sense, we
are witnessing the breakdown of the traditional distinctions
between a museum and all other sites of public exhibition.
Similarly, the newer ethnic-specific museums created during
the past three decades tend to blur the traditional boundaries
for the different types of museums: art, history, and science.
The ethnic group itself takes precedence over and unites the
various approaches to knowledge. Such museums are also more
transparently instrumental, since they seek transcendence within
the context of an exclusionary national culture rather than
within the universal realm of art, science, or history. Even so,
their demands have also become commodities.

By way of some examples, I would like to focus on the art
museum. I do so because the function of art in contemporary
U.S. society has been one of the major focal points for public
debate in the last decade, serving in many ways as the symbolic
battleground for underlying questions of community, citizenship, and identity.[5] Unfortunately, these complex issues are
now often defined by entrenched "us-versus-them" positions:
quality versus diversity, conservatives versus liberals, the art
world versus the state, and so on. Within this context, "minority" issues are seen not as an integral part of national categories and debates, but rather as an unsettling set of outside
demands. In the process, the exhibition spaces being fought
over are assumed to be homogeneous entities. Thus, debate
unfolds without a consideration of the wide range of exhibition
spaces, intended audiences, and aesthetic orientations. Indeed,

debate often unfolds as if it were limited to two sides—ours and theirs—that remain constant despite the shifting terrain of American politics. But in order to appreciate the complexity of these issues, we need to look at the museum through the filters of local and federal government and related social institutions.

In each of the three case studies that follows, I will clarify the different ways in which art museums engage with their political and economic contexts. In the first, I consider the struggle over the governance of a municipal museum in a city in which the predominantly nonwhite population has acquired political power. In the second, I examine a private institution and its periodic attempt to assess contemporary American art. Finally, I explore the tensions between private and public, museum and university, that were made visible during a recent site-specific installation. What makes these examples instructive is that they are not reducible to each other. If art participates in social conflicts, it does so in ways that are as different as the museums within which it appears.

OURS AND THEIRS

It is with this point in mind that I turn to the most radical Chicano artist, a *Chicana* artist, Carmen Lomas Garza, an artist so dangerous that she brought down a museum's cultural elite. Her example reveals the debate over aesthetic value as symptomatic of a power shift within local government and museum governance within minority-dominant cities since the late 1980s. Lomas Garza produces gouache paintings called *monitos* that provide a chronicle of communal, familial, historical, and cultural practices as refracted through personal memory. Her *monitos* respond to the institutional histories of Texas—of the Alamo and the Texas Rangers—although *not* at the level of documenting racial oppression or political resistance. Instead they tell of traditional customs, communal events, and local folk heroes. The *monitos* are the product of a *compromiso* or promise to remember for her community, a project that is by no means finished, and one whose pleasing and deceptively simple appearances bear the weight of more violent and exclusionary institutional histories. Her retrospective, then, provides a striking instance of an art exhibition that became the site of political struggle at the municipal level. Organized by the Laguna Gloria Art Museum in Austin, Texas, in the fall of 1991, *Pedacito de mi corazón* (a little piece of my heart) traveled first to the El Paso Museum of Art, where it was on display from December 14, 1991 until February 2, 1992.[6]

The exhibition came amid a national power shift regarding the role of the museum and the function of art in civil society, one aspect of which was publicly debated in terms of "cultural diversity" versus "aesthetic quality." What was less reported was how these changes—of demographics, of funding policies—impacted the internal structure of the art museum, such that the board of trustees, the museum director, and the various curatorial departments came to have different, and often conflicting, constituencies. And this is what happened in El Paso. The previous year, Becky Duvall Reese had been hired as the new museum director and was given a mandate to bring about change for the first time in twenty-five years. The museum was 100 percent municipally funded and yet was not responsible to the local community, especially the Mexican-Americans who made up 70 percent of the local population. Instead, the museum reflected the city's cultural elite, which oversaw the museum via the El Paso Art Museum Association. Duvall Reese set out to open up the museum to the general public, starting with an exhibition of Mexican colonial art from the permanent collection, followed in quick succession by three Chicano exhibitions: the Lomas Garza retrospective; *Chicano & Latino*, organized by the Daniel Saxon Gallery in Los Angeles; and the *Chicano Art: Resistance and Affirmation* exhibition.[7] These exhibitions turned around declining museum attendance, which averaged twenty people a day, boosting attendance to a hundred a day, with the Lomas Garza retrospective setting a record attendance of 6,500 people in its six-week run and the *Chicano Art: Resistance and Affirmation* exhibition attracting four thousand people to the opening alone.

The Lomas Garza retrospective, however, initiated an all-out public battle between the director and the Association. In a front page newspaper story published in late January of 1992, the president of the El Paso Art Museum Association announced that he had taken a personal survey of the show and found that no one liked it. "I've asked people to rate the exhibit from one to ten," he told the *El Paso Herald-Post*, "and didn't find a single person who rated it above a one. To me, it's an embarrassment."[8] Off the record, the Association complained about the "brown art" and "brown faces" that now filled the museum. Lomas Garza responded to the press statements, "There is a strain of racism in that attitude, which is also a form of censorship. I'm not threatened by it. I think it's sad."[9]

Were it to end there, this story would not be that unusual, a sad-but-true tale of thwarted ideals and expressions. But Duvall Reese and Lomas Garza went one step further. If the Association would take the high road of eternal values held by a cultural elite, they took the low road of political representation. They went to Freddy's Breakfast. That is where the town leaders would meet in the mornings before session. Lomas Garza worked the room, meeting with the mayor and council members, explaining her work, answering questions. To make a long story short, the city government moved to legally disenfranchise the Association. That is, while the Association continued to exist, it no longer governed the museum. Instead, the mayor and city council now appoint an advisory board, and the museum director reports directly to the mayor. For better or worse, the museum lost the facade of autonomy by which a public institution served private interests.

To look at this case strictly in terms of censorship or even something that could be called "reverse censorship" misses the point. It is not just a matter of expression, but about how expression can correlate to governance, that is, in relation to who gets to make administrative decisions. In this light, then, we need to ask why recent anticensorship struggles in the arts have proceeded on the assumption that expression and censorship are the mirror images of each other, not just in a given case, but in all instances. In other words, all would-be censors are alike and can be lined up on one side of the border, while the art "community" is all alike and can be lined up on the other. There is an epic and Manichaean quality to this scenario—and it is not without effectiveness in the subsequent struggles for control over exhibition spaces and federal funds.

But what happens in the process is that any censorship case is read as metonymic of the national struggle between the forces of censorship and free expression. The local and intra-institutional levels—and the possibility that these struggles can point in a number of directions—are lost except to the extent that local events can serve as an allegory of the nation. What happened in El Paso does not work as a *national* allegory, but it does provide an exemplary case of *local* struggle over the governance of public museums. The question of aesthetic value does not precipitate these struggles. Instead, it marks the boundary between their institutional and public manifestations, between governance and exhibition. Such a phenomenon is a local one; the situation is somewhat different at the national level.

ART AS CURATOR

For major museums that represent the nation to itself, questions about aesthetic value focus on the objects exhibited and reviewed, but their final locus resides in the museum's authority to select and present objects in the first place. Established in 1932, the Biennial Exhibition of the Whitney Museum of American Art represents the arbiter of "cultural value" for contemporary American art. While there are other and older annuals and biennials in the United States, the Whitney's has become, in art critic Roberta Smith's words, the "informative, if hardly infallible, barometer of contemporary art."[10] Indeed, within the art world, its existence is taken for granted. And yet each exhibition is the object of much contention, even scorn and ridicule. It is, as the press often notes, "The Show the Art World Loves to Hate."

The intense public debate over the Whitney Biennial must be read as a sign of the high stakes—both ideological and commercial—involved in the effort to define or otherwise measure the notion of "American" art. But it is, at the same time, also a sign of the impossibility of achieving consensus. Still, few will argue that no such thing as "American" art exists. And yet, ironically, the ensuing debate means that each definition of "American," each edition of the Whitney Biennial, inevitably becomes identified as a *particular* position or point of view. Thus, the Biennial can set the terms of the debate, but it cannot in itself occupy the *universal* high ground implied or assumed by that debate. That right is reserved for the museum itself.

In 1993, the Biennial presented itself as the first significant inclusion of sexual and racial minorities, while it also broke from the "painting and sculpture" dichotomy of past biennials, placing an emphasis on mixed-media installations, video, and performance. In fact, single-channel video was projected within a main gallery, while video installations were dispersed throughout the museum. The Biennial also featured fewer artists (about eighty as opposed to one hundred), many of whom were in their twenties or thirties. In addition, literary and cultural theorists such as Homi Bhabha and Avital Ronell were invited to contribute to the catalog, the first time outside writers had been solicited.[11] Indeed, it seemed as though an ascendant cultural studies had vanquished (or "hybridized") the art market, a position that the subsequent fire storm in the press seemed to confirm even further.

Dubbed the "Multicultural Biennial" in the press, the exhibition became the target of both conservative and liberal critics. In *U.S. News & World Report*, John Leo proclaimed a "Cultural War at the Whitney."[12] As in other critiques, two Latino artists—Daniel Martinez and Pepón Osorio—took the brunt of the author's criticism of the show's ostensible diatribe. Concluding with an account of the catalog's emphasis on "replacing the center with the margin," Leo mused on the avowed purpose of the Biennial: "In other words, it's a cultural war to destabilize and break the mainstream. The question is why institutions of the center should join this crusade to do themselves in."

Why, indeed? Though Leo did not offer any speculations, *Art & Auction* did, pointing out that the move toward diversity had as much to do with the contentious political climate as it did with the weak art market of the early 1990s.[13] As proof, *Art & Auction* pointed to an earlier "diverse" biennial that occurred under similar conditions twenty years before, providing a meeting ground of sorts for civil rights and the recession. In 1993, there was even speculation that Elisabeth Sussman, the museum's curator, had made her initial decisions and selections on the assumption that President George Bush would be reelected, and, hence, that the culture wars would continue unabated. Thus, the Biennial would emerge as a new focal point in the struggle against censorship and decreased government funding for the arts.

Beneath the accepted oppositions of political partisanship, however, a more subtle transformation was taking place in the Whitney Museum, one that required Latino theoretical and aesthetic concepts such as "border culture" and *mestizaje*, but not (necessarily) Latino artists or art works. Indeed, in the book-sized catalog, the articles give the impression of a larger Latino presence in the Biennial than was, in fact, the case. In the citation of Latino concepts, writers, and art *not* included in the exhibition, the catalog became a document for a future agenda. One year before the exhibition, the *New York Times* announced that "borders" had been selected as the theme for the Biennial.[14] While the exhibition never acquired an explicit theme, Sussman informed me that it would be quite apparent to people reading the catalog that "borders" served as an organizing concept for the exhibition, which she described to me (and in her catalog essay) as dealing with "the new sense of community emerging out of the plurality of cultures."

But why borders? The evolving role of the Whitney Museum had been the subject of much press in the three years prior to the 1993 Biennial, during which time the museum articulated three goals: (1) to dismiss the notion of a homogeneous national culture, (2) to place the revised (but unspecified) notion of American art against a "global" context, and (3) to achieve these two goals through the examination of international "influences." To go "global" suggests that one has undone the myth of a single American cultural identity. But if one has not done that, if the myth remains, then the international arena merely provides a chance to place that myth in a broader context. One ends up trying to define foreign "influences" for the same old categories, and "American" influences on other national arts. Nothing undercuts the notion of hybridity as much as an "aesthetics of influence" that, by its very nature, requires discrete and noncontingent categories in order to postulate that one affects the other. In other words, the exploration of "influences" reinforces rather than challenges the notion of a homogeneous "American" art, especially insofar as hybridity and heterogeneity are refigured as international phenomena that occur between nations rather than within them. That said, it also provides a rationale for exhibiting works from outside the United States as the museum adapts its original mission to a more competitive environment.

In the Whitney's move to exhibit non-American art, the concept of "borders" provided an intermediary step toward opening the door to international art, especially Latin American art. As a document toward that end, the catalog resituates the concept of "borders" within an international, global, if not *universal*, framework. In other words, if art critics feel that the Biennial has made "class, race, and gender" hegemonic within the art world, the catalog's renowned literary-cum-cultural theorists reassure us that such coherence of ideology and identity cannot be the case in our postcolonial, poststructural, postmodern moment. As Bhabha explains in the Biennial catalog, "The 'middle passage' of contemporary culture, as with slavery itself, is a process of displacement and disjunction."[15] True enough, I suppose, but within the pages of the catalog, such insights merely provide the groundwork for the curatorial agenda to reassert the museum's role in rebuilding the "social fabric" of a national "community of communities." In the end, the fabric itself—the 1993 Biennial—becomes less important than the sewing machine—the Whitney Museum—that takes up the task of binding together the "decentered whole."

These institutional maneuverings within cultural politics resulted in the expedient conflation of "new genre" art, political thematics, and notions of cultural diversity. Thus, rather than presaging the structural assimilation of sexual and racial minorities within the art world, this exhibition served to mark the ongoing struggles for cultural equity as a stylistic moment. In fact, the civil rights generation of minority artists was largely excluded from the exhibition, except in the area of film and video. Most of the minority artists were born after 1954, and, hence, came of age *after* Watergate, Vietnam, Stonewall, and the various civil rights movements. Without this historical continuity, the metaphorical "border crossings" of multiculturalism and postcolonialism could be refigured as the end of the swing of an aesthetic pendulum, soon to be replaced by something else—internationalism.

Critics should have asked why museums—seemingly antithetical to such political art—should suddenly embrace it in the early 1990s. Instead, the curatorial agenda was attributed to the art itself—not just the works in these exhibitions, but all "minority" art. And this response was not just a neoconservative one. Consider professor of art history Hal Foster's comments in a roundtable on the 1993 Whitney Biennial by the *October* editorial collective. He calls attention to a "pervasive [tendency] in contemporary art and criticism alike: a certain turn away from questions of representation to iconographies of content; a certain turn from a politics of the signifier to a politics of the signified."[16] Having just got the hang of the notion that all expression, all language involves a play of signifiers, a continual deferral of the signified (and by implication, the referent)—and that as goes language so go both the unconscious and society—we are now informed that, in fact, some art is attentive to this process, while other art is not. Apparently, this "other" art goes against the nature of language itself. While Foster raises this issue as an aesthetic observation, he does so as part of an academic group with deep ties to the Whitney Museum itself, a group whose semiotic and psychoanalytic definition of the "political" was seemingly ignored by the 1993 Biennial. So it is not too difficult to see the roundtable as more of an insider dialogue with other critics and curators than as an outside critique of the artists in the Biennial.[17] In addition, the few close readings undertaken in the roundtable are curious for their selective formalism—that is, they engage only selected portions of a work, deeming the rest "irrelevant."[18] Still, there is an assumption at work here that Foster shares with the curators and critics he takes to task (and even the neoconservative critics both sides oppose). It is an assumption of privilege that unites them across the ideological spectrum and various professional moorings. If we were to patch together a statement out of these different positions it would go something like this:

The barbarians are at the gate with their multicultural demand. We must tolerate their necessary inclusion, but at the same time their work is different—it is politically correct, identity-oriented, and, as an aesthetic matter, merely illustrative. In some ways, it is not really art as we have come to know art (as an aside, it is here that everyone's Greenbergian premises peek through), and, hence, it is work that cannot sustain a close reading.

The lines were drawn between the minority artist and everyone else in the art world, even as a civil libertarian overlay held everything together in a strategic coalition against the forces of censorship and reduced federal funding. If censorship served as the burning issue for the Biennial, it did so at the expense of a more informing national allegory found in the quality of the art world's own response. These arts professionals, while claiming to look at the art, were really keeping an eye on each other, bracing themselves against change.

AESTHETIC SPACES

As a final consideration, I would like to talk about an exhibition I co-curated at Cornell University's Herbert F. Johnson Museum and its consequences within the private university and public sphere. Of particular interest here is the structural relationship between museums and universities insofar as it informs recent debates over the public sphere. The exhibition, *Revelaciones/Revelations: Hispanic Art of Evanescence*, included eight Latino artists who work in the genre of site-specific installation, ranging from the personal to the cultural to the political.[19] In particular, I want to discuss Daniel J. Martinez's installation on the main Arts Quad at Cornell—a series of eight-foot-tall plywood walls painted with tar and lining both sides of the pathways. On the day before the opening, Martinez mounted Styrofoam statements on top of the walls. These were taken from his installation at the 1993 Biennial and included one by Greek philosopher Diogenes in 380 B.C.: "In the rich man's house the best place to spit is in his face."

Titled *The Castle is Burning*, and built over the course of Parents' Weekend, Homecoming, Alumni Weekend, and Halloween, it became the catalyst for heated debate on campus. Prior to its opening, art students repeatedly used the installation walls as a "blackboard" for their own expressions. Later on, the installation became the target of vandalism expressing class bias and racial hatred. In essence, Martinez's piece served as a blank screen that made visible many of the problems Latino students and faculty had complained about for years. The installation then inspired a Latino student rally against the vandalism. The students marched to the administration building seeking a meeting with the president in order to address the underlying issues. Upon being denied a meeting, they initiated an impromptu sit-in that lasted for four days. The sit-in ended with the administration promising to negotiate with the students. In the meantime, the students established contact with other Latino student and alumni groups across the United States.

In many ways, Martinez was a perfect catalyst for such a sequence of events. In the early 1990s, he emerged as a controversial figure in the "new" public art, drawing attention to racial and class discrimination through strategic interventions in public space. Michael Kimmelman, in the *New York Times*, refers to this as "a new paradigm for public art [in which] artists collaborate directly with communities that will come into contact with the work, the process of collaboration becoming, in many cases, as important as the end result."[20] Needless to say, this type of art is *not* new (consider, as two earlier extremes, the mural movement and the happenings), and, in fact, the current trend in public art is notable for its self-conscious dialogue with the political, process, and performance art of the 1960s.

In his public art, Martinez poses a simple question—"What is public?"—from within a site that should be its obvious answer: the streets and sidewalks of urban centers. What happens in the course of these installations, however, is that the public space is exposed as little more than a conduit or access between private or institutional spaces.[21]

At Cornell, Martinez turned to the quasi-public space of the Arts Quad, its pathways between classrooms metaphoric of the life path cut by a university, which provides not just knowledge, but a refined sense of class status and a lifelong set of social networks. Rather than focus on "public," Martinez raised the issue of "privilege" within spatial terms. Cornell was a unique site insofar as it is a hybrid private-and-public institution. In hindsight, it is interesting to note that few students and faculty members thought of the Arts Quad in terms of its pathways, although they are its predominant feature (and also the focus of Martinez's installation), with at least twelve distinct paths criss-crossing the otherwise "open" space.

As the numerous letters to the editor of the *Cornell Daily Sun* revealed, each critique relied upon an assumption about the essential spatial characteristic of the Arts Quad: Those who argued on the basis of a violated "beauty" assumed that they spoke about the quad-as-nature. Those who complained about the violation of majority rule assumed that the quad was a public space. Those who invoked the outrageous tuition their parents had paid assumed that the quad was a private space and that tuition granted them some basic property rights, or land-lease right. And, finally, those who pointed fingers or asked, "Who approved this? Who's in charge here?" assumed that the quad was an institutional space subject to administrative protocols and accountability.

Because the controversy surrounding the installation was so voluminous—with over three hundred articles, editorials, and letters to the editor in Ithaca newspapers alone—I will highlight aspects that give some insight into Martinez's work and its significance for the museum.[22] In the course of his installation, Martinez was a high-profile figure on campus, in large part because his project adapted mural-making techniques with their emphasis on large-scale collaboration and communitarianism. This adaptation resulted in a sense of shared ownership among the dozens of students who turned out each day to help Martinez paint the walls of his structure. But because Martinez withheld narrative or iconographic content until the last day, the students' sense of allegiance or patrimony rested not in a self-apparent artwork but in their participation in the project, in their encounter with Martinez, and in what he was saying to them about the artwork.

Thus, Martinez's words became the object of exegesis on the part of art students and others attempting to assign a meaning to the piece—in particular, a meaning that justified their active involvement and interaction with the installation. In short, Martinez's actions established him as someone able to deny permission within the university structure itself. This authority *was* an important aspect of his investigation of privilege. Nonetheless, this strategy also put him in a problematic position as an artist insofar as his heroic battle against the university and an earlier generation of earth artists—who had their first museum-sponsored exhibition at Cornell University in 1969—was itself placed in opposition to the up-and-coming generation that stood in the wings of his performance.[23] Several art students, mostly white women and black men, felt that Martinez had given them permission to use the tar-covered walls as a "blackboard" for their own artistic statements. Thus, what began as a question of privilege within an elite institution and art world also raised questions about class and generational conflicts among minority artists. In both instances, Martinez was at the center of these questions.

After the opening of the exhibition Martinez returned to Los Angeles. By the time of the sit-in, his position had changed in an unusual way. With Martinez gone, the university became the default steward of his installation and its "artistic integrity"— that is, of Martinez's intention. In this manner, "Martinez" (both the actual person and an idea of him based on exegesis) was incorporated into the decision-making loop as university officials attempted to respond to the vandalism against the piece. Martinez's physical absence, coupled with his troubling discursive presence (he seemed to have expressed just about every possible intention), brought university officials to a standstill.

In the midst of the sit-in, Larry Palmer, vice president for academic programs and campus affairs, put the issue of stewardship on public record: "We could not—given the conflicting messages of public art—take stewardship of the piece." As an act of symbolic politics, the initial rally must be seen as the students taking stewardship of the installation. The subsequent sit-in, then, became an act of expanding the students' stewardship to include the university curriculum. This act was done more to draw attention to an administrative vacuum than to effect an improbable power shift.

While Martinez defines his installation in terms of the viewer's privilege, he fails to mention its flip side—his own privilege, one that is based on getting permission to make the installation in the first place. During the installation, Martinez was the quintessential outsider, negotiating with officials who had some claim upon the space he occupied. In the end, his project made visible the organizational flow chart for the university, in which there were seven units under the vice president for academic programs and campus affairs, each with different claims to the space of the Arts Quad:

Hispanic American Studies Program (funding and implementation)
Herbert F. Johnson Museum of Art (aesthetics)
Risk Management (liability)
Grounds Department (maintenance)
Office of Environmental Health and Safety (safety)
Planning, Design, and Construction ("structural soundness")
Facilities of Arts and Sciences (access)

José Piedra and I, as the curators, were located in the Hispanic American Studies Program, from where we negotiated with the other six departments and, as things heated up, with Martinez himself. Finally, the vice president for university relations played a crucial role in framing the student takeover, especially before the regional and national press could reach Ithaca.

Ironically, Martinez's permission was based on the fact that no one ever asked what he was really up to in making the installation. The people involved remained within the limits set by their institutional position, their bailiwick. As long as Martinez and his installation satisfied the bailiwick of a particular department, that department was not about to assume the larger responsibility and ask, "Why?" And, as long as all of the seven departments were satisfied, the office of the vice president for academic programs and campus affairs was not about to ask "Why?" either. This situation seemed to come about *because* the project was undertaken in the name of art. (Earlier, students had been denied permission when they proposed a similar, albeit non-art, use of the Arts Quad.) As such, the larger responsibility—the holistic or synthetic level of control over the space—was refigured in aesthetic terms. In this instance, control worked from the bottom up, rather than the top down. What the installation did, then, was to bring to the surface not just deep-rooted social conflicts but the hierarchies and lines of communications that defined campus power relations.

In making visible both the racism *and* the decision-making structure that existed on campus, the installation and sit-in implicated the one in the other. Consider the following editorial in the *Cornell Review*:

> Mr. Martinez: we have a special message for you. You snot-brained fiend, you flighty, warbling, galavanting, strutting little twit. You whining, moaning, kvetching, sniggering, paste-and-construction paper excuse for an artist. You puerile non-entity, you prattling babe in the woods, you slobbering lapdog of the putrid international art establishment. You've ruined our campus, both with your pitiable attempt at aesthetic moment, and with the furies of political stupidity your troublemaking has released. Rot in hell![24]

While this excess is so laughable as to be beyond parody, its sentiments are not, especially as expressed in graffiti on the walls of *The Castle is Burning*: "Cesar Chavez is Dead" (with a smiley face drawn beneath), "Kill the Illegals," and "White Pride." Interestingly enough, the student protesters were grateful, because now it would be impossible for the administration to deny the racist climate that existed on campus.

Clearly, *The Castle is Burning* was effective within the university and public sphere. But is it art? In Martinez's piece, despite the overlapping and blurring of categories, there is a decisive moment when art ends and politics takes over—or, to be more precise, when his art ends, and the students' politics takes over. The installation was located midway between the museum and the administration building; it was produced under the auspices of the former, but aspired to impact the latter. And so, on November 29, 1993, Martinez sent a letter to President Frank Rhodes:

Given the response from the University students and all concerned, it seems there is a great need for the symbols that represent the freedoms of speech, thought, and expression and a forum that allows all voices to be heard. After the exhibition has concluded, I would like to offer in donation the artwork *The Castle is Burning* to Cornell University. I would like to make this temporary artwork a permanent public sculpture for generations of students and faculty to experience and feel proud of our great country and what it represents.

In the end, the museum declined the offer, while the university president negotiated with the students for some long overdue changes. A few weeks later, the installation was torn down. If it had an impact, it was because the museum already operated within institutional relationships that reached across the Arts Quad to the president's office and beyond. Martinez's installation made these connections material and, hence, visible within the public space.

In each of the above case studies, the aesthetic is as variable as the museum sites themselves. So, too, are the relationships between the art exhibition and a larger body politic. Perhaps these connections explain why there are never street signs announcing that you are *leaving* museum row. Arrival is everything in America! In the end, aesthetic value and the politics of exhibition are not the same thing. One cannot be reduced to the other. And the dynamic between them will be different across local and national, public and private, contexts. For its part, the museum provides the occasion by which they come together, as a product of and catalyst for dialogue, debate, and change. Such a process can never be pure. We will not have parity of representation and rights of access without having other complicating things, too.

ENDNOTES

[1] I examine these changes in greater detail, with attention to the role of the Ford Foundation, in Chon A. Noriega, *Shot in America: Telecommunications, Chicano Cinema, and the State* (Minneapolis: University of Minnesota Press, forthcoming).

²Tony Bennett, *The Birth of the Museum: History, Theory, Politics* (London: Routledge, 1995), 9.

³H. K. Colebatch, *Policy* (Minneapolis: University of Minnesota Press, 1998), 10.

⁴See Barbara Kirshenblatt-Gimblett, *Destination Culture: Tourism, Museums, and Heritage* (Berkeley: University of California Press, 1998).

⁵For an excellent anthology on science and technology museum exhibitions, see Sharon MacDonald, ed., *The Politics of Display: Museums, Science, Culture* (London: Routledge, 1998).

⁶Carmen Lomas Garza, *A Piece of My Heart/Pedacito de mi corazón: The Art of Carmen Lomas Garza* (New York: The New Press, 1991). See also Carmen Lomas Garza, *Family Pictures/Cuadros de familia* (San Francisco: Children's Book Press, 1990).

⁷See *Chicano & Latino: Parallels and Divergence/One Heritage, Two Paths* (Los Angeles and Washington, D.C.: Daniel Saxon Gallery and Kimberly Gallery, 1992); Richard Griswold del Castillo, Teresa McKenna, and Yvonne Yarbro-Bejarano, eds., *Chicano Art: Resistance and Affirmation*, 1965–1985 (Los Angeles: UCLA Wight Art Gallery, 1991); and *1993 Biennial Exhibition* (New York: Whitney Museum of American Art, 1993). For an insightful study of the *Chicano Art* exhibition, see Alicia Gaspar de Alba, *Chicano Art Inside/Outside the Master's House: Cultural Politics and the CARA Exhibition* (Austin: University of Texas Press, 1998).

⁸Robbie Farley-Villalobos, "Museum President Embarrassed: 'Personal' Survey Shows Public Doesn't Like Current Exhibit," *El Paso Herald-Post*, 25 January 1992, A1.

⁹Ibid.

¹⁰*New York Times*, 28 February 1993.

¹¹Elisabeth Sussman, ed., *1993 Biennial Exhibition* (New York: Whitney Museum of American Art and Harry N. Abrams, 1993).

¹²*U.S. News & World Report*, 22 March 1993.

¹³*Art & Auction*, March 1993.

¹⁴*New York Times*, 19 April 1992.

¹⁵Homi K. Bhabha, "Beyond the Pale: Art in the Age of Multicultural Translation," in Sussman, ed., *1993 Biennial Exhibition*, 67.

¹⁶Hal Foster et al., "The Politics of the Signifier: A Conversation on the Whitney Biennial," *October* 66 (Fall 1993): 3.

¹⁷I am not arguing for some sort of critical purity, as if inside and outside were discrete categories, but rather pointing to the failure of the roundtable members to locate themselves within their critique of the museum. To be fair, I was an "outside" advisor to the Biennial, while I had quite a different critique of the museum, not for including "minority" artists with a limited understanding of the signifier (as if the two were the same thing), but for the politics signified by the limited selection of "minority" artists. Chon Noriega, letter to Elisabeth Sussman, 5 September 1993.

[18]See especially Rosalind Krauss's reading of Lorna Simpson's installation *Hypothetical?* (1992) in which she essentially equates the catalog texts with the art itself. Simpson's piece consists of three walls: one wall covered with mouthpieces from various brass instruments opposite another wall with a photograph of the lips of a black person; on the third wall is a newspaper clipping in which Tom Bradley is asked whether, as a black man, he would be afraid after the Rodney King verdict if he were not also the mayor. Bradley replies, "No, I wouldn't be afraid; I'd be angry." Ironically, Krauss insists on attention to the "material level of the piece," and yet dismisses the third wall as "irrelevant to the piece" in order to redirect its "meaning" from "black rage" to "the play of the signifier." For Krauss, the former reading is "profoundly unpolitical," a point she extends later when she implies that blacks and other minorities should be grateful to modernism for ending (aesthetic) slavery: "The fact that modernism fought a battle to liberate images from a slavery to text, to a totally instrumental, illustrative task, doesn't occur to this generation." In the end, Krauss's repeated call for "multiplicity" becomes a code word for *not* talking about certain things, like race, no matter how material to a piece. Some signifiers are not allowed to signify. Foster et al., "The Politics of the Signifier," 4–6, 11.

[19]Chon A. Noriega and José Piedra, eds., *Revelaciones/Revelations: Hispanic Art of Evanescence* (Ithaca: Hispanic American Studies Program, 1993). A documentary on the exhibition is available through the Cinema Guild in New York City.

[20]*New York Times*, 26 September 1993.

[21]See Daniel J. Martinez, *The Things You See When You Don't Have a Grenade!* (Santa Monica: Smart Art Press, 1996).

[22]Exhibition documents and press clippings are archived in the Special Collections Department at the Stanford University libraries.

[23]*Earth Art* (Ithaca, N.Y.: Andrew Dickson White Museum of Art, 1969). Dickson was the precursor to the Johnson Museum.

[24]Editorial, *Cornell Review*, 29 November 1993.

In the 1990s, an unkempt crowd of terms, interpretive metaphors, and metonymies jostle in cultural studies in an effort to map out the contact zones of regions, local spaces, and cultures: terms such as Paul Gilroy's "the Black Atlantic," James Clifford's "traveling cultural intellectual," Fernando Ortiz's "transculturation," Jonathan and Daniel Boyarin's "Jewish, generative, diaspora identity," and Gloria Anzaldúa's invocation of "borderlands." Important new journals, such as *Diaspora* and *Transition,* as well as new cultural studies centers, such as the University of California at Santa Cruz's Center for Cultural Studies (directed by James Clifford), are devoted to the history and current production of transnational cultures.

José David Saldívar

From "Tracking English and American
Literary and Cultural Criticism"
Dædalus 126 (1) (Winter 1997)

Kathleen McLean

Museum Exhibitions and the Dynamics of Dialogue

MUSEUMS ARE NOT MUSEUMS without exhibitions. The most prominent and public of all museum offerings, exhibitions are the soul of a museum experience for the millions of people who visit them, as well as for many of the people who create them. As unique three-dimensional compositions, exhibitions show things, whether a work of art or a working machine, a history timeline or a bit of bone. This showing or exhibition is the one feature common to all museums, from institutions engaged in scholarly research for a small professional audience to large multidisciplinary organizations providing services for the broadest spectrum of people.

The act of showing brings with it an inherent dialectic between the intentions of the presenter and the experiences of the spectator. Even in the earliest temples of the muses, someone set forth some object for others to experience, and who selected what for whom is the question at the heart of all conversation about exhibitions. The objects may be trophies of conquest, curious things from the natural world, masterpieces, or constructed environments, but embedded in their presentation is material evidence of the presenter's intentions and values. Teasing out and uncovering this evidence has been an increasingly attractive activity for some museum professionals, critics, and social theorists, particularly since the intentions of exhibit creators are often opaque or hidden from public view, and sometimes even unconscious.

Kathleen McLean is director of public programs and the Center for Public Exhibition at the Exploratorium in San Francisco.

The belief in a universal truth made apparent through the research and scholarship of curators has given way in some circles to the notion that display is no more than the act of promoting some truths at the expense of others. As museums give more credence to the diversity of ideas, cultures, and values in our society, museum professionals are becoming increasingly conscious of the need to diversify the pool of curators, exhibit developers, and designers who have control of exhibition content and style of presentation. And those who traditionally have been doing the "talking" in exhibitions— with the often anonymous voices of curatorial authority—are increasingly expected to state their motivations and authorship up front.

On the other side of the equation are museum visitors—the people doing most of the "listening." Museums are getting to know them better, particularly since they have become more vocal in recent years, and possibly more discriminating. And museum professionals are coming to think of them less as passive spectators and more as active participants. Visitors now sit on exhibit-development committees, speak their minds in research and assessment programs, and even contribute to visitor-generated exhibits and labels in exhibition galleries.

As museums seek to attract and engage greater numbers of people, they are meeting, often for the first time, increasingly diverse audiences. People with different lifestyles and learning styles, cultural backgrounds and social perspectives are being enticed into museums. Whether they return will depend, to a great extent, on whether they can make personal connections and see something of themselves within. It will also depend on whether museums can keep up with the competition—the profusion of social, educational, and cultural activities vying for people's attention.

We have come a long way from the days when exhibitions were organized exclusively by and for collectors and curators. Nowhere will you find a museum closed on Saturdays, Sundays, and public holidays "to keep out the 'vulgar class,' such as 'sailors from the dockyards and the girls whom they might bring in with them.'"[1] Museums increasingly look to a general public audience for support, and competition for a market share of people's leisure time is a driving force that focuses the heat on exhibitions. In the rush to attract more visitors, exhibit professionals across the country are making profound changes in their exhibitions—expanding their range of exhibitable and often controversial themes and experimenting with new exhibition techniques and styles of development. Exhibitions are increasingly filled with interactive elements, multimedia and networked technologies, catchy and conversational labels, and objects out from under the glass.

The public nature of exhibitions makes them the obvious stage on which to play out the tensions of our times—tensions between access and exclusivity, common and expert knowledge, the prescribing and the challenging of meaning, and market and mission. The proposition that exhibition creators must pay attention to the interests and needs of their visitors still meets with resistance, particularly among those who hold to the notion of museums as temples and sites primarily of scholarship. They express concern about focusing on entertainment at the expense of learning and other high-minded museum experiences. Much farther along the continuum, a growing number of administrators are equating rigorous scholarship and depth of content with an outdated and elitist model of museum exhibitry, convinced that the public will not attend serious exhibitions. A majority of professionals stake their claim somewhere in between, characterizing museums and their exhibitions with metaphors like sanctuary, showcase, ritual, forum, and celebration.[2]

Profound social change has led museum professionals to an almost obsessive self-reflection: what value does the museum, as a civic institution, bring to the social mix? Where is our unique niche? When attempting to characterize and distinguish exhibitions, museum professionals naturally associate them with books and classrooms, comfortable with a resemblance to the academy. But they also, somewhat cautiously, compare exhibitions with television, motion pictures, and theme parks, acknowledging family ties to the world of entertainment. Like books and classrooms, exhibitions provide a framework for learning, and like good films, television, and books, exhibitions take us on revelatory journeys to destinations as close as neighborhood streets and as distant as the beginnings of life on Earth.

But books, films, and television are relatively uniform media that deliver an experience to physically passive individuals. Much more like the theme park, the multiformity of exhibitions ensures that museum visitors will interact in an almost endless variety of ways with the exhibits and with each other. In a contemporary exhibition of any discipline, it is not uncommon to find an introductory film; a collection of objects for viewing; elements to manipulate; labels and text panels to read (and sometimes even a reading area with books and comfortable chairs); photos, maps, and other graphics; a learning center with Internet stations and computers; embedded film and video loops; an "immersion environment"; and an adjacent gift shop. That same exhibition might house a quiet area for contemplation, a demonstration area for public programs, and even a conversation area for discussion with other visitors.

SCHOOLCHILDREN AND SCHOLARS, BABY-SITTERS AND PIPE FITTERS: WHO IS LISTENING?

Demographic and psychographic studies reveal that most museum visitors are well educated and value worthwhile leisure-time experiences that focus on learning and discovery.[3] While this is not new information, it is astonishing how little it seems to affect staff perceptions that visitors are less informed and knowledgeable than they. A 1974 survey of museum professionals and their attitudes toward their primarily college-educated visitors revealed that visitors were considered to be "untutored" or the "laity," "as if some great and sacred gap separated museum worker and the educated middle class visitor."[4] To some extent, this attitude is still with us today, although it gets played out in different ways.

While exhibit creators insist that their exhibitions are designed for the general public, empty museum galleries are evidence of pedantic or esoteric intentions at work. More often than not, the creators of these exhibitions ignore public interests, assuming they are out of line with their own. With a bit of investigation, they could probably find common ground, providing more relevant experiences for visitors while retaining intellectual depth. Conversely, the characterization of the public as "Joe Six-pack," espoused by an increasing number of marketing advocates, results in cheerful exhibitions that attract visitors in the short run, but may erode the quality and depth of the experience that the visitors ultimately expect.

Research on how and why visitors use museums has played a major role in helping to turn exhibitions into more connected two-way conversations. Although formal visitor research in museums had its start in the 1930s, it did not really begin to take hold until the 1980s, prompted by a sincere desire on the part of some professionals to better understand the effects of their exhibitions on visitors and by expectations of funding agencies that museums be able to back up with real evidence their claims of audience impact. For those exhibitions claiming to make an educational difference, visitor research and evaluation provide the tools by which to measure at least some aspects of their educational and communicative success.

While the science of visitor research has become an increasingly sophisticated art in recent years, many art museums have been reluctant to embrace the practice, perhaps out of a fear that by talking to visitors, they will lose the high ground. As one arts administrator put it, "The public does not know. Their responses will be anecdotal, so why are we asking them? Why can't we use creative intelligence and take intellectual risk?" A curator explained, "If we pander to what the public wants, we'll lose the poetry and beauty."[5] Besides raising the question of just what "public" these professionals are envisioning, it is clear that their attitudes come from a confusion of visitor research and evaluation with a "give-'em-what-they-want" style of market research not unlike Russian artists Komar and Melamid's nightmarish *People's Choice* paintings, which were based on the results of public-opinion polls about preferred elements in a work of art. (Visitor research, on the other hand, is a process of inquiry and discovery that can lead to new theories for practice, and evaluation helps us measure our own performance against our own goals.)[6]

Of course, with the increasing emphasis on articulating *easily achievable* research and evaluation goals, there is a danger in focusing goals too restrictively and reducing them to discrete subject nuggets that do not embody the potential depth of an experience or capture what is really important. In developing an exhibition for one of the nation's most significant natural history museums, for example, exhibit developers articulated the following goals: "Visitors will be able to name three different organisms on display in the hall, and a fact about each one," and "After attending this exhibition, visitors will be able to give one specific research scientist's name, research program name, or general area of research interest." Exhibitions resulting from such a process will suffer a dreary half-life. But good visitor research can lead to rich discoveries about visitor perceptions and the quality of their experiences and can encourage curators and designers to question their own assumptions about their intentions, their methods, and their audiences.

Exhibit creators focus a great deal of time on the ideas they are trying to convey and the forms their exhibitions will take, while visitor experiences are often inspired by more earthly constraints. Access to public transportation, ease of parking, and the availability of food services all have an influence on a person's decision to visit a museum. Once inside, a visitor may decide to attend a particular exhibition depending on its location within the museum, access to the restrooms, and other museum programs competing for attention. Exhibitions are places where people interact over time—an important factor in any exhibition experience—and people today never seem to have enough of it. On average, visitors usually spend less than 20 minutes in an exhibition, and a typical museum visit usually lasts from one-and-a-half to two-and-a-half hours.[7]

Visitors' experiences in an exhibition, over time and within a three-dimensional environment, will be as affected by the quality of air and the condition of their feet as the openness of their minds. And they are just as likely to have their most memorable encounter with another visitor as they are with an object or idea, no matter how intentional the presentation. Exhibitions provide a safe and interesting environment in which to bring people together, and the presence of people—whether they are visitors or staff—transforms a constructed exhibition setting into a dynamic public space. Staff explainers, docents, storytellers, artists, and actors enliven exhibitions, create context, and encourage people to interact with each other and with the exhibits. Even without staff, an exhibition designed to encourage face-to-face interaction and dialogue among visitors—often strangers—is arguably one of the most vital contributions museums can make to the social dynamics of our times.

THE CURATOR, THE EDUCATOR, THE DESIGNER, AND THE
COMMITTEE: WHO IS TALKING?

Traditionally, most museum exhibitions have been a one-way conversation "designed around the cognitive order in the minds of curators."[8] Curators assembled the objects, established the conceptual framework, and wrote the exhibition "statement" and labels. Designers then packaged the curatorial material in a three-dimensional form, usually embodying the curator's vision. Afterwards, educators prepared interpretive materials that could help visitors make sense of the exhibition experience. While this process ensured that the depth of a curator's passion and knowledge made it out into the galleries, it was fraught with problems, particularly when the curator's true affections were aimed at other scholars, leaving a majority of visitors in the dark.

In the challenging times of the 1960s and 1970s, the curator as the voice of authority was, of course, one of the first to be challenged. In some circles, this was characterized as wresting content and interpretive control away from curators and putting it firmly in the hands of educators. In the encyclopedic tome *The Art Museum as Educator*, editor Barbara Newsom reflects on the tenor of the times:

> For both observers and administrators of art museums, the curatorial-educational encounter has become increasingly bothersome in the last decade. Joshua Taylor, director of the National Collection of Fine Arts, calls the relationship between the curatorial staff and "the activity of the increasingly aggressive education department" in art museums of the 1960s "a major problem," noting that it grew "with the orientation of museums more and more towards the public." Hilton Kramer, who covered the 1975 meetings of the American Association of Museums in Los Angeles for the *New York Times*, has found the division between curatorial and education departments that exists in most art museums "an endless source of conflict."[9]

Art museums were not the only arena for this debate. In 1963, Albert Parr, then senior scientist at the American Museum of Natural History, suggested:

> Whenever two entirely different types of skill and creative imagination have to be called upon to act together with equal authority, administrative problems arise, but it is, in my opinion, quite impossible to maintain high standards of exhibition quality by placing the functions of design under curatorial command. On the other hand, it seems quite possible to make the entire execution of the exhibition program an autonomous function within the museum's organization by including one or more educators or educational designers on the staff of the exhibition department itself.[10]

This proposition was a radical one for its time, with Parr offering the disclaimer that his idea was not meant as a general recommendation but only as a possible solution in cases when educational aims were given short shrift by curators.

In response to a need for more professional dialogue, museum educators formed the Museum Education Roundtable in 1969, and in 1971 the American Association of Museums created the President's Committee on Education to provide a more formal venue for the voice of the educator. Some museums actually reorganized their management structures to accommodate an increased emphasis on education in exhibit development. The New York State Museum, for example, formed a division of museum services in 1968 that was staffed with exhibit developers who came out of the school system, ultimately focusing exhibitions on educational goals.[11]

At the same time, Frank Oppenheimer at the Exploratorium in San Francisco was creating a new kind of museum altogether, born from the philosophies of self-directed learning, interactivity, and individual discovery that were growing out of a burgeoning educational reform movement. At the heart of the new Exploratorium—"A Museum of Science, Art, and Human Perception"—was a fundamental mission to empower the public and "bridge the gap between the experts and the laymen" with exhibits and experiments that visitors could activate on their own.[12] Michael Spock, at the Boston Children's Museum, was on a similar mission to create a highly dynamic, hands-on learning environment where visitors took center stage. While this populist attitude was essential in opening up museums to a whole new model of public embrace, it was often taken to the extreme, with sometimes unpleasant side effects. In the redesign of the Brooklyn Children's Museum (the oldest children's museum in the world), the museum's collection objects, at the heart of a rich and successful tradition of teaching about nature and culture, were, for the most part, warehoused in favor of "The Learning Environment," an interactive construction based on the laws of the physical world.

> We do not want to have precious items but we want to have respect for precious children. . . . In museums the experiential component of learning is usually not present. Elements which are denoted as being interesting by their inclusion in the museum are placed behind glass or in textual or pictorial display which deny active participation and discovery. . . . Without arbitrary elements in the learning environment, without textual guidelines to the experiences, without objects behind glass that tell children that the objects' survival is more important than their own, without static pictorial explanations, without static human information sources, without fixed expectations of informational absorption, we will try and provide a learning environment for the children who arrive at the BCM.[13]

Although the underlying goals of open exploration and self-directed learning were admirable, the wholesale break with the tradition of using collection objects—a previously successful strategy for the museum—led to a more homogenous, less diverse program that eventually slid into neglect. Spock and Oppenheimer, on the other hand, understood the complexity of the public exhibit experience and worked at blending a variety of media—objects, text, images, and interactive experiences—to create richly textured multiform environments.

While educators were unrelenting in their pressure to influence exhibition perspectives, museum audiences were also getting into the act. Democratization of museums, at the heart of the struggle, focused on access and representation. In 1969, the landmark exhibition *Harlem on My Mind* opened at the Metropolitan Museum of Art, igniting a series of conversations that has continued to this day. The exhibition attempted, through a new immersion-environment technique of super-graphics and multimedia, to tell the story of the history of blacks in Harlem, from the early days at the turn of the century through the civil-rights movement and the unrest of the 1960s. What was perhaps most troubling was that in the rush to create a new type of exhibition, the museum went too far. The exhibition was designed with techniques and curatorial methods unlike any other display at the Met, exoticizing an already disenfranchised African-American community. To make matters more contentious, this black history exhibition was organized by a white curator. In a *New York Times* article twenty-six years later, Michael Kimmelman reflects, "From the distance of a generation it seems clear what went wrong with 'Harlem on my Mind.' Coming as it did in the midst of racial crises, the show was a Molotov cocktail of then-radical exhibition techniques and reckless social politics."[14]

On the other side of the country, the Oakland Museum in California opened its doors in 1969 to pickets over the blatant lack of representation of many in the community whose taxes had paid for the new institution. The museum's response was to create a Special Exhibits and Education Department with its Guild for Cultural and Ethnic Affairs, which organized its own exhibitions developed by designers working cooperatively with representatives from the community. Exhibitions like *Black Pioneers: Scientists and Inventors*, *Mine Okubo: An American Experience*, and *Three Generations of Chinese: East and West* were added to the traditional mix of art, history, and natural science exhibitions. Because these designers and community participants worked primarily outside curatorial terrain, they were free to organize themselves and their exhibitions in unusual ways. Juxtaposing diverse and often controversial points of view within theatrical environments, these exhibitions were more celebratory and dialogic than most of the exhibitions of the time.

Taking their cues from the educators, exhibition designers began to speak out. Despite the experimental exhibition designs of artists like El Lissitzky (in the 1920s) and Herbert Bayer (in the 1930s–1950s), most museum exhibitions were formulaic in their design and installation. And most exhibition designers were expected to be stylists at best, and more likely tradesmen, simply necessary for the building of walls, the application of plaster, and the positioning of furniture. During the 1960s and 1970s, innovative designers like James Gardner in England and Charles and Ray Eames in the United States were creating some of the more interesting exhibitions in museums. In the Eamses' exhibitions, *Mathematica: A World of Numbers and Beyond* and *The World of Franklin and Jefferson*, the designers replaced the curator as auteur, creating conceptual frameworks for the exhibitions and developing the content as well as the design. The exhibitions contained objects, models, dense collages of graphics, some of the first history timelines, and, in the case of *Mathematica*, a collection of participatory exhibits.[15]

Although these holistic designers had a salutary effect on the way some exhibitions were developed in museums, for the most part designers were considered extraneous to the development of ideas in exhibitions. In 1981, designers and other exhibit-focused professionals organized the National Association for Museum Exhibition (NAME) in order to have a voice in the professional arena and promote more designer involvement in the conceptual development of exhibitions. A major impetus in organizing was to "promote excellence in the creation and installation of museum exhibitions; to provide a means of communicating among museum exhibition professionals; and to organize workshops and seminars on design and all other aspects of museum exhibition."[16]

As museums struggled to create more effective frameworks for exhibit development, models employed in other fields provided alternatives for coordinating all of the people involved. While the auteur approach of film directors (and art museum curators) worked for some, the collaborative spirit of ensemble theater better suited those museums that emphasized community involvement and democratic representation. Additionally, the sensibilities of cross-functional business and industrial design "teams" infused exhibition practice with a market-driven emphasis. In the 1980s, museums embraced the "team approach" to exhibition development as a way of improving exhibit quality and ultimately diversifying exhibition presentations. In the team model, an assortment of specialists (usually a content specialist or curator, a form specialist or designer, an audience specialist or educator, and sometimes a process specialist or project manager) work together to create exhibitions, with the assumption that an equal relationship among specialists would produce exhibitions more cohesive, accessible, and richly textured than the curator-driven model. While team proponents consistently pointed to mutual appreciation among team members as a significant outcome of the process, there was no discernible improvement in the quality of exhibitions developed by teams. And pseudo-teams often generated a committee-style process that dulled creative vision.

ACKNOWLEDGING THE DIÁLOGUE

By the late 1980s, exhibition creators had become much more sensitive to the subjective representations inherent in exhibition display. In 1988, the Smithsonian Institution and the Rockefeller Foundation organized "The Poetics and Politics of Representation," an international conference on interpretation in exhibitions, culminating in a book of essays from the museum administrators, curators, historians, anthropologists, and folklorists who attended.[17] One of the most interesting and clarifying essays was by Stephen Greenblatt, who identified "resonance" and "wonder" as two conceptual models in art exhibitions (although these models can also apply to natural history, history, and science exhibitions):

> By *resonance*, I mean the power of the displayed object to reach out beyond its formal boundaries to a larger world, to evoke in the viewer the complex, dynamic cultural forces from which it has emerged and for which it may be taken by a viewer to stand. By *wonder* I mean the power of the displayed object to stop the viewer in his or her tracks, to convey an arresting sense of uniqueness, to evoke an exalted attention.[18]

As an example, Greenblatt described the then newly installed collection of late-nineteenth-century French art at the Musée d'Orsay, which was designed to present a social history by juxtaposing furniture, decorative arts, photographs, and sculpture with masterpieces as well as with paintings by lesser-known artists:

> The museum remakes a remarkable group of highly individuated geniuses into engaged participants in a vital, immensely productive period in French cultural history. . . . But what has been sacrificed on the altar of cultural resonance is visual wonder centered on the aesthetic masterpiece. Attention is dispersed among a wide range of lesser objects . . . many of the greatest paintings have been demoted, as it were, to small spaces where it is difficult to view them adequately, as if the design of the museum were trying to assure the triumph of resonance over wonder. . . .[19]

Greenblatt articulates the polarization of conceptual intent taking place in the exhibition-development arena, and he goes on to make the case that the triumph of one over the other is unnecessary, that "almost every exhibition worth viewing has elements of both" and that the goal "should be to press beyond the limits of the models, cross boundaries, create strong hybrids. For both the poetics and politics of representation are most completely fulfilled in the experience of wonderful resonance and resonant wonder."[20]

Heeding a recurring call for more experimentation in exhibit design (something that NAME had been proposing for some time), the Smithsonian opened its Experimental Gallery in 1991. Its mission was to "present techniques [that] are pushing the edges of our museum experience and/or take chances in their choice of subject matter or viewpoint . . . to celebrate and encourage innovation in exhibition technique and . . . the exchange and development of management styles and peer relationships across cultural lines."[21] The mission of the gallery was commendable, and a few of its exhibitions truly "pushed the edges" of practice, although most were focused on cultural resonance and rarely strove for the hybridization of resonance and wonder that Greenblatt encouraged.

One of the more memorable exhibitions at the Experimental Gallery was *Etiquette of the Undercaste*, a mazelike interactive installation that attempted to replicate symbolically the experiences of loneliness and alienation. In this highly resonant "social simulation," developed by Antenna Theater, visitors would lie down on a mortuary slab and get pushed into the exhibition. Once inside, people were "reborn" and forced to follow a constricted path through a series of tight corridors and claustrophobic rooms constructed of flimsy cardboard, tape, string, and glue. The prerecorded audio provided a voices-in-the-head narrative that was designed to give visitors "a sense of helplessness when faced by a series of disasters, where every solution attempted only leads to more problems."[22] What was, perhaps, most significant about this exhibition was that it was not created by museum professionals at all, but by artistic directors of a theater company.

Indeed, some of the most interesting and thought-provoking exhibitions were being created by artists, who played a major role in creating a new genre of self-reflective exhibitions that challenged the traditional values and interpretations of exhibit planners and the conventional contexts of museum display. Ripe for deconstruction, the environmental settings employed by many history, science, and natural history museums and the cultural interpretations in art museums—particularly when people of one culture interpret cultural objects of another—led to landmark exhibitions like *Mining the Museum* by artist Fred Wilson at the Maryland Historical Society. Wilson juxtaposed startling combinations of collection objects that called into question notions of context, value, and point of view. In the case labeled *Metalwork 1793–1880*, for example, ornate silver vessels were displayed with a pair of slave shackles. Wilson reflects, "Quite possibly, both of these could have been made by the same hand. To my mind, how things are displayed in galleries and museums makes a huge difference in how one sees the world."[23] Wilson's more recent installation, *Speaking in Tongues: A Look at the Language of Display*, at the M. H. de Young Memorial Museum in San Francisco, contained a thought-provoking room, "Secret/Sacred," that was "closed to the public and accessible only to members of indigenous groups who have cultural affiliations with the objects included in the collection," highlighting some of the behind-the-scenes tensions of museum ownership and access to collections.

Artist David Wilson, on the other hand, went even further and created his own museum. After moving his provocative installations from space to space, he finally settled on Los Angeles as the permanent site for the Museum of Jurassic Technology in the late 1980s. Wilson employs the traditional display elements of a natural history museum: specimens stuffed by a taxidermist, curious objects in vitrines, scholarly text, environmental recreations, and even a visitor-activated orientation slide show and a small gift shop. What is unusual about this museum is that, while the voice of museum authority rings out, the elicitation of wonder comes from a dense environment of semi-real and hoax-like tableaux. Destabilized, visitors certainly come away from the experience questioning the fixed nature of "truth" and are perhaps more wary of the creator's intent.

Artists were not the only ones deconstructing exhibition curatorship and display. In the exhibition *ART/artifact*, organized by art historian Susan Vogel at the Center for African Art in New York City in 1988, four different display environments for African objects over the past century—a 1905 curiosity room, a natural history museum presentation complete with diorama, a reverential art museum presentation, and a contemporary art gallery installation—were elegantly inverted into a critique of exhibition practice. As Vogel described it, "The exhibition stressed that these different styles reflected differences in attitude and interpretation, and that the viewer was manipulated by all of them."[24]

The most recent and ambitious in this self-reflective genre is the Museum of Modern Art's exhibition *The Museum as Muse: Artists Reflect*, organized by curator Kynaston McShine. More than sixty artists explored the notion of "museum" in all of its manifestations, as arbiter of culture and solicitor of patronage, as storehouse and funhouse. From Charles Willson Peale's iconic painting *The Artist in His Museum* to Hiroshi Sugimoto's photographs of museum dioramas, from Lothar Baumgarten's *Unsettled Objects* to Claes Oldenburg's *Mouse Museum*, the exhibition eloquently captured all that is poignant and problematic about museums and the exhibition medium.[25]

While one might assume that these exhibitions would appeal primarily to exhibition practitioners, museum administrators, and critics, many have attracted larger-than-average public audiences. *Mining the Museum*, for example, was extended from its original run of six weeks to one year, and during that time, attendance at the Maryland Historical Society increased tremendously. At the same time, these exhibitions have contributed to changing attitudes within the profession, as the *Excellence and Equity* report from the American Association of Museums indicates:

> Concepts of the "meaning" of objects and the way museums communicate about them are changing. Objects are no longer viewed solely as things in themselves, but as things with complex contexts and associated value-laden significance. Each visitor supplies yet another context and another layer of meaning by bringing individual experiences and values to the encounter with objects in a museum setting. Changing interpretive approaches will have a strong impact on museum collections and the public's understanding of them.[26]

Of course, many of these changes have not gone uncontested. In a 1997 article in *The New Criterion* about changes at the Smithsonian Institution, for example, the author declared:

> The Institution has been transformed by a wholesale embrace of the worst elements of America's academic culture. The staples of cutting-edge academic "research"—smirking irony, cultural relativism, celebration of putative victims, facile attacks on science— are all thriving in America's premier museum and research complex, its showcase to itself and to the world. The changes at the Smithsonian are not unique to that institution. Museums across the country have rushed headlong into what may be called the "new museology," based on a mindless parroting of academic fads.[27]

While this kind of hostility tends to make reasonable people dismiss it as a rant, it should at least sound a note of caution and inspire a more critical look at the quality and depth of exhibition enterprises.

As museum professionals have attempted to assess and appraise the quality of exhibitions, there has been an increasing need for a forum for exhibition critique or review. Historically, exhibition reviews have focused on curator-based content concerns with little or no analysis of form and experience, or design-based aesthetic concerns with no consideration of content and experience. Rarely were museum exhibitions held to the holistic scrutiny necessary to create a theoretical base and actually improve the practice. Since 1990, critique sessions at the American Association of Museums' annual meetings have attracted standing-room-only audiences, suggesting that exhibition professionals are hungry for a more substantial dialogue about the quality of museum exhibitions.

Exhibitions featured in these critiques have ranged from newly installed African galleries at the Seattle Art Museum to the Sixth Floor Museum, a historical display on John F. Kennedy's assassination in Dallas, to the Rock and Roll Hall of Fame and Museum in Cleveland. Critiques have focused on organizational clarity of exhibit concepts and elements, the ability of the exhibition environment to welcome and accommodate visitors while reinforcing themes and goals, the appropriateness of different media, and the overall effectiveness of communication between the exhibition and visitors.

An increasing body of academic literature on museum practice has been published over the last five years, much of it highly theoretical and not well-grounded in practice. While some of the discourse provides exhibition creators with a postmodern sociopolitical view from outside the field, one wonders how much the work will actually inform exhibition practice. On the other hand, museum curators, designers, and evaluators from the Standing Professional Committees Council of the American Association of Museums have recently developed "The Standards for Museum Exhibitions and Indicators of Excellence," and while there is always a danger in interpreting standards in too literal or concrete a fashion, they at least provide a more holistic baseline for exhibition practice and a window onto the current values and aspirations of the field.

Most exhibit creators agree that organizing a good museum exhibition requires the passion, intuition, scholarship, and expertise of a wide range of people, and more professionals are becoming multilingual (or fluent) in the languages of environmental psychology, aesthetics, learning theory, conceptual and spatial design, and interpretation. They are essentially "expert generalists," able to synthesize the variety of disciplines that inform the exhibit-development process—to recognize the importance of accurate and meaningful content, to comprehend and be able to manipulate the dynamics at play in the three-dimensional environment, and to be sensitive to the expectations and interests of a diverse audience. They are first and foremost communicators, dedicated to sustaining the relationships and enriching the conversations between exhibition and visitor.[28]

OF DIFFERENT PERSUASIONS

All exhibitions are three-dimensional experiences, compositions of images, objects, and architecture. But they are as varied as the subjects they examine. Art, history, natural science, and technology exhibitions may require different planning, design, and pedagogical considerations. Exhibitions designed for a number of locations will form around different constraints from those of exhibitions planned for one space, and exhibits that demonstrate the effects of natural phenomena may have different goals and require different development and design processes from those of object-oriented or topical exhibitions. But while museum professionals often view their exhibitions from within their own disciplinary boundaries, the current trend in exhibition development to provide a variety of visitor experiences is shifting exhibitions into multidisciplinary territory. Creators of art, history, and science exhibitions—traditionally strangers—would be well served to communicate with and learn from each other, since their collaborations should result in richer exhibit experiences for visitors.

In the recent *Memory* exhibition at the Exploratorium, exhibit creators intentionally combined scientific specimens, psychological models, and installations by artists with historical artifacts and interactive science exhibits in an effort to capture the notion of memory in its broadest sense. While each of these elements required different conceptual and display approaches in its development, when experienced by visitors the individual disciplines simply became pieces in the larger puzzle. Additionally, some exhibits were designed so that visitors created their own exhibits by adding their memories to the mix.

Temporary exhibitions have been the traditional testing ground for new exhibition philosophies and techniques, since they are usually open for only weeks or months and require lower development, design, and installation budgets than the permanent installations, which are often designed to last five to ten years (or longer). Blockbusters in the service of the box office are the exception, often lavished with big budgets and intense attention. "Big" is the key word here, and many professionals argue that too big a percentage of museum resources is spent on blockbusters, to the neglect of other programs and permanent exhibitions. In art and science museums alike, administrators dream of blockbusters as "cash cows," drawing huge crowds and generating a frenzy of activity. And when these dreams turn into reality, visitors will often find themselves spending more time in lines than in the actual exhibition.

While temporary exhibitions can focus more immediately on a theme of current interest, like the lighting of the Statue of Liberty, commemorations of the quincentennial, or reflections on the millennium, for example, permanent exhibitions—the core museum experiences—must remain relevant during the entire time they are open to the public, able to weather trendy viewpoints and fickle fashions. Additionally, permanent exhibitions require enough material to attract repeat visitors and provide them with opportunities for new discoveries on each visit. This means that while experiments on risky new techniques, interpretation, and subject matter, if attempted at all, find their home in temporary exhibition halls, the permanent galleries tend to prefer more traditional inhabitants.

PAYING THE PIPER

Each year, more museums open their doors while the money available for them does not increase proportionately. Since exhibitions are among the most expensive of enterprises in any museum, their costs come under greater scrutiny as administrators attempt to stretch limited financial resources. There is competition for funding from corporations and foundations, and funders often expect high visibility and high attendance in exchange for financial support. While some corporations, through their philanthropic foundations, still support museum exhibitions without any strings attached, funding today more often comes from corporate marketing departments, and it may be accompanied by the expectation of special treatment, such as exclusive use of particular products, direct access to exhibit audiences in order to advertise or distribute products and services, and, in some instances, influence in editorial decision-making.

The fund-raising practice of naming exhibits, facilities, and even museums after donors—euphemistically called "naming opportunities"—has long provided museums with an avenue for generating revenue. While generally a benign and gracious method of recognizing philanthropists, it can create identity and credibility problems when used indiscriminately. Perhaps the most extreme recent example is the Taco Bell Discovery Science Center, presenting "science Southern California Style . . . where science becomes a full-body contact sport."[29]

Limited resources have compelled museum professionals to improve efficiency, collaborate on a wide range of projects, and share the effort and expense of costly exhibition development, particularly for traveling exhibitions, interactive multimedia, and educational programs. More exhibits are available off the shelf, when one museum undertakes the costly research and development and then sells the plans or copies of exhibit units to other institutions. The advantage of using cloned exhibits is that they have been market-tested with visitors and are known to be durable and popular, but museum administrators must weigh the economic appeal of prepackaged programs against the risk of losing the distinct institutional voice essential in maintaining a clear public identity.

Shrinking pools of donated funds bring an increased reliance on "the gate" (admissions revenues) and other sources of earned income, shifting institutional emphasis even more towards the market. But broad public access may be jeopardized in the process. While museum exhibitions are being designed to provide for audiences with a wide variety of interests, learning styles, physical capabilities, and cultural and social orientations, they are also expected to increase gate revenues. Attendance fees at some museums may run as high as fifteen dollars per person, and, increasingly, museums are charging additional fees for entrance to special temporary exhibitions. In some museums, exhibition budgets are balanced against projected attendance revenues, and if revenues fall below projections, budgets are cut accordingly. For those museums attempting to attract new audiences, this makes life even more complicated.

At the same time that exhibition budgets are coming under greater scrutiny, museum marketing budgets are growing, in some cases dramatically. While advertising clearly keeps information about museum exhibitions in the public eye, too often museum administrators confuse marketing with audience development. Audience attraction is not necessarily audience development, and, in some cases, attracting audiences in the short run may actually work against building a visitorship that returns over and over again. The "spikes" in attendance for temporary exhibitions often translate into the unbearable crowds most of us like to avoid. (It is ironic to note that while some museum professionals are convinced that "spikes" in attendance are essential to the health of the museum, they also often prefer after-hours and special tours of other museums to avoid the crowds.) Building a sustained audience means building participation in decision-making and meaning-making, activities that must take place in many ways over an extended period of time.

EMBRACING THE TENSIONS

Our times seem to be framed by an increasingly complex and layered dialectic of privilege, expert knowledge, and prescriptive meaning-making on the one hand, and access, popular culture, and the negotiation of meaning on the other. The public spectacle of exhibitions makes them a particularly dynamic stage for this unfolding dialogue.

The current trend to create "public-program" and "guest-services" divisions, in which exhibitions and educational programs are combined and the research and curatorial functions are often separated out, has educators replacing curators and science educators replacing scientists. While this reorganization has been essential in making exhibitions more relevant, accessible, and "user-friendly" for a wider range of visitors, educators, in shifting away from the pedantic style of curators, have come up with their own style problems. Didactic, highly filtered "teaching tools" fill exhibition halls, and cognitive learning goals articulated with the reductionism of a multiple-choice test have begun to drive the exhibition-development process. Where museums once displayed a multiplicity of objects in their galleries, exhibit developers now favor the technique of selective display, with objects carefully selected to drive home a particular educational message. The hearts of these "audience advocates" might well be in the right place, but their exhibitions often suffer from an unnecessarily simplistic tenor.

As exhibitions pull away from the curator's grip, the momentum may have swung us too far in the other direction. The effects of splitting off the researchers and content creators from the public presenters have, in some instances, forced museum exhibitions to lose their essential relationship to the pursuit of inquiry and the world of mind in favor of a superficial and simulated experience much more connected to the world of mindlessness. This is particularly the case in science museums, in which elements like simulator rides and giant robotic insects are becoming de rigueur. While some of these techniques, if used intelligently, could contribute to the culture of learning that museums have traditionally embraced, for the most part the demeaning phrase "lowest common denominator" applies. In the traveling exhibition *Ice Age Mammals*, for example, a robotic woolly rhino and saber-toothed tiger were displayed alongside non-Ice-Age hominids, tossing scientific accuracy right out the window. Surprisingly, staff scientists at host museums either were ignored or shrugged off the exhibition as superficial entertainment, since the exhibition made its rounds to many of the nation's natural history museums. Defining "entertainment" with the mind-set of a scholar or "education" with the mind-set of a theme-park operator does a great disservice to the complexity and sophistication of our audiences. As Marshall McLuhan was fond of observing, "Anyone who does not understand the relationship between entertainment and education doesn't know much about either."

Many people, when recalling childhood museum memories, describe strange things in jars, sculptures larger than life, and chicken eggs hatching every few minutes. These unusual and amazing things have the powerful capacity to surprise, fascinate, and inspire people—something that may be overlooked in the rush to prove the educational and marketing values of exhibitions (values that can translate into funding). Some would argue that in shifting our emphasis from temple (a place of contemplation or wonder) to forum (a place for negotiation and experimentation), we have lost the essential qualities that make museums unique.

But museums are both temple *and* forum. Just as Greenblatt urged us to strive towards a hybridization of resonance and wonder, we—like genetics researchers—will need to select this element for one characteristic and that for another. Focusing entirely on either market or mission engenders a static sameness that no longer suits our relative world. It may be difficult to create dynamic channels for dialogue between those with expert knowledge and the visiting public (those with common knowledge), but it is also more interesting. By embracing the tensions inherent in a dialogue, we will better understand how each form of knowledge informs the other, and, most importantly, we will become better able to articulate our issues *in common*.

Like other cultural and educational media, exhibitions are about people communicating with each other. How this conversation takes place, and who is responsible for conversing with whom, will depend on museum missions and the visions of exhibit creators, administrators, visitors, and their constituencies. No matter how the dialogue is approached—a dialogue as diverse as lectures and stories, pronouncements and prayers—it is inevitable that exhibitions will be judged by the societies of which they are a part. Museums have long been places of inspiration, conversation, investigation, and celebration—places that feed our natural curiosity about the world. Our most important work lies in more fully articulating the quality and tenor of the dialogues museum exhibitions could be having with visitors.

ENDNOTES

[1]Kenneth Hudson, *Museums of Influence* (Cambridge: Cambridge University Press, 1987), 23.

[2]Although Duncan Cameron first juxtaposed the notions of temple and forum in the early 1970s, museum professionals still struggle with these dynamics today. See Duncan Cameron, "The Museum, A Temple or the Forum," *Curator* XIV (1) (1971): 11–24; for a description of one museum's metaphorical scope, see George MacDonald and Stephen Alsford, *A Museum for the Global Village* (Hull, Quebec: Canadian Museum of Civilization, 1989).

[3]John Falk, "Visitors: Toward a Better Understanding of Why People Go to Museums," *Museum News* 77 (2) (1999): 38–40.

[4]Barbara Y. Newsom and Adele Z. Silver, eds., *The Art Museum as Educator* (Berkeley: University of California Press, 1978), 77.

[5]In conversation with the author.

[6]Not all art museums are adverse to visitor research, and several, including the Cleveland Museum of Art, the Hirshhorn, the Denver Art Museum, and the Minneapolis Institute of Arts, have embraced it as an essential element of museum practice on some level.

[7]For more information on time spent in museums and exhibitions, see Beverly Serrell, *Paying Attention: Visitors and Museum Exhibitions* (Washington, D.C.: American Association of Museums, 1998).

[8]Sheldon Annis, "The Museum as Staging Ground for Symbolic Action," *Museum 151* 38 (3) (1986): 170.

[9]Newsom and Silver, eds., *The Art Museum as Educator*, 37.

[10]Albert E. Parr, "Curatorial Functions in Education," *Curator* VI (4) (1963): 290.

[11]Robert Sullivan, in conversation with the author, March 1993.

[12]Frank Oppenheimer, "A Rationale for a Science Museum," *Curator* XI (3) (1968): 206–209.

[13]Edwin Schlossberg, *The Learning Environment for the Brooklyn Children's Museum* (Brooklyn, N.Y.: Brooklyn Institute of Arts and Sciences, 1975), 24.

[14]Michael Kimmelman, "Culture and Race: Still on America's Mind," *New York Times*, 19 November 1995, p. 1, sec. 2.

[15]John Neuhart, Marilyn Neuhart, and Ray Eames, *Eames Design: The Work of the Office of Charles and Ray Eames* (New York: Harry N. Abrams, Inc., 1989), 254–259. The exhibition is still on view today at the Boston Museum of Science.

[16]"Exhibition Group Formed," *Exhibitionist*, October 1981.

[17]Ivan Karp and Steven D. Lavine, eds., *Exhibiting Cultures: The Poetics and Politics of Museum Display* (Washington, D.C.: Smithsonian Institution Press, 1991).

[18]Stephen Greenblatt, "Resonance and Wonder," in Karp and Lavine, *Exhibiting Cultures*, 42.

[19]Ibid., 54.

[20]Ibid.

[21]From a Smithsonian Institution press release, December 1990.

[22]From the exhibition catalog, February 1992.

[23]Ivan Karp and Fred Wilson, "Constructing the Spectacle of Culture in Museums," in Reesa Greenberg, Bruce W. Ferguson, and Sandy Nairne, eds., *Thinking about Exhibitions* (London: Routledge, 1996), 256.

[24]Susan Vogel, "Always True to the Object, in Our Fashion," in Karp and Lavine, *Exhibiting Cultures*, 198.

[25]The exhibition was on display at the Museum of Modern Art in New York from March 14 through June 1, 1999. For more information, see the catalog: Kynaston McShine, *The Museum as Muse: Artists Reflect* (New York: The Museum of Modern Art, 1999).

[26]American Association of Museums, *Excellence and Equity: Education and the Public Dimension of Museums* (Washington, D.C.: American Association of Museums, 1992), 11–12.

[27]Heather MacDonald, "Revisionist Lust: The Smithsonian Today," *The New Criterion* 15 (9) (1997): 17–31.

[28]Kathleen McLean, *Planning for People in Museum Exhibitions* (Washington, D.C.: Association of Science-Technology Centers, 1993), 37.

[29]From an invitation to the president's opening reception, 9 December 1998.

Is a library a collection of books, or is it a building? Historically, collections have needed buildings for storage, conservation, and access. The community has had need for a building—especially if it is a national library—to denote symbolically as well as literally the existence of a national published archive, announcing that the nation has a history of achievement, invention, exploration, and industry.

But do libraries still need buildings? It is apparent that our politicians believe so, to the extent that they are willing to commit very large sums of money to their construction.

The late twentieth century is a period of paradox for libraries. On the one hand, the closing decade will be recalled, in Europe at any rate, as a time of great new library buildings. The national libraries of the United Kingdom, France, Germany, and Denmark are all opening new buildings; some of them, as in Paris and London, are monumental in scale, the largest public buildings of the century in each country. On the other hand, libraries are living through an information revolution, the fruits of which could suggest that centralized book repositories are redundant.

Brian Lang

From "Bricks and Bytes: Libraries in Flux"
Dædalus 125 (4) (Fall 1996)

Harold Skramstad

An Agenda for American Museums in the Twenty-First Century

W E LIVE IN A CONTRADICTORY TIME. While Americans are increasingly impatient with any limitation on their individual rights, and loyalty to institutions such as the church, school, and community has been deeply eroded, they continue to seek out groups and institutions that can offer order, authority, and criteria that go beyond the imperatives of individualism. Those institutions that are able to recognize this contradiction and can help us find the required balance between our need for freedom and our need for authority are those that will be most successful in the next century.

One institution that is actively seeking that new balance is the American museum. Museums have helped shape the American experience in the past, and they have the potential to play an even more aggressive role in shaping American life in the future. They offer a powerful educational model that can help redesign and reform American education, and they can be important centers of community development and renewal. However, to accomplish these two things, museums must engage the world with a spirit of activism and openness far beyond what they are used to. They will have to reexamine and rethink some of the most fundamental assumptions they hold about what they do and how they do it. They will also have to reclaim the sense of bold entrepreneurship and experimentation that characterized the earliest days of the museum movement in America.

Harold Skramstad is president emeritus of Henry Ford Museum & Greenfield Village in Dearborn, Michigan.

109

Museums came early to America, and the story of America's first museums is one of lively entrepreneurship combined with a strong sense of educational purpose. In a nation characterized by Daniel J. Boorstin as creating and recreating new, transient, "upstart" communities, most museums were formed as voluntary associations that brought together civic boosters in an eclectic mix of collecting, education, and entertainment activities. Museums, like other community institutions such as colleges and universities, theaters and opera houses, were often built and in business before roads were named or paved. They functioned to anchor and stretch the communities for which they were created. Characteristic of these museum enterprises was a practical bias toward community values and a governance structure that reflected a blurring of private and public spheres.

If there was a distinguishing feature of American museums from the outset, it was their diversity. They might focus on one particular area such as art, history, science, or archaeology, or they might take a mixture of subjects, each represented by a mass of collection materials. One of the earliest museums in America was the Peale Museum in Philadelphia, established by Charles Willson Peale in 1786. Peale saw his museum as a commercial as well as an educational undertaking; he understood the need to connect his content to his audience's interests in a lively manner if he expected them to pay the admission fees that his museum required for its operation. Peale's museum was characteristic of a genre that saw its collections as representing the entire world. Its collections grew to over one hundred thousand specimens, collected and exhibited with two purposes in mind—to entertain and to educate. It is important to remember that early museums such as Peale's developed long before universal public schooling became common; they, along with the church and the library, were important institutions concerned with public education.

If we look at the history of nineteenth-century American museums, we find again and again bold and diverse patterns of museum development carried out against a backdrop of a society hungry for information and knowledge but wanting to get it in a digestible form. One of the most successful early museum pioneers was P. T. Barnum, whose American Museum was founded in New York City in 1841. Barnum's museum provides us with a vivid example of educational entrepreneurship. Materials from around the world were presented in displays designed to blend education and entertainment. Barnum's intent was to create a personal experience of exoticism and wonder. Visitors to his museum were stimulated by the displays to learn and to enjoy themselves in the process. They were comfortable in knowing they were in a place where discovery, dialogue, and conversation were encouraged. They took pleasure in uncovering and trying to discover for themselves whether the material on display was real or not, as Barnum was well known for his staging of elaborate hoaxes to boost attendance. In capitalizing on Americans' almost insatiable desire for knowledge, Barnum understood instinctively that learning and entertainment could exist comfortably in a museum setting. In this he was a genuine museum pioneer.

Later in the century, as cities such as New York, Chicago, Cleveland, and Detroit became dominant centers of commerce, one of the strategies for displaying their economic and cultural power was the creation of large art museums. Because of their size, scale, and social prominence, these art museums came to dominate the cultural assumptions about museums for the next century and to establish a new, more conservative model for museum creation. Most were founded with governance and operating structures that made them less dependent on earned admissions from the visiting public than the earlier museums, such as those of Peale and Barnum, had been. They depended instead on private subsidies by wealthy patrons for much of their financial support. Their founding missions combined the inspirational and the practical: to educate and uplift the public and to improve the skills and taste of those who worked with their hands. The founding patrons of such museums recognized that museums, like libraries, universities, and symphony orchestras, were prudent investments in both social control and civic pride, essential ingredients in the growth and success of America's emerging industrial cities.

Building the collections of these museums fell to a new group of America's business and civic leaders. Their rapidly growing wealth, created by the vast economic expansion of the American economy, meant they were able to accumulate masterpieces of the artistic and cultural patrimony of Europe and the Orient, and these treasures began to find a permanent home in America's museums. As a result, museums began to focus less on the care of audiences and more on the care of their valuable and quickly expanding collections. The result was a gradual yet profound culture change as museums shifted the direction of their energies from public education and inspiration toward self-generated, internal, professional, and academic goals. Museums began to see their primary intellectual and cultural authority coming from their collections rather than their educational and community purpose. The great art museums of New York, Chicago, Cleveland, and Detroit set the dominant tone of this inward movement of museum culture. They were the recipients of many of the artistic masterpieces collected by wealthy Americans. The visibility of their museum collections and exhibitions was symbolic of America's need to prove that American museums could and would reach a quality and scale equal to any in the world.

Because of their visibility as symbols of civic pride, art museums defined the popular perception of a "museum." Once seen as a place of curiosity, wonder, and delight, the "museum" became associated with quiet galleries where artistic treasures were displayed for contemplation. This perception remains today. When journalists and others outside the museum field speak of "museums," they are generally referring to art museums. It was art museums that first saw themselves as preservers of rare and beautiful objects of intrinsic value, and their view of collecting has subsequently shaped the collections of many non-art museums. Until relatively recently, history museums have tended to collect examples of rare and beautiful objects from the past rather than those most characteristic or emblematic of the historical period or locale that was their focus. The word "museum quality" is taken from the culture of art museums and assumes aesthetic quality rather than appropriateness of historical or scientific context.

The great success of the American public-education system in the nineteenth century also worked to strengthen the trend among museums to focus inwardly on the study and display of their collections. As schools began to take on the role of the monopoly providers of public education, the public-education role of museums received less attention. By the first decade of the twentieth century what had too often disappeared from museum culture was a concern about education and respect for the public audience. The expansion of knowledge through museum collecting was now considered by museums to be the primary focus of their work. The more knowledge that was accumulated through museum collections, the more useful that knowledge would be. It was no longer necessary for the museum to be a missionary force on behalf of popular education; rather, it would be a preserver and protector of the rare, the unique, the beautiful, and the special in the arts, the humanities, and the sciences.

There were many in the museum field who expressed concern about this inward-moving perspective. Among many there remained a belief that museums and museum exhibitions had the power to create memorable experiences that could stimulate and inspire people, especially the young. One of the most articulate proponents of this point of view was the aviation pioneer Samuel P. Langley, who was Secretary of the Smithsonian Institution at the turn of the century. Soon after assuming his position, he became concerned that the Smithsonian was doing little to address the educational needs of children who did not understand the arcane labels of the natural history displays designed by scholars. To solve the problem he appointed himself as Honorary Curator of a new "Children's Room" with instructions "to see that a room was reserved and properly prepared for such things as little people most want to know." In a letter to himself accepting the position, Langley wrote:

"The Secretary of the Smithsonian Institution has been pleased to confer upon me the honorable but arduous duties of the care of the Children's Room. He has at his service so many men learned in natural history that I do not know why he has chosen me, who knows so little about it, unless perhaps it's because these gentlemen may possibly not be also learned in the ways of children, for whom this little room is meant.

"It has been my purpose to deserve his confidence, and to carry out what I believe to be his intention, by identifying myself with the interests of my young clients. Speaking, therefore, in their behalf, and as one of them, I should say that we never have a fair chance in museums. We cannot see the things on the top shelves, which only grown-up people are tall enough to look into, and most of the things we can see and would like to know about have Latin words on them, which we cannot understand: some things we do not care for at all, and other things which look entertaining have nothing on them to tell us what they are about. . . .

"We think there is nothing in the world more entertaining than birds, animals, and live things; and next to these is our interest in the same things, even though they are not alive; and next to this is to read about them. All of us care about them and some of us hope to care for them all our lives long. We are not very much interested in the Latin names, and however much they may mean to grown-up people, we do not want to have our entertainment spoiled by its being made a lesson."[1]

In this letter Langley reveals an instinctive understanding of the educational power of museums and the degree to which that power is dependent on museum leaders' understanding of both their subject and their audience.

An important critique of the inward-moving trend in American museums appeared in a study done by Laurence Vail Coleman, commissioned by the American Association of Museums and published by the Association in 1939 as *The Museum in America: A Critical Study*. In his three-volume study, Coleman reminded museum workers that in America, "the museum, like the library, is a *community* enterprise in its very nature." He went on to criticize American museums as a "group of air-tight compartments" in which the "Instructors . . . are buffers between the public and the curatorial group that wants to be left alone. In large museums the instructors are gathered to a 'department of education' (named as though other departments might be dedicated to unenlightenment), and headed by a 'curator of education' (titled as though he had to take care of the stuff lest some of it get away)." Coleman's report remains an extremely insightful but too-little-read or -utilized artifact of American museum history.

The founders of America's first industrial museums, Julius Rosenwald and Henry Ford, provided another important counterforce to this inward focus among museums. Developed in the 1930s, Rosenwald's Museum of Science and Industry in Chicago and Ford's Edison Institute in Dearborn, Michigan, were driven by a strong sense of social purpose. The goal of their museums was to bring people into contact with new, educational, and potentially inspiring experiences. In describing his vision for the Museum of Science and Industry, Rosenwald argued:

> In an industrial center like Chicago there ought to be a permanent exhibit for the entertainment and instruction of the people; a place where workers in technical trades, students, engineers, and scientists might have an opportunity to enlarge their vision; to gain a better understanding of their own problems by contact with actual machinery, and by quiet examination in leisure hours of working models of apparatus; or, perhaps to make new contributions to the world's welfare through helpful inventions. The stimulating influence of such an exhibit upon the growing youth of the city needs only to be mentioned.[2]

This new type of museum was to be primarily a place of education, entertainment, and influence rather than research and scholarship. A formal, hands-on school was attached to Ford's museum; the experiences and artifacts in Rosenwald's Museum of Science and Industry would be chosen for their value in both entertaining and instructing its publics. For both men, the artifacts that formed their museum collections were of a different sort. Instead of focusing on the rare and the antiquarian, they focused on the vernacular and the everyday. Instead of focusing on artifacts that represented continuity, they focused on those that embodied and represented change. If original artifacts were not available, reproductions or models were commissioned. They created large and dramatic spaces and distinctive architecture to give a sense of theater and drama to the museum-going experience. Ford installed a dramatic eight-acre forest of technology behind a reproduction of the facade of Philadelphia's Independence Hall. Rosenwald focused on the creation of a number of vivid and theatrical exhibitions.

While the public responded positively to these new kinds of museums, other museums generally did not. The dominant focus of museum culture for most of the twentieth century remained the accumulation and management of museum collections and the professionalization of museum workers and museum work. The positive results of this focus are undeniable, indeed amazing. Extraordinary advances have been made in the building of new museum collections, the efficient management of existing collections, and the systematic study of those collections. Workers in the museum field have ceased to be seen as dilettantes or amateurs and are now for the most part well-educated and trained professionals. Yet this professionalism has too often widened the gap between museums and the publics who use and support them. Underlying much of contemporary museum culture is a fundamental belief that the collecting, research, and interpretation efforts of museums are intrinsic social goods and that members of the public who choose not to attend museum exhibitions and participate in museum programs do so because they are not quite up to the intellectual or aesthetic challenge. Museums have also increasingly adopted the conventions and privileges of academic culture, claiming the rights of academic freedom in both research and the production of museum exhibitions. In fact, in many museums the public is seen as a distraction from the study of the collection, the "real work" of the museum. The most cynical example of this is the way many museum professionals view "blockbuster" exhibitions. Blockbusters are often seen as little more than necessary pandering to the public rather than as opportunities to try to engage a broad audience in subjects and collections that in the long run benefit both the museum and the public.

Despite the inward focus that has dominated much of the museum culture during the twentieth century, there is no question that museums are almost universally acknowledged as an important part of the cultural landscape. The architecture of new museums has become an important source of civic pride and tourist dollars. Their collections have potency and their exhibitions are highly visible and can be important statements. For this reason, museums have begun to hear more clearly and bluntly from audiences that feel they have been either neglected or badly treated. These audiences are far more diverse and vocal than ever before in their expectations of museums. And because of their political power, they cannot be ignored. For example, when a broad coalition of American Indian groups objected that American museums were housing and studying the remains of their ancestors in a way that conflicted with their own beliefs, they forced federal legislation that gave hegemony to Indian values over museum collecting and research values.

Other groups have begun to look to museums to legitimize and validate their special claims or grievances and have found to their dismay and anger that their accomplishments and struggles are undocumented in museum collections and remain neglected in museum exhibitions and scholarship. Their response has often been to start their own museums so that their interests will not be diluted in the interests or purposes of larger museums. The continuing plethora of new museums (it is estimated that over one-half of the museums in America have been started since 1960) reminds us all that museum founding continues to be an important activity in the building of American communities. The extraordinary proliferation of these special-purpose museums, many of them focused around the history and story of a particular subject, community, or special interest group, is a vital sign of strength in the American museum movement.

THE MUSEUM AS A NEW EDUCATIONAL MODEL

Imagine the prototypical elementary school of the twenty-first century. It is an educational environment in which young children come together to learn about real subject-matter content and to develop critical thinking skills. They work with the real things and ideas of science, art, and the humanities. They work in a setting of participatory learning, led and mentored by adults who are themselves skilled practitioners of the particular craft or discipline the children are learning. The work is rigorous, involving projects that require team-based inquiry and demanding a variety of complementary learning skills. The rewards come in the form of recognition of the individual intellectual and emotional strengths of the learners as well as recognition of the strength of the working teams. All of the activities undertaken require basic skills in thoughtful and critical reading, analytical thinking, problem-solving, clear writing, and computer understanding. The measurement of learning comes in a variety of forms, including standardized tests, teacher assessment, and student self-assessment.

Although this schooling model is rare today, it describes very closely the kind of learning that goes on presently in many American museums, especially children's museums and science and technology centers. These new types of museums developed out of community concerns that more traditional, collection-focused museums were not meeting the learning needs of their audiences. Most of these museums do not have large collections of objects, or if they do, the objects function as stimuli for the exploration and discovery of larger ideas or concepts, not as icons in themselves. During the past several decades, these two classes of museums have been great pioneers in improving the process of learning by the young. Their lead is now being followed by museums whose collections are rich in content and who have gained a renewed understanding of the potential of those collections as educational tools.

The museum educational model pioneered by children's museums and science and technology centers focuses on experiential and content-based problem-solving activities working with the real objects of art, history, and science; on participatory, "hands-on" learning; on apprenticeship under the tutelage of people engaged in real-world intellectual activity; and on learning experiences designed to engage all the senses. Its emphasis on educational experiences that address the diverse learning styles of students could, with a relatively small investment, take place in every museum of reasonable size. This model recognizes that education in tomorrow's world needs to be truly different from what it is today. Even the most disadvantaged child now has access to an extraordinary range of experiences in a variety of media. To respond with an educational model designed for a motivated and compliant middle-class student for whom the traditional rigor and rote learning of the classroom is an accepted form of education just will not work.

Yet too often museums are dismissed as institutions of "informal" education, which is taken to mean a less important and less powerful form of education than traditional schooling. The formal educational potential of the museum has been undervalued and greatly underestimated. Some important experiments are already underway in this area. A number of museums have close partnerships with schools so that work and study projects in the museum and at school are seen as a seamless educational experience. At Henry Ford Museum & Greenfield Village in Dearborn, Michigan, a new public high school based on the theme of innovation and focused on the development of critical thinking and problem-solving skills is actually located in the museum. A very diverse student body, chosen by lot, uses all of the facilities of the museum as a giant learning classroom and laboratory. Standardized tests of these students have shown very positive results. In a very different setting, the American Museum of Natural History has developed an extraordinarily ambitious, $25 million national program to educate children and adults about science. It will do this by making the research and discovery process of the museum "transparent" through sophisticated electronic technology available both on-line and through a variety of hardware and software packages. As these and other museum educational models become more fully developed in a variety of settings, it will be important to test and compare outcomes with those of more traditional models of schooling.

But the museum model of education should not be limited to the younger years. Museums can and should provide educational experiences for adult learning that are just as powerful. In museums adults can learn at their own speed and in their own way in a setting that is multisensory and engages the emotions as well as the intellect. With no mandated curriculum, learners can organize themselves by almost any criteria of interests. The mixing of education, age, gender, and race can become a strong asset in a shared learning process. The museum can provide a place that encourages and enables intergenerational learning. The closely controlled environment of the school, open during very limited hours and not available to all members of a family or community-based group, cannot match the environment of the museum for encouraging groups of all kinds to learn together.

THE MUSEUM AS A MODEL COMMUNITY INSTITUTION

Museums in America have been and remain the creations of diverse and distinctive communities. The pattern of civic enterprise that has brought and continues to bring museums into being needs continual nurturing and development. The dominant governance model of museums, the independent nonprofit organization led by lay citizens in service of broad community objectives, can provide an important center of leadership in a community. Changes in a community may well mean the need to reexamine a museum's mission, goals, and strategies. It may also involve the need for changes in the bylaws and other forms of self-regulation by the organization. Museums offer in their organizational model ample room for either minor course correction or major change. If the governing authority of the museum is not able or willing to make the necessary changes in the museum's mission, direction, or strategies to meet community needs, there is a good possibility that another leadership group will organize to form a new museum with a new mission and direction that more directly meet those community needs. While this is often seen by established museums as a wasteful dilution of community resources and leadership, it remains a critical element in the process of museum and community renewal.

But just as important as the organizational model of the museum is its focus on real content. Many community-based organizations such as service clubs, community centers, and fraternal organizations focus on very practical issues—i.e., how to solve a specific community problem. Other community-focused organizations, primarily social-service agencies, focus on how to deal with human problems at either the individual or the group level. These organizations must inevitably neglect what is even more important for any community—its need to create and sustain successful human beings who are capable of integrating their own lives into larger traditions of civic responsibility. To do this requires institutions that go beyond the immediate and practical concerns of people's lives and communities. In a museum, content, made real by contact with objects, stories, ideas, and lives from the realms of science, art, and the humanities, can offer a gathering point for exploration of an inexhaustible store of topics. The museum is a place for tactile, emotional, and intellectual contact with people, ideas, or objects that have the potential to inspire. It is a place where people can meet and make friendships with others who share similar interests or where they can be a part of something larger and more important than their own individual lives. In order to develop the community potential of museums, museums have much work to do in developing new metaphors for their work that will emphasize their "caregiving" as well as their "collection-getting" focus.

THE MUSEUM AS A DESIGNER AND DELIVERER OF EXPERIENCES

Effective development of a much expanded educational and community role for museums in the next century will require museums to develop a much deeper competence in designing powerful and engaging educational experiences and delivering them to broad public audiences. More and more Americans expect that their social, economic, and cultural activities, though shaped by a variety of sources, will engage them in a way that is vivid, distinctive, and out of the ordinary. This is even more the case for children who are being brought up in a world of interactive media, which sets up new expectations of active participation. They expect to be treated as individuals who have a significant capacity to influence as well as be influenced by any experience in their lives. This means that in the world of the next century, these experiences will have to be developed with close interaction between their producers and their consumers. This interaction and the resulting relationship of trust is what increasingly will give authority to any experience. Organizations of all kinds, from theme parks to retail stores to restaurants, are beginning to structure their products and services in this way. The goals are always to make a connection with an audience, to establish a relationship of trust, and to cause some specific outcome, whether it be knowledge, fun, insight, or the purchase of a product or service. Museums need to recognize that they are in the experience business and that it is the distinctive theme, context, and value of the experiences they bring to a particular audience that will increasingly define their success.

There exists for museums great potential to orchestrate new and distinctive experiences that can give value to their audiences in a way that meets their individual needs. The key is that whatever is presented must offer an opportunity to go beyond passive learning to active involvement in the experience itself. This experiential dimension was a constant among the visionary and forward-thinking museums of the past. The displays in Barnum's American Museum were attempts to create an environment of the extraordinary, the wondrous, or the exotic. Langley's Children's Room at the Smithsonian was designed to inspire delight and discovery rather than convey specific information. The American museum experiences that are among the most memorable and influential tend to be those that are experientially rich, that have a sense of engagement, that have more similarity to a theatrical performance than a lesson plan. The pioneering dioramas of the American Museum of Natural History and other natural history museums, the planetarium as a new form of museum experience, the coal-mine exhibit at the Museum of Science and Industry, and the affecting exhibitions of the United States Holocaust Memorial Museum are examples of museum experiences that remain underutilized as models for future museum development. The producers of these museum experiences instinctively recognized that a museum's content or collections were not self-revealing guides to knowledge but were ingredients for the creation of special settings for undertaking exploration and discovery that acknowledged and respected the audiences' lives and experiences.

The refocused educational and community agenda for museums that I am advocating would make experience design and delivery central to the museum mission and would view artifacts and content as means rather than ends. It assumes that the content and collections are not the mission of the museum's work but powerful tools that enable it. It recognizes something that we all know through both common sense and research in museum learning: museums are not effective or efficient communicators of large amounts of information. People do not read very well standing up, and every study of the outcomes of museum experiences tells us that people remember very little of a museum's content. However, that same research reminds us that they do vividly remember museum experiences that somehow have a connection to their own lives. I am not suggesting here that museums create content to fit the needs of their audience, but rather that they create mission-related experiences to fit those needs.

Many museums recoil from this idea. The usual argument is that to focus on experience rather than on content is to pander to the audience and to attenuate the subtlety and nuance of what is being communicated. What is really being said in this argument is that the museum only wants to communicate to those people for whom nuance and subtlety will be an essential part of the experience. This is fine for internal discourse among professionals and connoisseurs but hardly acceptable for public museums. Experience design is a new and special skill, and it will be in great demand in the future. Museums need to better understand and develop this skill now, in collaboration with filmmakers, game creators, artists, poets, storytellers, and others who can bring necessary skills and talents to the process. In developing experiences, museums have an advantage over their competitors, whether they be electronic media, theme parks, or other entertainment venues. The real and authentic objects, stories, ideas, and lives that are the subject matter of museum experiences have a resonance that is more powerful than all but the most compelling imaginary experiences.

A focus on experience design and delivery will also allow museums to be more effective participants in the rapidly evolving field of cultural tourism. Travel and tourism are among the world's largest, most important, and fastest-growing industries. As tourism continues to rise, there will be an increased interest in what is unique and special about each tourist destination. Museums will be extremely important organizations in defining the specialness of a place, the "there" of a specific locale. Their ability to design and package powerful, content-rich tourist experiences will increasingly be critical not only to their educational success but to their economic success as well as the economic success of their communities.

A MODEL FOR SUCCESS

But more than conceptual and imaginative skills are required for museums to reach a central place in the American agenda. To become a forceful model for American education and a vital center for American communities, museums must develop three characteristics in their institutional culture in order to fully succeed. These characteristics are authority, connectedness, and trustworthiness.

Authority

Traditionally, museums have defined their authority primarily through the uniqueness of their collections and the special skills of their content specialists. Yet today all manner of resorts, hotels, casinos, restaurants, banks, and retail establishments have acquired collections of art and artifacts and engage in exhibitions and other collection and content-related activities that at one time would have been seen as the exclusive domain of museums. For example, the Hard Rock Cafe chain of restaurants has an important collection of artifacts related to its "core" content consisting of Elvis Presley, the Beatles, the Rolling Stones, U2, and Madonna. Its staff travels around the world soliciting donations and making purchases related to its "permanent" collection. Every artifact to be added to the Hard Rock Cafe's collection must be authenticated by a staff with special knowledge and training. And no artifact acquired for the core collection is ever sold. The recently opened Bellagio casino and resort in Las Vegas is developing heavily publicized art exhibitions from its own collections. The Rain Forest Cafe chain of restaurants has appropriated many of the elements of the interpretive programs of zoos. In each case, these commercial businesses have adopted the conventions of museum practice to lend a sense of deepened authenticity to their commercial experiences.

In addition to coming from the collections themselves, the authority of museums has come in large part from the larger and more transcendent ideas and values embodied in those collections and understood by traditional patrons, staffs, and audiences as intrinsically good and worthy of transmission to everyone without fear of controversy. More recently, museum exhibitions and other programs have become subject to increasingly sharp criticism from a variety of sources for a variety of reasons. This is not surprising. As museums engage the interest of more diverse and pluralistic audiences, they have become battlegrounds for larger cultural and historical debates. The contentiousness of the debate surrounding exhibitions mounted by institutions as varied as the Smithsonian Institution, the Library of Congress, and the Museum of the City of New York are recent examples. The most well-publicized example in recent times was the debate surrounding a Smithsonian exhibition that focused on the decision of the U.S. government to drop the atomic bomb on Japan during World War II. The curators of the exhibition did not fully understand the emotional issues that were at the root of the concern over their exhibition script, which questioned the need for dropping the bomb. The resulting controversy pitted the Smithsonian against a variety of outraged groups, some of which were both savvy and politically ruthless adversaries. The outcome, the canceling of the originally planned exhibition and the substitution of a much-simplified display, reflected badly on all parties to the debate. The lesson of this failed exhibition is that the development of the authority of museum exhibitions and experiences in the future will require continuous conversation and negotiation between museum staff with their specialized skills and knowledge and audiences now used to playing a more active role in the planning and development of the experiences in which they have an important stake. This is not to say that the skills of the specialist and the expert are no longer important in establishing the authority of a museum program or exhibition, but that a museum is not a university and that to expect audiences to yield to an absolute respect for and deference to the museum's cultural authority is no longer a reasonable expectation.

Connectedness

The controversy surrounding the Smithsonian exhibition on strategic bombing during World War II also evolved out of a lack of connectedness. Connectedness is nothing more than the process of a close, continuous, long-term connection between an organization and its audience. It is only through being connected to audiences in a close and continuous way that the museum will be trusted. In order to achieve connectedness in an ever more pluralistic society, both the governance and the staff makeup of American museums are going to have to become a lot more diverse. It will be impossible for museums to retain any sense of authority with the more pluralistic America outside museum walls unless there is diversity inside those walls. Connectedness also means that museums will have to master the skill of listening as well as the skill of talking—that is, how to listen and what questions to ask. And, most importantly, they will need to know what to do in response to the listening. The process of systematically listening to consumers and potential consumers goes against the grain of traditional museum practice, which assumes that the museum is teacher and the audience is learner and that the museum cannot allow its audiences to play a role in defining its programs. But if the museum has defined its mission clearly and if this mission is connected to the value the museum can give to its audiences, this is a false concern. Increasingly, museum mission statements are going to have to contain not only a concise statement of what the museum does but also a description of the outcome of what it does and of the value of that outcome to the community it serves. If there is nothing special about its work, nothing that connects what it does to people's lives, then what is the point of its existing and who should care? If we look at the museums that are most successful in their ability to carry out their public missions, we see those that work hardest at carrying on a continuous conversation of mutual respect with their audiences.

Trustworthiness

Museums could learn much about trustworthiness from the business world. There is among the best companies an almost fanatical concern about "brand" and "brand management." The result of good brand development and management over a long period of time is that the consumer can reasonably expect that any product or service carrying that brand will live up to or exceed expectations. The product or service will be seen as trustworthy, even before it is experienced. It also means that from time to time a mistake or a poor product or service will be forgiven in the marketplace. However, a string of poor-quality or unresponsive products or services results in an erosion of trust. Once eroded, this trust is very difficult, if not impossible, to rebuild. Whether in the more traditional world of organizations or in the new world of electronic connectivity and e-commerce, people always seek information, knowledge, and insight from people and organizations they trust. This is why businesses invest so much time and money in establishing a "relationship" with consumers and potential consumers, and work so hard at making a commercial transaction an "experience" that is positive and memorable. Establishing a relationship of trust requires both a great deal of time and an attitude of mutual respect between the producer and consumer of a product or service. This is nothing new. Anthropologists remind us that in traditional societies, language was used less for communicating content than for establishing bonds of trust and understanding. It is only in modern societies that language is primarily used to communicate content, but at the risk of reducing the bonds of communication and trust. It is no different for museums. Trustworthiness and authority in a museum grow directly out of skill and expertise well exercised as well as out of continual connection to the audiences served. In the new world of the new century, the authority that a museum claims will be built not primarily through its collections nor on its specialized expertise, but through those resources engaged in conversation and dialogue with those audiences the museum serves. Relentless focus on establishing continuous and direct connection to the audience will, over a long period of time, result in the museum being seen as worthy of authority, affiliation, support, and trust.

CONCLUSION

As the distinctions between nonprofit and profit, education and entertainment, form and content, and product and service become less clear, our view of institutions will inevitably change. The ability of any institution to give meaning and value to people's personal and collective lives will take on even greater importance than it has today. This is why American museums have so much to offer American life. The great age of collection building in museums is over. Now is the time for the next great agenda of museum development in America. This agenda needs to take as its mission nothing less than to engage actively in the design and delivery of experiences that have the power to inspire and change the way people see both the world and the possibility of their own lives. We have many practical institutions to help us work through our day-to-day problems. We have enough educational institutions that focus on training us to master the skills we need to graduate from school and get a job. Yet we have too few institutions that have as their goal to inspire and change us. American museums need to take this up as their new challenge. Up to now much of their time has been devoted to building their collections and sharing them through "outreach" to the larger world. Now they must help us create the new world of "inreach," in which people, young and old alike, can "reach in" to museums though experiences that will help give value and meaning to their own lives and at the same time stretch and enlarge their perceptions of the world. This will not be an easy task. It will require major changes in focus, organization, staffing, and funding for museums. But the potential benefit to America is tremendous. Working in partnership with each other and with their communities, America's museums remain one of America's best hopes for realizing the possibilities of the American future.

ENDNOTES

[1] Albert Bigelow Paine, "The Children's Room in the Smithsonian Institution," *Smithsonian Institution Annual Report 1901* (Washington, D.C.: Smithsonian Institution, 1901), 553–554.

[2] Letter from Julius Rosenwald to Samuel Insull as quoted in Victor J. Danilov, "Science and Technology Museums Come of Age," *Curator* 16 (3) (1973): 30–46.

Maxwell L. Anderson

Museums of the Future:
The Impact of Technology
on Museum Practices

RESEARCHING AND RECONSIDERING THE ORIGINAL OBJECT

ANYONE'S FIRST ENCOUNTER with the eminent classical archaeologist Dietrich von Bothmer is always memorable; I was witness to that of the lady who arrived in the Metropolitan Museum's Greek and Roman Department offices in the early 1980s with a small vase neatly wrapped in tissue paper. Dr. von Bothmer picked up the parcel and instantly handed it back to her. He explained that he had no need to unwrap the object since its weight revealed it to be modern.

In the early days of the digital age, many are concerned that there will not only be no need to unwrap the object thanks to the magic of networked technology and digital imaging, but that audiences in the future will become impatient with the static nature of works of art and material culture and seek nourishment elsewhere. Even in the preparation of this essay I found myself interested in pre-1993 (pre-Web) publications about technology and art primarily out of nostalgia, rather than out of a sense that they might hold indispensable wisdom. What was possible before 1993 and what is today possible are two entirely different propositions. The instantaneous retrieval of information globally, in authoritative and systematic ways, is transforming the experience of the original object as well as

---

Maxwell L. Anderson is director of the Whitney Museum of American Art in New York.

129

the prefatory and subsequent experiences of learning about it. While advanced research used to involve the uncertain courtship of a card catalog by a reader in a particular library, any end user anywhere is likely to resort to identical information from a limited number of databases, which are in turn communicating with each other. Thus, research, which used to involve searching, now involves a far easier combination of searching and linking—a much less laborious, thoroughly automated, and the cynical would say unintellectual enterprise at best.

It should be disclosed at the outset that while I am persuaded of the enormous potential of networked information for museums, and not fearful that it will prove a disincentive to visiting them, I am also leery of its impact on our attention spans and curiosity. Baby boomers now predisposed to using library resources on-line rather than in a reading room are primitives next to an emerging generation reared in chat rooms and accustomed to communicating with each other and with the rest of the world through their own home pages. The free time of today's youth is less often spent in what we defined as experimentation. The manufacturers of software-based games have defined the limits of interactivity, while the leisure-apparel industry has enough variety to render self-definition through clothing an effortless and uncreative act. Other traditional realms of teenage expression have been market-researched and tested to the point that patience is no longer required—if one is impatient with one thing, the marketplace offers a dozen instantaneously consumed alternatives, at the mall, on the set-top box (television-top computer box), or on the Web. We are all being converted into unwitting participants in focus groups simultaneously predicting and fulfilling our every need. Consumer society will be radically redefined by intelligent agents in the coming years, and museums have yet to grasp that the sanctity of the original object must be defended in the wake of a commercial tide created by comfort-peddling merchandisers.

In keeping with this larger order of change, today's potential museum-goers and lovers of art and artifacts will actually be less often bombarded with information, because that is the way mass communication works, but not the way robotic "intelligent agents" work. Instead, the "cookies" spawned by our

Internet address when jumping onto a site can be used to track patterns of interest and spending with cheerful but unnerving accuracy. Rather than pursuing every potential consumer, advertisers are learning how to identify the vulnerable, one consumer at a time. This turn of events is paradoxical: information is becoming more centralized and authoritative while the seduction of surfing the Web for its own sake makes centralized, authoritative information potentially stultifying. Thus, only five years after this intoxicating resource was introduced, it is too soon to tell if America Online is right to move away from its heavily filtered environment to a more open-ended one. The American consumer likes the appearance of variety without the increasingly aggravating need to choose. Museums will be forced to confront the fact that the competition for leisure time demands a more aggressive case for the experience of the original. If we increasingly paint ourselves as destinations indistinguishable from malls, we will be forced to compete with malls, and the absence of a price tag on our paintings, sculptures, and photographs will not always provide us with an advantage.

The reinvention of research and the consequences for examining objects are inseparable. Museum curators and administrators have struggled for a few decades to make the inscrutable more easily understood. The majority of museum professionals are deeply concerned about how to ensure the primacy of the visitor's encounter with the original object, and hope to engage the attention of the viewer without unduly prejudicing what he or she finds rewarding in it. The examination of an object in a museum is akin to an imagined conversation between observer and artist or context, mediated by the object. Among the most satisfying features of high-flying conversation is the effortless allusion to fact in order to support judgment. The wily individual equipped with a clear memory has the advantage. He or she may also be the person with greater quantities of the unconnected assets of imagination, creativity, or curiosity, all of which are essential to making use of memory to achieve something more fruitful than mere recitation, connectivity, or, in the phrase of the Internet, hyperlinking. If scientific discoveries are often arrived at partly by chance or error, if artistic innovation is not always a reaction to what has gone before, and if great fiction is born of the circumstances of the present rather than laboriously referential to the past, then a different kind of memory may be required of us in an age of networked databases.

As children we were rewarded for exercising our capacity for memory. Young students today use pocket calculators to compute what we had to memorize, rely on the spell checker instead of a dictionary, use a keyboard instead of mastering good penmanship, and consult the Web rather than a card catalog. As the knuckle-rapped denizens of schools where long division, spelling bees, and index cards were the norm, baby boomers and our predecessors naturally bemoan the decline of our children's education, now seeming to be a form of socialization with diminishing expectations of rigor, discipline, and memory. But that sentimentality is typical of any generation that senses its raw deal being traded in for a better one.

An alternative to decrying changes in educational technology as the beginning of the end would be to concede that time previously spent learning how to perform functions that are increasingly made possible by networked technology might now be devoted more directly to problems of reasoning, development of independent judgment, language training, artistic exploration, and the like. If dissecting a frog remains a more fruitful enterprise than examining the living frog's biology through a microcamera the width of a catheter tube, we need to understand why. If the alphabetical acrobatics of algebra are an ideal path to reasoning, many boomers are still at a loss to reason why.

Memory is invisible, and what we today call technology will likely become largely invisible in the future. Not literally so—but figuratively. As the author and technology prognosticator Don Tapscott observed, his teenage children ridiculed his appearance on a nationally televised Canadian program in 1996 showing how to "surf the Web."[1] They asked whether he next planned to show how to inspect their refrigerator's contents. For the young, networked information is not a novelty or a luxury; it is a consumable like any other. As we move into a postwired era of air-fed Internet access, when switching on a laptop, raising an antenna, and pulling down a connection to the network through the ether seems normal, the nostalgia of the baby boomers and our parents is out of place. We can choose to inhabit an indexed world instead of a hyperlinked one, but the penalties will be the compromised accuracy of our findings, their dated quality, and our potential absence from the consciousness of other researchers who ply their trade on-line.

The ways in which historical, art historical, and scientific studies are changing through the use of digital technology are legion. The difficulty of recalling past research on a given topic is problematic and mounts with each passing year. We are, as researchers, inured to the fact that a vast proportion of our time is spent in reconstructing the factual evidence of past discoveries. It is taken as axiomatic that a thorough familiarity with the history of history is a first step to membership in the company of educated men and women. Yet computerized memory should see to it that such information is easier to retrieve, which will reduce the amount of time we must spend recalling what others have discovered or ventured and will allow us to honor past research that had the misfortune to be published in an obscure journal or in Cyrillic.

The quantification of scholarly achievement in a networked world is ever more challenging. The "original" idea, observation, or conclusion appears to be both original and finite when presented in a bound volume like this one. But when scanned into a database, the constituent elements are separable and can be altered with dizzying ease. As future generations of scholars modify the findings of our teachers and our students through new discoveries, the autonomy of one scholar's achievement stands to be compromised. Implicit in the temporarily free-trade zone of the Web is a new form of currency, which values various kinds of resourcefulness over originality.

The demise of mass communication presages the arrival of a new communicative and intellectual milieu. The wired world promises to be more challenging and probably more rewarding than the relatively brief era of radio and television, and to return to us a framework of fewer prescribed certainties than that we have inherited from logical positivism. With voice-recognition technology, it is the spoken word, not the newspaper or even broadcast television, that will once again become the most powerful information broker—live and interactive, not spoon-fed. The re-villaging of our sensibilities, independent of physical location, will draw us toward an experience with which we are inextricably involved: no longer as passive viewers, but as, at the very least, "viewsers"—viewers and users of information.

Instead of sitting under an Athenian olive tree, students are today sitting in front of the Web, where questions lead to questions, as with Socrates, instead of leading to the pabulum of textbooks with prescribed certainties about the natural world and history. Fact comes into question as multiple information sources compete for an analytic mind, while previously single sources demanded fealty to single interpretations. Sitting under the olive tree or sitting before the screen, students have the whole world before or above them, whereas sitting in a conventional classroom, they have prescribed learning paths and rote. The challenge ahead will be to assure that the surfeit of easily retrievable information does not let students off the hook from mastering it.

Hyperlinking (digital), rather than indexing (analog), is changing the way that we conduct research. Indexing retraces countless closed circles of knowledge, whereas hyperlinking engages the infinite spectrum of fact and imagination. Similarly, we might claim that the Internet, in replicating, however reflexively, associative powers of the brain, has more promise than information organized in discrete publications. It is as unfettered as the human imagination, whereas books are convenient precisely because they confine speculation and information into prescribed routes—unlike conversation, which is the most natural way to learn. The apparent decline in the writing skills of America's youth began long before the Web, and it remains to be seen what effect this new world of voice recognition will have on the quality of thinking and of formal communication.

Museums as centers of research, experience, and publication will be reshaped by this world. With regard to research, the benefits are obvious: access to databases and shared postings, on-line inquiries, imaging techniques for identification, morphing to complete elements of damaged or incomplete works or contexts. Expertise will have a new character: intuition and relational thinking will play a larger role than experience. The academic world will face the inevitability that human memory will indeed be less highly prized than before, which will certainly have a profound impact on the motivation to acquire a command of a particular area. The nature of a museum visit will be palpably different, since the visitor will have at his or her command a massive database delivered at levels appropriate to schoolchildren or to scholars. The experience of the original object, at least, stands to be richer, relatable to other experiences, and more easily recalled.

The sorting and comparison of works of art and artifacts of natural history is an enterprise requiring a combination of memory, reasoning, and intuition. Were the scanning of images of artworks and their uploading to a centralized database of works of art to be undertaken by every museum in a position to do so, the first requirement, that of memory, would be answered in part. Until three-dimensional scanning is effortless, the results will be haphazard to some extent. But the advantage of even this fledgling effort is that a collective database can be established, accessible instantaneously and globally, and forever refined, rather than haltingly advanced in coincidence with new editions of scientific texts inconsistently available in various languages.

Reasoning involves the application of memory to the purpose at hand; it requires that we sort objects in such a database among like types and shapes, such as portraits to portraits, skull types to skull types, or found objects to found objects. It is also exercised in sorting by subject and period, or even by artist, if the attribution seems obvious. At this point, rank amateurs in the likening of objects can insert themselves with riotously implausible pairings, which is where intuition is certainly indicated. As conclusions are proposed for general review, the collective intelligence of the field may aspire to contribute to the task significantly. It is in the voids separating works of art where intuition is most in demand, and the provision of rudimentary animation tools will allow for a variety of rapid-fire potential solutions to millennia-old puzzles. The exclusion of improbable or unhelpful associations can proceed with relative ease.

More significant than the networks' ability to sort categories of images by subject, as simple as that may sound, is the potential of image mapping and retrieval, which is the computer's version of intuition. With image mapping, the computer quite effortlessly reduces digitized images to their constituent ones and zeroes and retrieves them in combinations as required. Such opportunities for new kinds of research are already blossoming and would most naturally find their place in museums.

In the realms of publication and communication, museums must work to become centers more broadly based and community-oriented than universities, and more focused in content creation both for the educational community at large and for the mass audience. As we move toward the site licensing of images of artworks on the Web, the next issue confronting us is how willing we will be as a profession to share "unpublished" information. Publication has already been transformed by electronic communication. The stirring of a bear market in intellectual property—partly hastened by court decisions challenging the copyright of images—may threaten the most natural course of events in art history, which would favor the provision of data and images at the earliest possible convenience, so as to gain from the taxonomic skills of scholars in every field worldwide. The creation of chat forums should provide a jumbled but open path to consensus and accelerate the mid-course corrections of flawed assumptions, rendering vengeful book reviews a less frequently served dish. That will represent a privation of sorts, since, in the academy as elsewhere, the vindication of one's own divergent point of view is best expressed in the ostensibly objective forum of the review—although it is often a vehicle for self-rehabilitation rather than for the revelation of factual error.

Museums demand credible art historical and scientific inquiry and often turn to scholars in universities to bolster the research value of their own monographs and exhibition catalogs. That alliance will become increasingly problematic if museums are impelled toward greater openness through electronic publishing. We have seen of late the emergence of a paradoxical standoff within the academy. Tenure committees continue to demand evidence of scholarly credentials and capacity through published books, while academic presses are increasingly declining to publish texts of such limited potential readership that their production costs can no longer be justified. The logjam will only be broken if university presses no longer have to be profitable (which seems unlikely), if tenure committees abjure the published evidence of candidates as the primary criterion of conferring entrance into the guild (improbable but perhaps moot in that tenure itself is coming under scrutiny as an outdated system), or if electronic publishing is deemed acceptable as a conduit for scholarship (which seems inevitable). The day is probably not far off when the young scholar's proving ground is electronic, and his or her research is no less easily retrievable by both tenure committees and colleagues.

The largest obstacle to realizing the full potential of electronic publishing is neither the tenure system nor our affection for books. It is the proprietary instinct of the scholar. Since St. Jerome the scholar's reputation has been that of the intelligent being at work in isolation. It is paradoxically when "on leave" from work that the scholar is believed to do his best work. But a networked world is challenging the logic of our approach to the enterprise of research and thus to the ways that museums can foster research and learning. If indeed a primary goal of scholarship in the museum profession is the uncovering of fact, followed by greater understanding and appreciation of the achievements of artists, then the prompt reporting of partly digested information, more akin to journalism, may increasingly replace solitary investigation undertaken in relative secrecy until a completely reasoned argument can safely be aired among one's peers.

This model of scholarly productivity is not consistent with the behavioral norms of the for-profit world, where innovation and creativity bring financial rewards when they are achieved in teams or in isolation and presented as a market-oriented, income-generating, and often unanticipated result. In that universe, collaboration would be fatal to competition, since there is a finite amount of disposable income to be invested in consumer-oriented products. The world of ideas, by stark contrast, operates without such financial goals or cerebral constraints, and gains little from "cornering" a market of information outside of fulfilling the needs of a career-reward system prescribed by the academy today.

The gap between the first culling of information and the polished presentation of one's personal conclusions is the topic here in question. The matter is not trivial; that arena can sometimes extend for generations, as is the case with the Dead Sea Scrolls or with an artist's overprotective heirs. Thus, the true test will soon be upon students of the humanities with regard to their ultimate motivation in research. If the thrill of the chase is the stimulus for the life of mind, then surely openness on networks, even with partly digested evidence disclosed in hopes of a better purchase on the problem at hand, could ensue. Given the ineluctable accumulation of research, the "original" idea in a dissertation may well be original, but also spectacularly trivial. When an individual's originality is not necessarily more highly prized than his or her ability to distill the vast quantities of information contributed by many simultaneously, the likelihood is that a new reward system will have to acknowledge this shift to associative achievement and editing in place of innovation for innovation's sake.

It is all too easy to take such a position from the administrative recesses of a museum, and far harder to do so as a scholar implicated in the academy's reward system. But ultimately a technological imperative will likely lead us to adapt to new communicative norms, and this would constitute a truce in advance of our probable accommodation to one of the coming conflicts between the stewards of intellectual property *qua* property and the staggering permeability and informational elephantiasis of the Internet.

The first phase of networking among museums is now emerging. By way of example, the Art Museum Network (www.amn.org) is a resource that links the scholarship, educational resources, and interactive potential of art museums throughout North America. It operates on the premise that *networked* information is the greatest untapped potential of the Internet; amalgamates the exhibition calendars of dozens of museums in a single searchable database; hosts the web site for AMICO, the Art Museum Image Consortium; and is exploring the potential of an on-line scholarly journal and public-oriented publications as well. Only by implementing a site-licensing approach to images, text, and multimedia encounters will the museum profession be in a position to achieve true collaboration of the sort that the *disiecta membra* of our collections demand. The joining of disparate objects stands to be accelerated by the Web and its successor's successor. The hardest part of the next phase of collaboration among museums is how to assure a financial return for licensing access to images and text purveyed by those institutions, a step that will move museums from being fledgling players in the world of intellectual currency to more significant ones. Museums are, after all, a field in which the work of the solitary scholar or the networked community of scholars has enormous potential visibility. There scholars may reap rewards from the presentation of their research results that can enhance their reputations among those in fields beyond their own, let alone in the public at large. A globally networked effort involving thousands of graduate students and scholars in museums and universities can accelerate the Herculean labors of the hundreds of scholars who have heretofore set the table at which learners dine.

The post-structuralist fashions of literary criticism long ago permeated the discipline of art history and even its older sibling, archaeology. Dressed up with exotic vocabularies, they often constitute a rejection of the primacy of the artist as a human agent with free will. Each variant will likely take its place among other theoretical seductions that seek to subsume the fertile creative act into a tidy biological, political, social, or semiotic schema. To ensure the survival of connoisseurship as a skill essential to the museum trade, the criteria that underpin it need to be made explicit and learnable. Only then can a new generation of scholars, more self-assured about methods of attribution and iconographical precedent, be encouraged to venture outside the comfortably unprovable purview of theory and into the risky enterprise of exposing a hypothesis to collective on-line scrutiny—with the intention of assigning a painting or intended allusion to an artist, a decorative element to a building, a bone to a dinosaur, or indeed making any other association.

VIEWING THE ORIGINAL IN THE MUSEUM:
TECHNOLOGICAL ENHANCEMENTS AND INTRUSIONS

Long before Warhol found rich irony in subverting the concept of the unique gesture through reproduction, art historians wrestled with the implications of replication for historical art. Ernst Gombrich, former director and professor of the History of the Classical Tradition at the Warburg Institute, University of London, speaks of the "beholder's share in the reading of the artist's image."[2] He also writes, now anachronistically: "One may admit that the creation of indistinguishable duplicates is of greater interest to the forgers of banknotes than to artists. . . ."[3]

A succession of nineteenth-century writers had a love affair with photographic reproduction. In 1860, referring to the twenty-year-old invention of photography, *Scientific American* made a bold claim about the potential simulacrum of experience to be obtained through this new medium: "With a pile of pictures by their side, which cost almost nothing, [even the humblest Americans] can make the European tour of celebrated places, and not leave the warm precincts of their own firesides."[4]

The critic Murat Halstead, writing in 1894, concurred, describing the "extension of picture galleries" as surpassing "all of the treasures of art in Rome and Florence and Paris and Dresden, and the feast is spread by the sitting-room window or under the fireside lamp."[5] Referring that same year to a series of photographs of the Chicago World's Fair, James William Buel described the portfolio accompanying the Columbian Exposition as follows:

> In some respects, this splendid portfolio is better and more to be desired than an actual visit to the Exposition, for through the magic agency of photography the scenes are transferred in marvelous beauty and permanent form to the printed pages, while the accompanying historical descriptions make plain and clear myriads of intricate and wonderful things, many of which were not comprehended by those who saw them.[6]

Against the backdrop of how the experience of objects has been framed by critics, technocrats, scholars, and museum professionals, we now turn to the visitor, who for all intents and purposes is detached from the aforementioned Swiftian battles among Marxists, postmodernists, connoisseurs, and wireheads. Museum-goers today are invited by the museums themselves to think of museums the way they think of other destinations intended to cajole and entertain. They have certain expectations of comfort and convenience, and unlike malls and amusement parks, museums often fall below their expectations. Thus the original object, cared for by the same people who subject the visitor to poor directional signage, infinitesimal and inscrutable labels, minimal restroom facilities, a shortage of elevators, inadequate seating, hard stone floors, and overpriced eateries, will suffer guilt by association. It may prove less remarkable than it appeared in the brochure, television program, or Web page, and that is among the first problems that museum administrators face in answering the needs of the visitor. The art historian and critic Donald Kuspit is unflinching on this topic:

> How do we get to see and really experience art? It is certainly not by going to galleries and art museums, in search of a direct relationship with original works. This is confirmatory, after the fact of the art we have known and come to love, a vindication and verification of it—the assurance that it exists, in however attenuated, objective form, i.e., as a specific, one might say terminal, object. To really see and experience art we look for it in its mass media image.[7]

The narrowing of the gap between expectation and reward in front of the object should be a primary quest of the museum professional. The temptation to animate the motionless object in a museum display for the general public is not new. It dates at least as far back as the Capitoline Museums, which were founded in 1471 but extensively renovated in the nineteenth century. Numerous classical statues there and in the Vatican Museums to this day have brass spindles that allow the visitor to turn the work on a cylindrical pedestal so as to see it in the best possible light. Few visitors today would think to avail themselves of this mechanism, but it was originally of use to art students who sketched the masterpieces of antiquity. Today's visitors are more often led in forced march through sequences of galleries, with their eyes fixed not on the vanishing point of Ghibertian perspective but on the colored umbrella held aloft by their tour guide.

The visitor's increasing separation from the object has reached new proportions, to be sure. Larger numbers of museums are now shielding their most prized oil and panel paintings from the potential of accidental damage or vandalism with tempered glass. Railings are now the rule in major traveling exhibitions and often in permanent galleries as well. Light levels have been dimmed down at the behest of conservators who see incremental damage in exposure to ultraviolet radiation. Alert guards will usually caution the visitor who approaches a work too closely. Motion detectors sometimes emit piercing sounds when a gesture strays into an invisible beam. Visitors to major exhibitions are the beneficiaries of invisible tactics to move them through expeditiously, by avoiding long labels or handouts that might cause them to linger, the elimination of culs-de-sacs to assure free-flowing traffic, the careful orchestration of stops on recorded tours to impel them onwards, and the design technique of making the next gallery even more appealing than the one they are in.

All of these precautions are sensible, of course, and no one familiar with the travails of museums that have failed to make use of most or all of them would begrudge the museum administrator. But their cumulative effect is so far from the brass spindles of Italian museums that the uninitiated visitor may question how welcome he or she is. While the museum professional's ready response is that visitors are of course welcome, the messages inherent in the presentation of objects is a different one.

In stark contrast to this increasingly protectionist instinct, attractions like the Las Vegas casino Bellagio are being built as an alternative context for the enjoyment of great art. There the message is far clearer to the potential visitor: this art is being shown because it has value, and that value will not be hidden from you beneath layers of demanding information; if you gamble here you are combining a seductive inner-directed experience with a rewarding voyeuristic one; you can wear what you want; and no one will expect you to be an expert on the paintings. Similarly, the Wonders Exhibition series in the American South has for the last several years promised blockbuster exhibitions packaged and sold as all-inclusive experiences in convention centers, with only the best art at fair prices, harnessed to recognizable figures in history (Ramses, Catherine the Great), bearing superficial resemblance to museum exhibitions but without their modest shops, arcane interpretive strategies, and intimidating ambience.

Concomitant with the visitor's increasing isolation from the original in the museum is a tendency to provide a place of honor for the replica. Not since the era of the plaster-cast-filled Metropolitan Museum of Art of the 1870s have replicas—albeit electronic ones—had such visibility in American museums. The problem that next presents itself occurs when museums seek to produce compelling virtual experiences as opposed to mere representations of objects. The cultural historian Walter Benjamin's simple formulation of the perils of reproduction is obsolete; the persuasive, trompe l'oeil simulation of objects or contexts in which objects are placed can now indeed become a substitute for the encounter with the original. We might single out two kinds of simulacra: the imitation of a dinosaur in a natural history museum and the visitor's immersion in a sensory environment that renders the original object inert by contrast.

The actual-scale reconstructed dinosaur is an example of the challenges that museums are setting themselves up for as they seek to respond to the dizzying growth of the entertainment industry. By changing observation from a contingent experience—one requiring that there be authentic bones admixed with plaster or plastic skeletons—to being an autonomous experience—one in which the simulation of an authentic context is seen as sufficient—museums are on a collision course with the monolithic entertainment industry. That industry has no shortage of marketing money, operating income, indifference to accuracy for its own sake, or appetite for competition. The technologies that enable large-scale reproductions of long-extinct creatures are no less valuable to Hollywood filmmakers and theme-park executives—now one and the same—than they are to research scientists seeking to assemble puzzles of biology. A critical difference between the museum and the theme park is that the young consumer choosing between them knows where the better toys, faster food, state-of-the-art interactive games, and comforting amenities are. And the endgame for museums that have been forced to provide not only simulations of settings in natural history but settings akin to theme parks is not likely to be a happy one.

Younger visitors may become as impatient with the unmediated encounter as they are with an inadequately responsive interactive tool. In their disdain for those who would separate new media from old media, they warm to various enhancements to the museum experience. These might include physical contact with objects to see just how hard marble is, or whether a section of redwood is cool to the touch, at least as much as they expect a multimedia explanation of how objects may be situated in their culture or context. For the Nintendo generation, the immersive simulation of a real context—one in which dinosaurs roam or painted triptychs are situated in seicento chapels—is an autonomous experience, equally satisfying in a museum orientation gallery or a child's toy-packed room.

The situation need not be as bleak as we might fear. Just as slides, postcards, and posters of famous works of art have encouraged generations of college students and members of the public to visit art museums, the promulgation of digital images and information about works of art should encourage future audiences to visit art museums. No less importantly, the growing surfeit of "virtual" experiences in daily life is likely to result in a growing appetite for the authentic, and especially for encounters with those priceless touchstones of human creativity that cannot be adequately experienced in a virtual medium, provided that museums do not accede to the impulse to satisfy the lowest common denominator.

Of course, the commercial destinations offering only merchandise or experiences that are replicable at home through digital technology are finding themselves reinvented through the Internet. Whereas many of today's generic destinations— the shopping mall, movie theater, and even library—may be challenged by the efficiencies of networked commerce, entertainment options, and communications, the hunger for social interaction in the attractive, safe, and unique settings provided by museums may well grow as a result of these efficiencies. Museums should be working now to make the museum visit the easiest and most attractive option possible, through networked collaboration, the use of webcasting, the availability of up-to-date information on activities in museums, and the provision of services including on-line ticketing, reservations, and interactivity, in preparation for and in the aftermath of a visit.

The impact of new media is already ubiquitous and barely discernible, like tiny meteoric depressions on the surface of the moon. It can be examined in isolation, but the visitor's experience is no longer one of different kinds of encounters ranging from seeing a slide in a classroom to browsing a catalog in the shop to glancing at an image in a brochure to planting him or herself in front of the original. In a digital environment, what were discrete encounters are no longer isolated from each other, and can be simultaneous with, prefatory to, or subsequent to the experience of an object at a laptop or desktop anywhere, any time. Because of the surfeit of communications sources everyone endures today, we now occasionally forget whether we learned something from a newspaper, book, memo, fax, voice mail, e-mail, Web page, or even conversation, and in a larger sense, as long as the information is retrievable, the conduit is decreasingly significant. The growing transparency of information technology will lead to its ultimate invisibility, and the conduit will be completely irrelevant. That is a laudable goal if one is hoping to encourage an encounter not with information about the original but with the aura of the original, seamlessly mediated by authoritative and rewarding information. But the younger visitor may lack interest in the aura, because an aura doesn't move, play music, or interact.

Those concerned about the potential demise of books are disconsolate about the resulting discounting of sources. Some of us may take the long view, according to which the oral tradition—here transmogrified into the innovation of voice-recognition technology—is the venerable one, and according to which books have for several centuries proved welcome but not indispensable. The cultic creation of lavish temples to books in the form of marble libraries, beginning with that in Alexandria, began when the amount of information worth exchanging exceeded the capacities of human memory. Now that human memory is under fire from the potential of networked information, the pre-Alexandrian model of information exchange seems somehow more civilized than adapting to reserve lists, the absence of books from shelves, the heroic but time-consuming analog search for kernels of ideas, and the inconvenience of closing hours.

The ease of encountering didactic information about the object in a networked world is at the crux of our inquiry. The less motivated potential museum-goer—anyone in the majority of people—might find him or herself seduced into visiting a museum on the strength of a chance encounter with an image and associated information, and that is the hope of all museum professionals engaged with new media. Repeat visitors or museum members, on the other hand, may resort to networked information as a way of deepening their understanding of the works they plan to see or have seen, and this is a variant of the kind of experience had by a researcher. The converted, as we might call them, delight in making new associations, expanding their understanding of something about which they already have at least rudimentary knowledge. And they are more likely to see new media interpretations as an enhancement of rather than a substitution for the authentic object.

That, at least, is the hope of the museum administrator. The concomitant concern is that the potential visitor may elect not to make the pilgrimage described above, because of anecdotes from disgruntled peers who made the effort, a sense of intimidation at the perceived sanctity of the surroundings, or a genuine, heartfelt lack of interest. The last cause of nonattendance is the most difficult one for museum administrators to accept. As members of the body of the converted, we cannot imagine why someone would not want to project him or herself into another time and place, or experience the delight of being in the presence of a very precious, beautiful, or rare thing from the past or the present. But lack of interest on the part of nonvisitors

DÆDALUS invites you to

escape the labyrinth . . .

Subscription Order/ Gift Order Form

☐ Please enter my subscription to *DÆDALUS*:

☐ Please send *DÆDALUS* as my gift, preceded by a gift announcement in my name:

	One Year	Two Years	Three Years
☐ Individual	☐ $33.00	☐ $60.50	☐ $82.50
☐ Institution	☐ $49.50	☐ $82.50	☐ $110.00

(U.S. dollars only. Canadian rates: $42, 1 year individual; $60, 1 year institution. All other foreign subscribers add $7 per year to the price of U.S. subscriptions. All orders must be prepaid.)

_____   _____
MY NAME   *GIFT TO*

_____   _____
ADDRESS   *ADDRESS*

_____   _____
CITY/STATE/ZIP/COUNTRY   *CITY/STATE/ZIP/COUNTRY*

☐ *My check is enclosed*
☐ *Charge to:*   ☐ *VISA*   ☐ *MasterCard*

Card No. ——————————   *Expiration Date* ——————

Signature ————————————————————————
Please fold and seal this card to ensure your privacy.   **SU99**

is a legitimate sentiment, like lack of interest on the part of an academic attending a monster-truck competition.

The experience of standing reverentially before the object is the primary construct in museological value systems that the staff seeks to protect in art museums. The passion with which we defend this construct is directly proportional to our belief that this experience actually occurs on a regular basis. We labor intensively to strike the perfect balance between labels brief enough not to detract from the experience of the object and long enough to provide the intelligent but potentially uninformed visitor with a metaphorical spindle with which to turn the object into something apprehensible. But we would do well to acknowledge that most museum administrators who toil to preserve the encounter with the original would never think of attending a major exhibition when open to the public if they can find a way around it. Having sat for an extended period on a bench in a museum in Los Angeles, weary from the demands of my two-year old and of the day, I was witness to what we all know in our hearts: that the reverential encounter is such a rare event as to border on a miracle. The vast majority of our visitors are pleased to be in the museum, relieved that the amenities are available even if below par, and may happen upon some combined experience of looking and reading that connects with a higher order of understanding—but we cannot count on it. The most the visitor obtains on a regular basis is the confirmation and elucidation of a fact that they were already privy to, or the discovery of something that is novel but not intrinsically connected to any other facts of consequence to them.

Although we of course maintain that the design of museum settings has a palpable effect on the experience of objects displayed therein and spend vast amounts of money and energy planning these settings, the results are no more predictable than those of an acoustician testing a music hall. The visual cues and notes may ring false in the finished product, and no end of baffles and muffling tactics may disguise the failed effort. The neutrality of the white wall is, for example, among the fictions in the story that museum professionals tell themselves.[8] The white wall is, of course, another interlocutor, masquerading as

an unobtrusive feature of the museum experience. The artist
and scholar Brian O'Doherty speaks of the evolution of the
white wall as "a sort of strip-tease, in which art in the white cell
became more and more naked, while the wall became richer in
meaning."[9] Museums showing contemporary art tend to favor
white walls, not only because they are part of a Bauhaus-
inspired modernist tradition, but because commercial galleries,
where new art incubates, are slavishly committed to white
walls and unfinished floors. The use of color on walls is seen as
what separates the historical from the contemporary.

Multimedia kiosks were the first digital devices implanted in
museums and continue to be installed. Those that are connected
to the Internet are the newest variety, but the tried-and-true
models of the late 1980s allow the visitor to retrieve information about collections in an environment reminiscent of a language lab. "Microgalleries," to use the term promulgated by
American Express when subsidizing these high-tech reading
rooms in London, Washington, Ottawa, and elsewhere, welcome the visitor into a world apart from art and culture, which
might just as well be in a classroom or library. Studies undertaken by London's National Gallery suggest that visitors using
the Microgallery spend more time in the art galleries rather
than substituting time in front of screens for time in front of art.
Other museums, like the Carlos Museum in Atlanta and the
Minneapolis Institute of Arts, have taken the step of placing
kiosks right in the gallery, allowing the visitor to glance up
from workstation to pedestal without missing a beat.

Museums are today experimenting with digital audio players—a more literal interlocutor. These devices allow the visitor
to tour a collection making random selections of desired information, and thereby level the playing field for the intelligent but
uninformed observer. While they tend to be popular in conjunction with traveling exhibitions, sometimes reaching 30 percent
of ticket-buyers, they rarely reach more than 4–5 percent of
visitors viewing a permanent collection. This compares even
less favorably with another sobering statistic: that only 5–8
percent of visitors to special exhibitions at American art museums buy catalogs. Although it is hard to speak of digital audio
yet having a major impact on visitors to permanent collections,

most museum administrators are completely devoted to providing such systems to that small percentage of visitors that finds them useful. As museums experiment with universal distribution of such players attached to the ticket cost, and as Nintendo users grow up, the percentage may grow.

The next chapter being explored as of this writing is the portable tablet allowing the visitor to recall not only sound but also text and images. While the notion is heretical to some in that it risks taking more time away from looking at objects, others hazard the guess that with more information at hand than a label, the visitor is likely to spend more time gazing at the object in question. Since the device is only in its earliest stages of development, it is too soon to predict its impact. But it is safe to imagine that it might change the experience of visiting museums in the near future, and that this mention will be seen as a delightfully anachronistic reference like the observation that the Model T might have some impact on American society beyond providing an alternative to the horse.

The ways in which such innovations have changed or will materially change museum practice are difficult to measure. Each model has a traditional equivalent—the reading room or the docent—and in that sense, they have perhaps enhanced the opportunities for the visitor to retrieve information that might otherwise have eluded him or her. But whether they have altered the basic quality of the experience for the visitor is open to question. Only the curmudgeon decries these as intrusions into the art museum—and that curmudgeon is likely to delude him or herself into believing that he or she is adequately informed about every work on display and in storage.

Three-dimensional imaging is another innovation that holds promise in multimedia explanations of the context of the object. The projection of images in free space, which is now being used in the promotion of merchandise and for training the defensive forces of the United States, has potential in the visual arts and in museum orientation as well. The hologram has been surpassed now that the laser-projected object is liberated from the vacuum tube and can be seen as if in front of the viewer. Artists who are being commissioned to explore the potential of this technology will doubtless produce startling and rewarding results, and the concept of a floating docent will doubtless be explored by the more adventurous science museums.

It is essential to take the temperature of those experiencing museum-based technology on a continuing basis. Walter Benjamin famously prophesied where we were heading:

> Even the most perfect reproduction of a work of art is lacking in one element: its presence in time and space, its unique existence at the place where it happens to be. . . . The presence of the original is the prerequisite to the concept of authenticity. . . . The authenticity of a thing is the essence of all that is transmissible from its beginning, ranging from its substantive duration to its testimony to the history which it has experienced. Since the historical testimony rests on the authenticity, the former, too, is jeopardized by reproduction when substantive duration ceases to matter. And what is really jeopardized when the historical testimony is affected is the authority of the object. . . . [10]

He was right to speculate that the authority of the object would be jeopardized but failed to predict that many contemporary artists, like their Dadaist predecessors, would revel in that jeopardy, which leaves his definition of art somewhat exposed. He also opined that "that which withers in the age of mechanical reproduction is the aura of the work of art. . . ."[11] Here we have yet to see much evidence. The assessment of the extent to which a work of art has an aura—through an aurometer, as it were—is a difficult task at best. The construct of an aura is under continuing fire from postmodern sophisticates, who find risible the proposition that a work of art has some overarching power independent of the biases of the observer. The rest of us, who would prefer to inhabit a world in which certain works of art are precious, others derivative, and yet others completely undeserving of our attention, may yet prevail, as a new generation of art-history students demand a renewed connection to objects.

Even after countless millions of reproductions of the *Mona Lisa,* there is an undiminished appetite to be in its presence. Whether this is a function of its being seen in reproductions or the power of the aura of the original, however, is unclear. For the visitor who is offered the choice of braving the crowds or flipping on the monitor, the museum's impulse toward "edutainment" may unintentionally make the choice easier—and not in ways that the museum would celebrate. Thus, somehow museums must find a way to inspire or rekindle the potential visitor's belief in the power of authenticity. If museums find themselves seduced by the infinitely variable and ever-changing realm of electronic simulation, they risk draining the original object of its power. If they fail to exploit the potential of electronic simulation, they just as surely risk losing audiences drawn to the virtual experiences on screens and in theme parks. The only way out for museums is to pursue their original educational mission with determination while attempting to ride the rapids of multimedia innovation, staying as close as possible to the shoreline of their mission.

In 1923, Nikolai Tarabukin, flush with Bolshevik victory, adopted a critical view of museum interpreters at the moment that Paul Sachs was training Harvard's chosen few to carry out the fullest potential of curating:

> Museum workers are confronted with the task of sorting this material which was visionary in its time into an historical order and to bury it "beneath numbers" on inventory lists as dry as the "artistic storehouses." And for the art historians, those inexhaustible, dry as dust archaeologists, there awaits a new work in the writing of explanatory texts for this sepulchral crypt so that the descendant, if only he doesn't forget the way to them, can worthily evaluate the past and not confuse the landmarks of "historical perspectives."[12]

Tarabukin's zeal to prevent formulaic research and interpretation from stifling the power and joy of the original object is little different from that of museum educators who toil in the shadow of their more visible colleagues in curatorial departments. In the tradition of John Dewey, they are always at pains to avoid the imaginative sclerosis that attends fact recited for its own sake, connections of interest to the learned but not the many, and obscurantist vocabulary. Collections management vendors are now struggling to keep up with an ever-more sophisticated and demanding museum-based clientele, for whom Tarabukin's admonition is both legitimate and still fresh. As more museum staff become involved in creating collection-related information, the tyranny of bean- or bug-counting is giving way to a still structured but more broad-based obligation to authoritative documentation. And that documentation is no longer available only to the registrar and occasional researcher, but increasingly to anyone with a modem. The consequent reshuffling of responsibilities will have registrars continue to care for the original objects while a team of experts—from curators to educators—will take on the preparation of collection-related content for broad public consultation.

Larger issues loom in the inquiry about how replication is affecting the museum experience. The critic Markus Brüderlin notes that in relation to the artist Sherrie Levine's works reproducing works by other artists:

> While . . . [the] strategy of "open piracy" [Don Cameron] was mainly regarded as subversive criticism of art-market mechanisms in the eighties, its effects are open to interpretation in broader terms today. As the reproductions "suctioned" from circulation in the media are placed in a museum context they find rest. This process of recycling turns out to be a loop leading to a potential encounter with the original. The duplicated artwork leaves the endless chain of simulacra and enters the circulation of a new recycling culture in which the burning issue is not only the recreation of the aura, but also the collective commitment of communication. . . . Hans-Peter Feldmann's "double and triple copies" and Sherrie Levine's recycling strategy lend themselves well to illustrate a closer look at the two main aspects of criticism about Benjamin's aura theory. One aspect is that the original does not lose its aura by reproduction, but multiplies it, with La Gioconda and its "déjà-vu" aura being a case in point. Some artworks have actually become unique through photographic reproduction and duplication. The second, more significant point of criticism tries to prove that the aura disappears in the copied and mass-distributed original, but is by no means lost because it re-appears in the reproduction. As pointed out above, this is especially the case when the original vanishes behind its multiplied versions. Adorno may have had this in mind when he criticized Benjamin in terms of a negative dialectic: "Every work designated for many is already a reproduction in terms of its idea."[13]

Artists using the Web are of course changing not only what art refers to and how it is experienced but how it is collected and distributed as well. This area of art-making can put the museum to the side and reach the observer directly, with the only intermediary being an Internet browser. While the market for such work has yet to be defined, it clearly constitutes a challenge to both the art dealer and the curator, and if artists in this medium find a way to achieve acclaim and a market, we will have to rethink a great deal in the role of the art museum. Already museums have begun to move from just linking to Web art to commissioning and purchasing it, and the next two frontiers are to understand how the artist and museum negotiate the intellectual property implications of acquiring Web art and how increased bandwidth will affect the work of Web artists.

INTRANETS AND OPEN MUSEUM MANAGEMENT

The for-profit world has been swift to explore the full benefit of networked communication to the corporate environment. File-sharing and electronic mail have improved the productivity of the "road warriors" who stake out customers, connect with the home office several times a day, and are never out of touch with the basic information that keeps them competitive, on the road or back at their desks. Museums, by contrast, have predictably invested enormous resources in the microcomputing environment—the power of individual desktops—and the Internet-based environment: how museums connect with their (potential) audiences on-line. Thus, each staff member with a computer on his or her desk is likely to have a state-of-the-art software environment with a unique filing system on the hard drive, and the department responsible for managing the web site is likely to have reasonable support for its efforts. The missing step has been connecting museum staff members with each other to maximize the free flow of information and break down communication barriers among departments. But that should not surprise us. The museum culture is one of spirited competition, not only among curators, but also among departments competing for limited resources with little perceived reward for collaboration. While the corporate environment mandates streamlined planning and cross-departmental information retrieval, the museum environment leaves ample room for fiefdoms and favorites, a system that rewards individual entrepreneurship over teamwork.

Those museums that have been able to harness the potential of an Intranet-like environment have begun to see a shift in management style. Memoranda that were formerly sent to a select few are now available for browsing in a fileshare environment. Electronic mail that was formerly the preserve of "key" staff is now an indispensable tool for regular museum-wide communication. Standing and ad hoc meetings are more often prepared in advance or substituted with emailed updates and action steps. And access to the World Wide Web, which was in 1994 painted as a potentially devastating drain on productivity, has begun to be seen as a valuable resource that can connect staff with information not otherwise available, leading to a less isolated institutional culture. As a consequence, the staff at large now see an open information structure as an entitlement, not a privilege, and the hierarchical communication environment of un-wired museums is seen by staff already steeped in a networked culture as quaint at best and needlessly autocratic at worst.

The effect of this management change can be salutary for the public—once accustomed to the freer exchange of information within museum walls, staff members are likely to see less harm in making information more widely available outside. The pressure to make individual staff members and departments accessible to the public through e-mail is changing the traditional communications paradigm of the telephone operator as the museum's most accessible employee, with the remainder of the staff (apart from the guards—the second most accessible employees) cloistered in their offices. The results will of course provoke demands for more support staff to answer queries, while administrators will struggle to find less costly solutions. Among these are the provision of answers to frequently asked questions on the museum's web site and electronic newsletters aggregating and answering inquiries.

Other than cost, the primary obstacle to the widespread implementation of Intranets in the museum environment is the belief by administrators that information is best carefully controlled through a prescribed hierarchy. While that may be true in various cases, including official publications and donor and budget details, as well as agreements in a state of delicate negotiation, like certain exhibitions, the vast majority of busy work in our museums is not sufficiently salacious to command the interest of hackers, even those on staff. And even hackers are not so difficult to track down in such a finite group of end users—easier, perhaps, than identifying those who abuse the privilege of the photocopier. Furthermore, if museum staff rejoice in publicly undermining the institution by means of computer networks, the problem may not lie with technology but with management.

COLLECTIONS MANAGEMENT:
FROM THE CARD CATALOG TO THE WEB

The most impenetrable preserve of every museum has for many years been not the vaults, the storerooms, or the loading dock, but the registrar's office. There, long before the advent of automation in the 1970s, those records detailing the provenance, publication history, conservation treatments, and other essential information about the collection have been carefully guarded by the staff entrusted with their accuracy. The near-fetishistic care accorded these files was altogether appropriate before they became electronically replicated as well as available in a printed version. But since the invention of the microprocessor and the provision of easily accessible versions of authoritative data, the culture of the registrar's office has not always changed with the technology. If anything, the easy replication of collections data has created an understandable fortress mentality among some members of the profession.

In 1996 the Association of Art Museum Directors launched the Art Museum Image Consortium (www.AMICO.org), which has changed the dynamic of collections management in almost thirty of the leading art museums in the United States. Each museum formerly pursued its own approach to collections management and even tolerated proprietary solutions among curatorial departments. The premise of AMICO is that a central database of collection information culled from dozens of museums would allow for numerous improvements. These include enhanced educational opportunities by means of the Internet, greater record-keeping efficiency through the adoption of standard descriptive vocabularies, the possibility of shared income from a single licensed resource, and a diminished risk of obsolescent solutions.

The initial skepticism about sharing collection information was overcome by the logic of collaboration behind AMICO. Because museums have spent their history protecting their collections and information about them, the sea change implied by networked technology is just beginning to have an impact on their policies and procedures. The inter-institutional merging of information has changed museum culture forever. What was formerly the near-private preserve of the registrar is fast becoming the most widely available information furnished by a museum. This portends the beginning of several changes in how museums manage themselves and consider cooperating.

While the for-profit world organizes itself along clearly demarcated lines, staking out areas for competition (market share) and collaboration (lobbying), the museum community is new to the potential of thinking outside of its walls for any purposes other than mounting traveling exhibitions and comparing professional practices. Networked information will doubtless stimulate both more competition and more collaboration, in ways that can only be imagined today. The potential is likely to alter the landscape considerably. Just as the broadcast rights accorded network television prompted sports teams to find new opportunities in leagues and franchises, it is possible that museums will find themselves entering into new relationships in the coming years through the power of the Internet. These will be based not only on shared collection information but on many other aspects of the museum's mission as well, including educational outreach, publishing, marketing, and merchandising.

PROGRAMMING THE CONTENT FOR THE
COMPUTER-TURNED-TELEVISION

The prevailing ways in which museums will connect with audiences over phone lines and airwaves in the future have yet to be determined. It is pointless to speculate about how computer and television manufacturers will work together to assure that the average American household has some form of screen delivering a high-end interactive multimedia experience. The outcome is preordained. It is increasingly clear that the biggest challenge ahead in distance learning is not how telecom companies will achieve adequate and cost-effective bandwidth to deliver multimedia to the home, but how the quality of the content can be assured. Museums are beginning to grapple with the possibility of reaching audiences beyond their walls but have yet to organize themselves to achieve the best possible results. This is clearly another area in which collaboration among institutions holds great promise. Their natural inclination to proceed autonomously makes less sense in this field of endeavor than in almost any other.

Among the possibilities in collaboration ahead is the development of curriculum-based learning modules applicable state by state and school district by school district. If museums have a chance to defend themselves against the onslaught of commercial edutainment, it is through a concerted effort to work in tandem with teachers. The plethora of resources available to fuel education in an affluent America is unprecedented, but the native suspicion of teachers and school administrators about the for-profit sector, whether because of Chris Whittle's early Channel One experiment or Disney's likely forays into edutainment, is slowly being eroded. Nonprofits are standing by the wayside developing individual efforts, web site by web site, instead of working together to compete with the market-savvy solutions of entertainment conglomerates. Consortia of like institutions, such as history, science, art, and natural history museums, should recognize their potential as allies instead of squandering resources on vanity projects that have no promise of longevity or broad application.

Museum directors thus have another role demanded of them: that of television producer. The many-to-many communication model of the Web promises exciting rewards in reaching audiences that have hitherto seen museums as obscure or intimidating fortresses. Through astute video programming on networked web sites, museums need no longer accede to being passed over because of the relentless onslaught of powerful commercial interests that have directed the audiovisual stimulation of the mass audience. With networked digital technology available through the set-top box, it will be a battle of wits to get our multiple messages across as well as to cajole audiences to communicate with each other through our museums by means of wireless keyboards and, soon enough, voice-recognition systems—which will require the advent not only of a sequel to this monograph, but of a new kind of museum.

E-COMMERCE: RESHAPING THE BUSINESS MODEL

The blurring of boundaries between the for-profit and nonprofit worlds will accelerate with the spread of electronic commerce. Museums are slowly coming to appreciate the ways in which on-line ticketing, merchandising, and the licensing of intellectual property might produce income that can help bolster their ability to serve the public. The results are going to transform museums' ways of connecting with their current audiences and open the possibility of connecting with new ones.

The American Association of Museums documents museum attendance in periodic surveys and routinely turns up the statistic that more people visit American museums than attend sporting events. This arresting fact is always surprising to those not in the museum community, and is taken for granted but not exploited by those in the community. The largest industry in the world is tourism, and among the largest tourist attractions in major markets are museums, but unless and until these museums harness their collective potential, the statistic will continue to be contested by the uninformed and only mentioned in passing by those in the field. The opportunities presented by electronic commerce are potentially powerful and should allow museums to assume greater control of their destiny. That control can be exercised by the extension of existing models of income generation on-line, and the development of new models of revenue creation for an on-line audience.

Existing models include the provision of access to museum shop inventory, whether through the museum's own web site, that of a commercial provider, or that of a consortium. The museum's own web site may attract tens of thousands of user sessions (as opposed to hundreds of thousands of hits) annually. Even if a healthy percentage of end users elected to make purchases from the site, such as 5 percent, which would be a remarkable return on investment, the sales volume would not be enough to do more than provide incremental growth for the existing yearly sales average. If the museum resorts to a commercial provider, the skimming of income can erase whatever advantage the museum might otherwise realize from having its content more easily retrievable from a single known address rather than its institutional one. A consortium of museums, even one arranged in partnership with the for-profit sector on an equitable basis, is a surer strategy, since it puts the museums in the position of strength and control. Such enterprising efforts as exCALENDAR, an on-line exhibition calendar built on the Art Museum Network (www.excalendar.net), are developing as museums come to recognize the exploding market share of on-line commerce. There is also the discouraging fact that the millions of consumers on-line are no more likely to visit the museum's web site in the future than they are to pick up the phone today and find out what is potentially engaging about it.

CONCLUSION

The impact of the computer chip and networked databases is radically reshaping the on-site museum experience as well as providing remote access to information and commodities and inviting participation in the museum's mission. The museum community is slowly awakening to the potential of networked information, in merchandising, ticketing, and licensing content. It must pick up the pace, not only in order to prevent obsolescent experiments, but also to stave off commercial alternatives masquerading as educational ones. The only viable course is for like institutions in the museum community to come together and examine how these new tools can be used to collaborate. Spirited competition among web sites is a myopic approach to combating the tidal wave of commercial interests that are channeling their energies into the so-called leisure industry. Museums are places of leisure for the public, but behind the gallery walls they are an amalgam of research institutes, scientific laboratories, storage facilities, educational facilities, community centers, and small businesses providing dining and merchandising alternatives. The sooner they harness their collective potential through new technologies, the better equipped they will be to serve their educational mandates while navigating through a world of diminishing attention span and free time. Let us hope that a considered examination of the impact of technology on museums in a decade is not a tale of splintered pilot projects but one of intrepid and collective self-preservation.

BIBLIOGRAPHY

Adorno, Theodor W. *Aesthetic Theory.* Trans. C. Lenhardt. Ed. Gretel Adorno and Rolf Tiedemann. London and Boston: International Library of Phenomenology and Moral Sciences, 1984.

Art and Technology. Guest edited by Johan Pijnappel. London: Academy Editions, 1994.

Aura: die Realitat des Kunstwerks zwischen Autonomie, Reproduktion, und Kontext (the reality of the artwork between autonomy, reproduction, and context). Ed. Allan McCollum et al. Wien: Wiener Secession, 1994.

Benthall, Jonathan. *Science and Technology in Art Today.* New York: Praeger, 1972.

Bijvoet, Marga. *Art as Inquiry: Toward New Collaborations Between Art, Science, and Technology.* New York: Peter Lang, 1997.

Bredekamp, Horst. *The Lure of Antiquity and the Cult of the Machine: The Kunstkammer and the Evolution of Nature, Art, and Technology* (*Antikensehnsucht und Maschinenglauben*). Translation from German by Allison Brown. Princeton: M. Wiener Publishers, 1995.

Brüderlin, Markus. "The Rise of the Aura." Excerpted from Brian O'Doherty, "Inside the White Cube: Notes to the Gallery Space" [Part 3]. *Context as Content,* in *Artforum.* New York: November 1976. In Allan McCollum et al., *Aura: die Realitat des Kunstwerks zwischen Autonomie, Reproduktion, und Kontext.* Trans. Elisabeth Grossebner and Camilla Nielsen. Wien: Wiener Secession, 1994.

Brunette, Peter and Wills, David. *Deconstruction and the Visual Arts: Art, Media, Architecture.* Cambridge: Cambridge University Press; Cambridge Studies in New Art History and Criticism, 1994.

Danto, Arthur. "The Artworld." *Journal of Philosophy* (1964): 571–584.

Davis, Douglas. *Art and the Future: A History-Prophecy of the Collaboration Between Science, Technology, and Art.* New York: Praeger, 1973.

Druckrey, Timothy, ed. *Iterations: The New Image*. New York: International Center of Photography, 1993.

Fopp, Michael A. "The Implications of Emerging Technologies for Museums and Galleries." *Museum Management and Curatorship* 16 (2) (1997): 143–153.

Franke, Herbert W. *Wege zur Computerkunst*. Wien: Edition die Donau hinunter, 1995.

Freedberg, David. *The Power of Images: Studies in the History of Theory and Response*. Chicago: University of Chicago Press, 1989.

Gablik, Suzi. *The Reenchantment of Art*. New York: Thames and Hudson, 1991.

Gombrich, E. H. *Art and Illusion: A Study in the Psychology of Pictorial Representation*. Princeton: Princeton University Press, 1972.

Goodman, Cynthia. *Digital Visions: Computers and Art*. New York: H. N. Abrams; Syracuse: Everson Museum of Art, 1987.

Grana, César. *Meaning and Authenticity: Further Essays on the Sociology of Art*. New Brunswick: Transaction Publishers, 1989.

Graubard, Stephen R., ed. *Art and Science*. Lanham, Md.: University Press of America, 1986. Originally appeared as *Dædalus* 115 (3) (Summer 1986).

Graubard, Stephen R., ed. *The Artificial Intelligence Debate: False Starts, Real Foundations*. Cambridge: MIT Press, 1988. Originally appeared as *Dædalus* 117 (1) (Winter 1988).

Grieder, Terence. *Artist and Audience*. 2d ed. London: Brown & Benchmark, 1996.

Haapala, Arto, Jerrold Levinson, and Veikko Rantala. *The End of Art and Beyond: Essays after Danto*. New Jersey: Humanities Press, 1997.

Heidegger, Martin. *Der Ursprung des Kunstwerks*. Stuttgart: Reclam, 1935.

Josephson, Susan G. *From Idolatry to Advertising: Visual Art and Contemporary Culture*. 1st ed. Armonk, N.Y.: M.E. Sharpe, 1996.

Kemp, Martin. "Perspective and Meaning: Illusion, Allusion and Collusion." In *Philosophy and the Visual Arts: Seeing and Abstracting*, ed. Andrew Harrison. Dordrecht: Reidel Pub. Co., 1987.

Kuspit, Donald. *The Critic is Artist: The Intentionality of Art*. Ann Arbor: UMI Research Press, 1984.

Lippmann, Walter. *Public Opinion*. 1922 reprint. New York: Free Press, 1965.

Mumford, Lewis. "Culture and Machine Art." In *Annual of American Design 1931*, ed. R. L. Leonard and C. A. Glassgold. New York: Ives Washburn and the American Union of Decorative Arts and Craftsmen, 1930.

O'Doherty, Brian. "Inside the White Cube: Notes to the Gallery Space" [Part 3]. *Context as Content*, in *Artforum*. New York: November 1976.

Orvell, Miles. *The Real Thing: Imitation and Authenticity in American Culture, 1880–1940*. Chapel Hill: University of North Carolina Press, 1989.

O'Toole, Michael. *The Language of Displayed Art*. London: Leicester University Press, 1994.

Stoessel, Marleen. *Aura, das vergessene Menschliche: Zur Sprache und Erfahrung bei Walter Benjamin*. Munich: C. Hanser, 1983.

Tarabukin, Nikolai. "From the Easel to the Machine." Ed. and trans. Christina Loder. From "Ot mol'berta k maschine." Moscow: n.p., 1923. In Francis Frascina and Charles Harrison, eds., *Modern Art and Modernism: A Critical Anthology*. London: Harper & Row, 1982.

Walker, John A. *Art in the Age of Mass Media*. London: Pluto Press, 1983.

Woodfield, Richard. *Gombrich on Art and Psychology*. Manchester: Manchester University Press, 1996.

ENDNOTES

[1] Don Tapscott, *The Net Generation*, aired in 1996 on the national Canadian broadcast of the *Pamela Wallin Live* show on CBC. Don Tapscott, *Growing Up Digital: The Rise of the Net Generation* (New York: McGraw-Hill, 1988), 39–40.

[2] Gombrich, *Art and Illusion*, 182.

[3] Ibid., 307.

[4] *Scientific American* (2 June 1860).

[5] Murat Halstead, *Camera Mosaics: A Portfolio of National Photography* (New York: H.C. Jones, 1894).

[6] James William Buel, *The Magic City: A Massive Portfolio of Original Photographic Views of the Great World's Fair* (Philadelphia: Historical Publishing Company, 1894).

[7] Kuspit, *The Critic is Artist*, 387.

[8] Wolfgang Meisenheimer, "Die Weisse Wand," *daedalus* (30) (Berlin 1988): 88.

[9] As quoted in Brüderlin, "The Rise of the Aura," 70.

[10] Walter Benjamin, "The Work of Art in the Age of Mechanical Reproduction," trans. Harry Zohn, in Francis Frascina and Charles Harrison, eds., *Modern Art and Modernism: A Critical Anthology* (London: Harper & Row, 1982), 218.

[11] Ibid., 219.

[12] Tarabukin, "From the Easel to the Machine," 141.

[13] Brüderlin, "The Rise of the Aura," 70.

Elaine Heumann Gurian

What is the Object of this Exercise? A Meandering Exploration of the Many Meanings of Objects in Museums

"WHY DID THE SERBS AND CROATS shell each other's historic sites when they had so little ammunition and these were not military targets?" I routinely ask my museum-studies graduate students this question when I lecture. "To break their spirit," is always the instantaneous answer. Museums, historic sites, and other institutions of memory, I would contend, are the tangible evidence of the spirit of a civilized society. And while the proponents of museums have long asserted that museums add to the quality of life, they have not understood (as the graduate students did when confronted by the example of war) how profound and even central that "quality" was.

Similar examples reveal the relationship between museums and "spirit" in sharp detail. Why did the Russians proclaim, one day after the Russian revolution had succeeded, that all historic monuments were to be protected even though they most often represented the hated czar and the church? Why did Hitler and Stalin establish lists of acceptable and unacceptable art and then install shows in museums to proclaim them while sending the formerly acclaimed, now forbidden, art to storage? Why did the Nazis stockpile Jewish material and force interned

Elaine Heumann Gurian is acting director of the Cranbrook Institute of Science in Bloomfield Hills, Michigan.

curators to catalog and accession it, intending to create a museum to the eradicated Jews? Why, when I was in the rural mountains of the Philippines, was I taken to hidden closets that served as museums, curated by tribal members, holding the material of the tribe's immediate past, secreted from the dealers who were offering great sums for the same material?

In adversity it is understood, by antagonists and protagonists alike, that the evidence of history has something central to do with the spirit, will, pride, identity, and civility of people, and that destroying such material may lead to forgetting, broken spirits, and docility. This same understanding is what motivates cultural and ethnic communities to create their own museums in order to tell their stories, in their own way, to themselves and to others.

Yet neither the museum profession nor its sibling workers in the other storehouses of collective memory (archives, libraries, concert halls, and so forth), makes (nor, I would contend, understands) the case clearly about its institution's connectedness to the soul of civic life. In cities under duress you can hear the case being made better by mayors and governors. Dennis Archer, the mayor of Detroit, said recently while being interviewed on the radio, "Detroit, in order to be a great city, needs to protect its great art museum, the Detroit Institute of Art." It was Archer and his predecessor, Coleman Young, who championed and underwrote the latest incarnation of Detroit's Museum of African American History. And it was Teddy Kolik, the fabled former mayor of Jerusalem, who was the chief proponent of the creation of the Israel Museum (and who placed one of his two offices within the building). Mayors know why museums are important. Citizens, implicitly, do too. A recent survey in Detroit asked people to rate the importance of institutions to their city and then tell which they had visited. The Museum of African American History was listed very high on the important list and much lower on the "I have visited" list. People do not have to use the museum in order to assert its importance or feel that their tax dollars are being well spent in its support.

The people who work in museums have collectively struggled over the proper definition and role of their institutions. Their struggle has been, in part, to differentiate museums from other near relatives—the other storehouses of collective memory. The resulting definitions have often centered on things—on objects and their permissible uses. I believe the debate has missed the essential meaning (the soul, if you will) of the institution that is the museum.

OBJECTS ARE NOT THE HEART OF THE MUSEUM

The following discussion will attempt to capture that soul by throwing light on the shifting role of museum objects over time. It will show how elusive objects are, even as they remain the central element embedded within all definitions of museums. This essay will also postulate that the definition of a "museum object" and the associated practices of acquisition, preservation, care, display, study, and interpretation have always been fluid and have become more so recently. Objects did not provide the definitional bedrock in the past, although museum staffs thought they did. I will show that museums may not need them any longer to justify their work.

But if the essence of a museum is not to be found in its objects, then where? I propose that the answer is in being *a place* that stores memories and presents and organizes meaning in some sensory form. It is both the physicality of a place and the memories and stories told therein that are important. Further, I propose that these two essential ingredients—place and remembrances—are not exclusive to museums. And, finally, I contend that the blurring of the distinctions between these institutions of memory and other seemingly separate institutions (like shopping malls and attractions) is a positive, rather than negative, development.

Not meaning to denigrate the immense importance of museum objects and their care, I am postulating that they, like props in a brilliant play, are necessary but alone are not sufficient. This essay points out something that we have always known intuitively: that the larger issues revolve around the stories museums tell and the way they tell them. When parsed carefully, the objects, in their tangibility, provide a variety of stakeholders with an opportunity to debate the meaning and control of their memories. It is the ownership of the story, rather than the object itself, that the dispute has been all about.

This essay suggests what museums are not (or not exactly) and, therefore, continues the dialogue about what museums are and what makes them important, so important that people in extremis fight over them.

WHAT IS AN OBJECT?

"Ah, but we have the real thing," museum professionals used to say when touting the uniqueness of their occupation. When I began in museum work, in the late 1960s and early 1970s, the definition of museums always contained reference to the object as the pivot around which we justified our other activities.[1] Although there were always other parts of the definition, our security nonetheless lay in owning objects. With it came our privileged responsibility for the attendant acquisition, its preservation, safety, display, study, and interpretation. We were like priests and the museums our reliquaries.

The definition of objects was easy. They were the *real* stuff. Words were used like "unique," "authentic," "original," "genuine," "actual." The things that were collected had significance and were within the natural, cultural, or aesthetic history of the known world.

Of course, *real* had more than one meaning. It often meant "one of a kind," but it also meant "an example of." Thus, artworks were one-of-a-kind, but eighteenth-century farm implements may have been examples. Things made by hand were unique, but manufactured items became examples. In the natural history world, almost all specimens were examples but had specificity as to location found. Yet some could also be unique— the last passenger pigeon or the last dodo bird. Objects from both categories, unique and example, were accessioned into the collections. Museums owned the objects and took on the responsibility of preserving, studying, and displaying them.

Yet even within these seemingly easy categories there were variations. In asserting uniqueness (as in made-by-hand), specific authorship was associated with some objects, such as paintings, but not with others, most especially utilitarian works whose makers were often unknown. Some unique works were thought of as "art" and some as "craft"; with some notable exceptions, art was individualized as to maker but craft was not. This practice, which is now changing, made it possible to do research and mount shows of the work of particular artists in some, but not all, cultures.

WHAT ARE COLLECTIONS?

In the early 1970s the American Association of Museums (AAM) established an Accreditation Commission. As its members deliberated, they discussed whether groups of living things could be called collections and whether institutions that so "collected" should be classified as museums. Heretofore, "museums" were conserving things that had never been, or now were no longer, alive. The field debated if the living things in botanical gardens, fish in aquaria, or animals in zoos were "collections"; if so, were those institutions, *de facto*, museums? It was decided that, yes, at least for funding and accreditation purposes, they *were* museums, and the living things they cared for were likewise to be regarded as collections, and hence objects.[2]

Yet there were other institutional repositories that cared for, protected, preserved, and taught about "objects" but were not called museums nor necessarily treated by museums as siblings. Archives and libraries, especially rare-book collections, were considered related but not siblings even though some museum collections contain the identical materials. There were also commercial galleries and private and corporate collections that were considered by museum professionals to be different and outside the field, separated supposedly by an underlying purpose. A legal distinction of "not-for-profit" was considered an essential part of the definition of a museum. It was clear that while objects formed the *necessary* foundation upon which the definition of a museum might rest, they were not *sufficient* in themselves.

CAN NONCOLLECTING INSTITUTIONS BE MUSEUMS?

The Accreditation Commission of the AAM next sought to determine if places that resembled collections-based museums but did not hold collections (i.e., places like not-for-profit galleries and cultural centers) were, for purposes of accreditation, also museums. In 1978, they decided that, in some instances, galleries could be considered museums because, like museums, they cared for, displayed, and preserved objects even though they did not own them. Ownership, therefore, in some instances, no longer defined museums.

There was also the conundrum brought to the profession by science centers and children's museums, mostly of the mid-twentieth century. Earlier in the century, these places had collected and displayed objects, but by mid-century children's museums and science centers were proliferating and creating new public experiences, using exhibition material that was built specifically for the purpose and omitting collections objects altogether. How were these "purpose-built" objects to be considered? They were three-dimensional, often unique, many times extremely well made, but they had no cognates in the outside world. Much of this exhibit material was built to demonstrate the activity and function of the "real" (and now inactive) machinery sitting beside it.

The Adler Planetarium, applying to the AAM for accreditation, also caused the AAM to reconsider the definition of a museum. The planetarium's object was a machine that projected stars onto a ceiling. If institutions relied on such "objects," were these places museums? Had the profession inadvertently crafted a definition of objects that was restricted to those things that were created elsewhere and were then transported to museums? That was not the case in art museums that commissioned site-specific work. Certainly the murals of the depression period applied directly to museum walls were accessionable works of art—an easy call! Portability, then, did not define objects.

In 1978, the Accreditation Commission of the AAM, citing these three different types of noncollections-based institutions (art centers, science and technology centers, and planetariums), wrote specific language for each type of museum and, by amending its definition of collections for each group, declared these types of organizations to be . . . museums! They elaborated: "The existence of collections and supporting exhibitions is considered desirable, but their absence is not disabling. . . ."[3] In response, many museums set about creating more than one set of rules—one for accessioned objects, and another for exhibitions material—and began to understand that the handleable material they used in their classes (their teaching collections) should be governed by a different set of criteria as well.

Nevertheless, there were often no easy distinctions between the handleablity of teaching collections' objects and those others deserving preservation. The Boston Children's Museum loan boxes, for example, created in the 1960s, contained easy-to-obtain material about Northeast Native Americans. But by the 1980s, the remaining material was retired from the loan boxes and accessioned into the collections because it was no longer obtainable and had become rare and valuable.

Even purpose-built "environments" have, in cases such as the synagogue models in the Museum of the Diaspora in Tel Aviv, become so intriguing or are of such craftsmanship that they, decades later, become collections' objects themselves. So, too, have the exhibitions created by distinguished artists, such as parts of Charles and Ray Eames's exhibit *Mathematica: A World of Numbers and Beyond*.

Dioramas were often built for a museum exhibition hall in order to put objects (mostly animals) in context. These display techniques, which were considered a craft at the time they were created, were occasionally of such beauty, and displayed artistic conventions of realism (and seeming realism) so special, that today the original dioramas themselves have become "objects," and many are subject to preservation, accession, and special display. The definition of objects suitable for collections has, therefore, expanded to include, in special cases, material built for the museum itself.

WHAT IS REAL? IS THE EXPERIENCE THE OBJECT?

In the nineteenth century, some museums had and displayed sculptural plaster castings and studies. The Louvre and other museums had rooms devoted to copies of famous sculptures that the museum did not own. The originals either remained in situ or were held by others. People came to see, study, and paint these reproductions. They were treated with the respect accorded the real thing. For a long time, museums and their publics have felt that though there were differences between the "original" and reproductions, both had a place within their walls.

Similarly, reconstructed skeletons of dinosaurs have long appeared in museums. They usually are a combination of the bones of the species owned by the museums plus the casting of the missing bones from the same species owned by someone else. Sometimes museums point out which part is real and which is cast, but often they do not. "Real," therefore, takes on new meaning. Curators recognize that the experience of seeing the whole skeleton is more "real," and certainly more informative, than seeing only the authentic, unattached bones that do not add up to a complete or understandable image.

Likewise, multiples or limited editions were always considered "real" as long as the intention of the artist was respected. Thus, the fact that Rodin and many others authorized the multiple production of some pieces did not seem to make each one any less real or less unique. The creation of additional, though still limited, copies, using the same etching plates, but after the death of the artist, caused more problems. But often, while acknowledging the facts of the edition, such works also hung in museums and, if the quality was good, were accessioned into their collections.

IS THE IMAGE THE OBJECT?

The twentieth century's invention of new technologies has made multiples the norm and made determining what is real and what that means much more difficult. While original prints of movies, for example, exist, it is the moving image that the public thinks of as the object rather than the master print of film. Questions of authenticity revolve around subsequent manipulation of the image (e.g., colorization, cutting, or cropping) rather than the contents of any particular canister.

Printed editions with identical multiples are considered originals, and become more valuable, if signed; unsigned editions are considered less "real" and certainly less valuable. In such cases one could say that the signature, rather than the image, becomes the object. Photographs printed by the photographer may be considered more real than those using the same negative but printed by someone else. With the invention of digital technology, many identical images can be reproduced at will without recourse to any negative at all. So the notion of authenticity (meaning singularity or uniqueness) becomes problematic as images indistinguishable from those in museums are easily available outside the museum. It is the artist's sensibility that produced the image. It is the image itself, therefore, that is the object.

IS THE STORY THE OBJECT?

Of the utilitarian objects of the twentieth century, most are manufactured in huge quantities and therefore could be termed "examples." Which of these objects to collect often then depends not upon the object itself but on an associated story that may render one of them unique or important.

The objects present in the death camps of the Holocaust were, in the main, created for use elsewhere. There is nothing unique in the physicality of a bowl that comes from Auschwitz-Birkenau. These bowls could have been purchased in shops that sold cheap tableware all over Germany at the time. However, when the visitor reads the label that says the bowl comes from Auschwitz, the viewer, knowing something about the Holocaust, transfers meaning to the object. Since there is nothing aside from the label that makes the bowl distinctive, it is not the bowl itself but its associated history that forms importance for the visitor.

DOES THE CULTURAL CONTEXT MAKE THE OBJECT?

As Foucault and many others have written, objects lose their meaning without the viewer's knowledge and acceptance of underlying aesthetic or cultural values. Without such knowledge, an object's reification even within its own society cannot be understood. Often the discomfort of novice visitors to art museums has to do with their lack of understanding of the cultural aesthetics that the art on display either challenges or affirms.

By accessioning or displaying objects, the creators of museum exhibitions are creating or enhancing these objects' value. Further, society's acceptance of the value of museums themselves likewise transfers value to their objects. When museums receive gifts or bequests from a major donor's holdings, they are inheriting—and then passing on—a set of value judgments from someone who is essentially hidden from the visitor's view. A particular aesthetic pervades such museums because of the collections they house and the collectors who gave the objects in the first place.

This issue of values determining choice comes into sharper focus when museums begin acquiring or presenting collections from cultures whose aesthetic might be different. When installing a show of African material in an American art museum, should the curator show pieces based on the values inherent in the producing culture (i.e., focusing on the objects that attain special aesthetic value within that culture), or should the curator pick objects that appeal more to the aesthetic of his or her own culture? This question, the source of much debate, arises when museums attempt to diversify their holdings to include works created by a foreign (or even an assimilated) culture quite different from that which produced the majority of their holdings. For example, the selection of which African or Latino art to accession or show has to do not with authenticity but with quality. The notion of quality has been sharply debated between the scholar within the museum and the peoples representing the culture of the maker. So the question becomes: who selects the objects and by what criteria?

In material created by indigenous artists, the native community itself sometimes disagrees internally as to whether the material is native or belongs to a modern tradition that crosses cultural boundary lines. Some within the native population also argue about the birthright of the artist; blood quantum, traditional upbringing, and knowledge of the language sometimes have considerable bearing on whether artists and their creations are considered native. In such cases, the decision about what is quality work that should be housed in a museum may have little to do with the object itself and more to do with the genealogy of the producer.

WHAT IF YOUR STORY HAS NO OBJECTS OR DOES NOT NEED THEM? IS THE ABSENCE OF OBJECTS THE OBJECT?

Most collections were created by wealthy people who acquired things of interest and value to themselves. The everyday objects of nonvalued or subjugated peoples were usually not collected. Often the people in the lowest economic strata could hardly wait to exchange their objects for those that were more valued, giving no thought, at the time, to the preservation of the discarded material. So it goes for most peoples during their most impoverished historical periods. Accordingly, their museums must choose among a narrow band of choices—do not tell that part of their history, recreate the artifacts and environments, or use interpretative techniques that do not rely on material evidence.

The Museum of the Diaspora in Israel, struggling with this issue more than twenty-five years ago, decided to tell the complete story of five thousand years of Jewish migration without using a single authentic artifact. It elected to create tableaux that reproduced physical surroundings in an illustrative manner based on scholarly research into pictorial and written documentation of all kinds. The museum did so because its collection could not accurately or comprehensively tell the story, and a presentation of settings that appeared "like new" honored the history of Jewish migration more than an assortment of haphazard authentic artifacts showing their age and wear. The experience, wholly fabricated but three-dimensional, became the object. It presented a good public experience, many argued, but still did not qualify as a "museum." Ultimately, this total re-creation was accepted as a highly distinguished museum. The Museum of the Diaspora also presented movies, photos, and recordings in a publicly accessible form, arguing that a comprehensive presentation required material that was non-artifactual.

The U.S. African-American and Native American communities have suggested, in the same vein, that their primary cultural transmission is accomplished through oral language, dance, and song—vehicles that are ephemeral. Their central artifacts, or objects, if you will, are not dimensional at all, and museums that wish to transmit the accuracy of such cultures, or display historical periods for which material evidence is not available, must learn to employ more diverse material. It may be the performance that is the object, for example. And the performance space might need to be indistinguishable from the exhibit hall. As museums struggle to do this, one begins to see videos of ceremonies and hear audio chanting. Such techniques, formerly thought of as augmentation rather than core interpretation, have increasingly taken on the role and function previously played by collection objects.

Even in museums like Cleveland's Rock and Roll Hall of Fame or the soon-to-be-opened Experience Music Project, it is the sound and performance of the artists that is the artifact much more than the stationary guitar that, say, Jimi Hendrix once used. Indeed, musical instrument archives at the Boston Museum of Fine Arts and other places have long struggled with the proper presentation of their "artifacts." "Silent musical instruments" approaches an oxymoron.

HOW IS THE OBJECT TO BE PRESERVED?
IS THE OBJECT TO BE USED?

The museum, in accepting an object for its collection, takes on the responsibility for its care. In doing so, collections managers follow rules organized for the safety and long-term preservation of the objects. Climate control, access restrictions, and security systems are all issues of concern to those who care for objects. Institutions devoted to music or performance transform the notion of collections and certainly the notion of preservation, because while it is true that most things are preserved better when left alone, some musical instruments are not among them. They are preserved better if played, and so, for example at the Smithsonian's Museum of American History, they are.

Likewise, many native people have successfully argued that accessioned material should be used in the continuance of ceremony and tradition. Artifacts, rather than being relinquished to isolated preservation (and losing their usefulness), are stored in trust waiting for the time when they must again be used. In the 1980s, when native people from a specific clan or group asked for an object to be loaned for a short-term use, this was a radical notion for most natural history museums. That request now is more common and often accommodated. For example, at the end of the 1980s, the Dog Soldiers of the Northern Cheyenne requested their pipe, which the Smithsonian's National Museum of Natural History holds, and used it in their ceremonies, after which it was returned to the museum.

Now, native museums and, less commonly, some general museums that hold native material accept objects into their collections with the express understanding that they will be loaned out and used when needed. The notion of a museum as a storehouse in perpetuity has, in these instances, evolved into the museum as a revolving loan warehouse. A long-standing and easily understood example predates this relatively new development. The Crown Jewels of the British monarchy, which are displayed in the Tower of London, are worn by the monarch when he or she is crowned. And so it has been for many centuries.

WHOSE RULES ARE USED FOR OBJECT CARE?

There are other fundamental rules of collections care that are successfully being challenged worldwide by native people's involvement. Collections care has been predicated on the basic notion that objects are inanimate. Though some objects were once alive, they now are no longer, and most had never been alive. Thus, collections-care policies proceeded from the assumption that objects should be preserved in the best manner possible, avoiding decay from elements, exposure, and use. Protective coverings and storage cases were designed to do just that. Extremes in the exposure to light and temperature, and all manner of pest infestation, were to be avoided. But when the museum was recognized to be neither the only nor the absolute arbiter of its material holdings, accommodation to the beliefs of the producers of the materials or their descendants became necessary.

These beliefs often included a lack of distinction between animate and inanimate. Thus, spirits, "mana," fields of power, and life sources could live within an object regardless of the material from which it was made. And that being so, the care for these living things, it was argued, is, and should be, quite different from the care of dead or never alive things. So, for example, bubble wrap, while an excellent protector of objects, does not allow for breathing or "singing and dancing at night." Those working with native populations in good faith have come to respect native understanding of their own objects and now provide for the appropriate life of the object. Some objects need to be fed, some need to be protected from their enemies, some need to be isolated from menstruating women. Collections are no longer under the absolute province of the professional caregivers. Storage facilities that accommodate the native understanding of their objects require new architectural designs that allow for ceremony for some and isolation from the curious for others.

WHO OWNS THE COLLECTIONS?

This change in collections use and care alters the notion of the museum as owner of its collections and opens the door to multiple definitions of ownership. These new definitions have far-reaching implications. If tribal communities can determine the use, presentation, and care of objects "owned" by museums, can the descendants of an artist? Can the victims or perpetrators of a war event? In the recent Smithsonian National Museum of Air and Space *Enola Gay* exhibition controversy, it was the veterans who flew the plane and their World War II associates who ultimately controlled the access to, presentation of, and interpretation of the object. Ownership or legal title to an object does not convey the simple, more absolute meaning it did when I began in the museum field.

The notion that if you buy something from a person who controlled it in the past, then it is yours to do with as you wish is clearly under redefinition in a number of fields. What constitutes clear title? Under what rules does stolen material need to be returned? What is stolen, in any case? Do the Holocaust victims' paintings and the Elgin Marbles have anything in common? The issue is so complex and varied that countries forge treaties to try to determine which items of their patrimony should be returned. Similarly, museums in countries like New Zealand, Canada, and Australia have developed accords that, in some cases, give dual ownership to collections. Museums and the native populations then jointly control the presentation, care, and even return of the objects, or museums give ownership to the native populations, who, in turn, allow the museum to hold the objects in trust. Ownership has developed a complex meaning.

IF I OWN IT CAN I HAVE IT BACK, PLEASE?

Some of this blurring of ownership began with native people maintaining that some items should not be in the hands of museums regardless of their history. That this would be claimed for human remains held in collections was easy to understand. Almost all cultures do something ceremonial and intentional with the remains of their people, which, in almost all instances, does not include leaving bodies for study in boxes on shelves. So when native people started to call for the return of their ancestors' remains, there was an intuitive understanding of the problem in most circles. This, however, did not make it any easier for the paleontologists and forensic curators whose life work had centered on the access to these bones, nor for the museumgoer whose favorite museum memories had to do with shrunken heads, mummies, or prehistoric human remains. The arguments that emanated from both sides were understandable and difficult to reconcile. It was a clear clash of world views and belief systems. To the curators it seemed that removal of human remains within museum collections would result in the unwarranted triumph of cultural tradition and emotionalism over scientific objectivity and the advancement of knowledge.

As it turned out, the Native American Grave Protection and Repatriation Act (NAGPRA)[4] made clear that Native American tribes had rights to the return of their sacred material and to their ancestors' remains and associated grave goods, regardless of the method by which museums had acquired the material. However, the emptying of collections into native communities, as predicted by the most fearful, did not happen. Rather, museums and native communities, working together in good faith, moved into an easier and more collegial relationship, as between equals. In most cases, the objects returned are carefully chosen and returned with due solemnity. Some tribes have chosen to allow some forensic samples to be saved, or studied prior to reburial, and some have reinterred their ancestors in ways that could allow for future study should the native community wish it.

NAGPRA struck a new balance between the world view of most museums and their staff (which endorsed a rational and scientific model of discourse and allowed for access to as much information as could be gathered) and the spiritual interests of traditional native peoples. A variety of museum practices were broadened, and visitors began to see the interpretation of exhibitions changed to include multiple side-by-side explanations of the same objects. For example, *Wolves*, an exhibition created by the Science Museum of Minnesota, presented scientific data, native stories, conservation and hunting controversies, and physiological information together in an evenhanded way. An argument for multiple interpretations began to be heard in natural history museums whose comfort level in the past had not permitted the inclusion of spiritual information in formats other than anthropological myth.

HOW OLD IS AN OBJECT?

The scientific dating of artifacts used in religious practices often holds little relevance to the believers. When an object such as the Shroud of Turin, for example, is carbon dated and shown to be insufficiently old, the problem of writing its museum label becomes complex. An object held in TePapa, the Museum of New Zealand, was returned to an iwi (tribe) that requested it, with all the solemnity and ceremony appropriate. So too went records of its age and material composition, at variance with beliefs held by the Maori people. But if, as the Maori believe, spirit or mana migrates from one piece to its replacement (rendering the successor indistinguishable from its more ancient equivalent), then what relevance is the fact that dates or materials are at variance? The object's cultural essence is as old as they say.

Similarly, when restoration of landmarks includes the replacement of their elements (as is routinely the case in Japanese shrines), the landmark is said to be dated from its inception even though no material part of it remains from that time. That does not upset us. So even something so seemingly rational and historical as dating is up for interpretation.

THE OBJECT IS OFF-LIMITS. IT IS NONE OF YOUR BUSINESS

Museums, even in their earliest incarnations as cabinets of curiosities, were available to all interested eyes or at least to those allowed to have access by the owners of the cabinets. In fact, part and parcel of conquest and subjugation was the access to interesting bits of the subjugated. This assumption that everything was fair game held currency for a long time. Though the notion of secret and sacred was also understood (for example, no one but the faithful could enter Mecca), this concept did not attach to museums nor to the holdings thereof. If a museum owned it, the visitors could see it if the curator/ staff wished them to.

So it came as a surprise to some curators that contemporary native peoples began to make demands on museums to return not only human remains but material that was sacred and once secret. Accommodations negotiated between the museums and the native people sometimes led to agreements to leave the material in the museum but to limit viewing access. The notion that one people, the museum curators, would voluntarily limit their own and others' access to material owned by museums came initially as a shock to the museum system. But under the leadership of sympathetic museum and native people and, further, under the force of NAGPRA, museums began to understand that all material was not to be made available to all interested parties.

It was the beginning of the "It is none of your business" concept of museum objects. It held that the people most intimately concerned with and related to the material could determine the access to that material. In many cultures sacred ceremonies are open to all, and the objects in use are available for view in museum settings, but that too may change. For example, in Jewish tradition, Torahs once desecrated are supposed to be disposed of by burial in a prescribed manner. Yet some of these are available for view, most notably at the United States Holocaust Memorial Museum. There may come a time when such artifacts are petitioned to be removed for burial even though the statement they make is powerful.

WHO SAYS ALL OBJECTS NEED TO BE PRESERVED?

Ownership is not always an issue; sometimes it is the preservation of the object itself that needs examination. Museums have felt their most fundamental responsibility extended to the preservation of the object, yet in returning human remains to the earth, artifacts are being intentionally destroyed. That was difficult to reconcile for those trained in preservation. Even more difficult was the belief that not all things made by hand were intended to be preserved; perhaps some should be allowed to be destroyed. The Zuni war gods preserved by museums were returned to the Zuni tribe when it was successfully proven that these could only have been stolen from grave sites. But even more difficult was the Zuni's assertion that these objects were created to accompany the dead, and that preservation of them was therefore anathema. The war gods were returned to the Zuni, who watched over the gradual decay of these objects as they returned to the earth. In effect, the Zuni were entitled to destroy the objects that the museums had so carefully preserved.

The notion of preservation has, therefore, also been blurred. Museum personnel began to wrestle with the notion that all people do not hold preservation of all objects as a universal good. The Tibetan Lamas who create exquisite sand paintings only to destroy them later would certainly understand this.

THE OBJECT SPEAKS

I would be remiss if I did not also acknowledge the power of some objects to speak directly to the visitor, for example, in the sensual pleasure brought about by viewing unique original objects of spectacular beauty. But the notion that objects, per se, can communicate directly and meaningfully is under much scrutiny. The academicians of material culture, anthropology, history, and other fields are engaged in parsing the ways in which humans decode objects in order to figure out what information is intrinsic to the object itself, what requires associated knowledge gleaned from another source, and what is embedded in cultural tradition.

In some ways, it is because of this parallel contemporary inquiry into the "vocabulary" of objects that I can inquire into the object's changing role in the definition of museums.

WHAT ARE MUSEUMS IF THEY ARE LESS OBJECT-BASED?

Museum staff intuitively understand that museums are important—an understanding that the public shares. However, especially for the public, this understanding does not always revolve around the objects, though objects are, like props, essential to most museums' purposes: making an implicit thesis visible and tangible. The nature of the thesis can range from explanation of the past to advocacy for a contemporary viewpoint to indication of possible future directions—in each case through a medium that presents a story in sensory form.

Museums will remain responsible for the care of the objects they house and collect, but the notion of responsibility will be, and has already been, broadened to include shared ownership, appropriate use, and, potentially, removal and return.

The foundational definition of museums will, in the long run, I believe, arise not from objects, but from "place" and "storytelling in tangible sensory form," where citizenry can congregate in a spirit of cross-generational inclusivity and inquiry into the memory of our past, a forum for our present, and aspirations for our future.

Coming back to definitions, the current definition of museums used by the Accreditation Program of the AAM encompasses all museums and no longer separates them by categories. Museums, in this definition, ". . . present regularly scheduled programs and exhibits that use and interpret objects for the public according to accepted standards; have a formal and appropriate program of documentation, care, and use of collections and/or tangible objects. . . ."[5]

For the visitor, it is the experience of simultaneously being in a social and often celebratory space while focusing on a multisensory experience that makes a museum effective. Virtual experiences in the privacy of one's home may be enlightening but, I think, are not part of the civilizing experience that museums provide. It is the very materiality of the building, the importance of the architecture, and the prominence that cities give to museum location that together make for the august place that museums hold. Congregant space will, I believe, remain a necessary ingredient of the museum's work.

The objects that today's museums responsibly care for, protect, and cherish will remain central to their presentations. But the definition of "objectness" will be broad and allow for every possible method of storymaking. These more broadly defined objects range from hard evidence to mere props and ephemera. I hope I have shown that objects are certainly not exclusively real nor even necessarily "tangible" (even though the AAM uses that word). For it is the story told, the message given, and the ability of social groups to experience it together that provide the essential ingredients of making a museum important.

Museums *are* social-service providers (not always by doing direct social-service work, though many do that), because they are spaces belonging to the citizenry at large, expounding on ideas that inform and stir the population to contemplate and occasionally to act.

Museums are not unique in their work. Rather, they share a common purpose with a host of other institutions. We need museums and their siblings because we need collective history set in congregant locations in order to remain civilized. Societies build these institutions because they authenticate the social contract. They are collective evidence that we were here.

ENDNOTES

[1]"For the purposes of the accreditation program of the AAM, a museum is defined as an organized and permanent non-profit institution, essentially educational or aesthetic in purpose, with professional staff, which owns and utilizes tangible objects, cares for them, and exhibits them to the public on some regular schedule." American Association of Museums, *Museum Accreditation: Professional Standards* (Washington, D.C.: American Association of Museums, 1973), 8.

[2]". . .owns and utilizes tangible things animate and inanimate." Ibid., 9.

[3]An art center "utilizes borrowed art objects, cares for them and maintains responsibility to their owners . . . [its] primary function is to plan and carry out exhibitions." Ibid., 12. A science and technology center ". . . maintains and utilizes exhibits and/or objects for the presentation and interpretation of scientific and technological knowledge. . . . These serve primarily as tools for communicating what is known of the subject matter. . . ." Ibid., 12. A planetarium's ". . . principal function is to provide educational information on astronomy and related sciences through lectures and demonstrations." Ibid., 11.

[4]Native American Grave Protection and Repatriation Act (25 U.S.C. 3002).

[5]American Association of Museums, *A Higher Standard: The Museum Accreditation Handbook* (Washington, D.C.: American Association of Museums, 1997), 20.

What can the study of literature tell us about suffering? It is, of course, an impossible question, a sinkhole, a yawning chasm that dissertation directors warn against. It is also a question that opens up special difficulties because debates in contemporary theory have forced us to ask hard questions about such basic issues as the nature of interpretation, the boundaries of literature, and the relations between texts and the world. Literature, for example, is now routinely described as an ideological category that did not exist before the Enlightenment—its status threatened by such postmodern upstarts as discourse, *écriture*, and grammatology. A loose alliance of new academic disciplines has shown how once-canonical works of Western literary tradition relegate minority figures—i.e., women, blacks, and Asians—to, at best, marginal status. What literature has to tell us about suffering, in short, depends on basic decisions about what counts as literature and whose suffering matters.

David B. Morris

From "About Suffering:
Voice, Genre, and Moral Community"
Dædalus 125 (1) (Winter 1996)

Willard L. Boyd

Museums as Centers of Controversy

W E THINK OF MUSEUMS as places of objects. In fact they are places of ideas. The objects of nature give rise to human ideas about nature. Ideas give rise to the objects created by humans. Ideas are the principal means by which humans interact with objects in museums. Too often our different ideas lead to conflict rather than to understanding. Our ideas about objects change over time as our knowledge and attitudes about them change and our research techniques improve. Changing ideas are controversial because they contradict what we have previously believed.

In some instances, the simple display of an object can be controversial. When exhibits go beyond the "wonder" of the object standing alone and are designed to inform and stimulate visitor learning, they consciously invite controversy—as they should.

In ancient Egypt and Greece, museums were centers of speculation and research, the places where Plato, Aristotle, and Ptolemy engaged their students in learning about the natural world.[1] Most American colleges and universities were organized around collections of art, material culture, and natural science. Indeed, it is to cabinets of natural history that the roots of the Darwinian revolution can be traced. In the nineteenth and early twentieth centuries, museums were at the forefront of challenging our accepted ideas about the world.

By 1969, however, Dillon Ripley wrote:

Willard L. Boyd is president emeritus of the Field Museum, and professor of law and president emeritus at the University of Iowa.

The nineteenth century is the epoch of the rise of public museums. It is also the period during which museums first created the public impression which has been so disheartening in subsequent years to museophiles. The word museum, instead of seeming to imply a center of learning, came to mean something ponderous, dull, musty, dead, a graveyard of old bones of the past.[2]

At the beginning of the twenty-first century, museums once again see themselves as centers of learning about the world in which we live. Even though many Americans have complained that museums are boring, they do not want their museums to be controversial. Nevertheless, in a pluralistic society, what and how museums collect, and what and how they exhibit, are matters of increasing controversy. If museums are to be on the frontier of public appreciation and learning about their subject matter, they will be involved in controversies arising from new discoveries, new creations, and new interpretations about which there will be conflicting and forcefully articulated views. Museums are no longer perceived as infallible; they can no longer presume the privilege of issuing unquestionable pronouncements. Recognizing this new era, Harold Skramstad has said:

> We have all followed the heavily publicized questioning of the intellectual authority of established museums, which are under attack by groups with very diverse views and very different interests . . . .
>
> Our universalist claims of value and authority—which gave us such a strong, almost religious sense of calling, and which have done so much to improve the quality and professionalization of everything we do—now seem to be a barrier to preparing us to address legitimate expectations of a more pluralistic society. In retrospect, it appears clear that we have based much of our appeal upon our belief that the appropriating, holding, and exhibiting of the material record of the human and the natural world is an intrinsic social good, which is understood and valued by all, and not solely the particular groups that have both governed and staffed our museums.
>
> It is in [our claim to the expectation of authority] where much of the present controversy over the role of museums has been centered. Like most institutions in modern American life, the museum has been, to use Neil Harris's term, "deprivileged". . . . Today,

museums have an assumed authority that makes them vulnerable to attack in the way that any influential source of authority is. . . . Our response to these attacks is too often retreat or arrogance. Properly managing and continuously renegotiating our authority will be a major and time-consuming responsibility of the future.[3]

Museum "expertness" does not trump public concerns about what is collected and how it is exhibited. Nobody—especially an expert—likes to have his or her views challenged. Yet we live in an era of public challenge, often strident and inflexible. Museums and museum professionals cannot dismiss criticism as uninformed. If we can challenge the views of others, others can challenge our views. In a pluralistic world it is too much to expect that we will find a consensus—either among museum professionals or across museum audiences. Museums can and should serve as fora for these differing perspectives.

Museum professionals need to hear and reflect on the diverse opinions of others in a pluralistic society. This takes time, patience, and an open mind, often under trying and unpleasant circumstances. The idea of listening to and considering other points of view is often dismissed by some as politically correct pandering, or naively embraced as a means of magically producing consensus. But pursued genuinely, listening and consulting can generate deeper understanding of the divergent perspectives that are inherent in a pluralistic society.

Museums, like all institutions, look inward. Museum professionals look to their peers for evaluation, guidance, and innovation. Looking beyond ourselves is demeaned as unprofessional. But is it? Does good museology nowadays require museum professionals to listen to and consult with others both within and outside the museum, both professionals and laity? Should we go further and involve outsiders in museum decision making about collections and exhibits? Should we include hostile as well as friendly outsiders in the process? Do museums have a special responsibility to consult and involve affinity groups whose cultures and environments are represented in our collections and exhibits? Given that no such group is monolithic, how broadly should we consult within an affinity group?

Should we consult beyond the affinity group to the broader public?

Consultation must be real, not cosmetic. We consult to learn. We must listen to others with a mind open and willing to change when merited. The purpose of consultation is to expand both professional and public knowledge and understanding. Visitors should be made aware of differences of opinion. Ultimately, however, those responsible within the museum must make decisions with respect to collections and exhibits. And we must vigorously and openly defend those decisions on their merits.

Museum decisions will be critiqued by both experts and the public. We should not be surprised by negative reactions to decisions made in shaping and presenting collections and exhibitions, including charges of censorship for what has been omitted and of cultural bias for what has been included. We live in an era of intense and acerbic criticism. Our objective in openness is to engage and consider other perspectives, both professional and public. In doing so, we can learn much, but we cannot abdicate our responsibility to make decisions. We must be prepared to live with the controversial consequences of well-considered decisions.[4]

WHAT AND HOW MUSEUMS COLLECT

In the museum profession the questions of what and how museums collect are properly considered the province of the curator, whose professional judgment should be conclusive or at least accorded great weight. Increasingly, however, curatorial judgment is being called into question, even formally curtailed by government regulations and peer ethical standards to which museums as institutions are primarily held responsible. Informally, the curator's professional judgment may also be subtly and not so subtly affected by public opinion.

In contrast to the unfettered collecting of the 1890s, collecting in the 1990s is considerably restricted. While museum and curatorial ethics codes are still struggling to articulate specific restrictions on museum collection practices, governments at the national and international levels are actively promulgating collection restrictions. In doing so, governments and the publics they represent often consider museums and curators major culprits in depriving a people of their cultural and environmental heritage. Museums are also seen as duplicitous for acquiring objects plundered in wartime or stolen in peacetime by either governments or private parties.

Given the varying types of possible possession, museums need to think through the possible ramifications of each. What are the different legal and ethical responsibilities of the museum as owner, as borrower, and as bailee? What are the respective implications of a museum's role as curator, registrar, collection manager, and conservator with respect to owned, borrowed, and bailed collections? In order to make museums more accountable, such responsibilities must be more clearly delineated.

Where a museum engages in field work, permits are usually now required for on-site studies as well as for export and import of cultural objects and biological specimens by museum staff. If field-study objects or specimens are brought into a museum, there is now a question as to whether the museum has possession as owner or as borrower. Increasingly, the ownership of field-collected objects remains with the government or an agency or individual at the place of collection. Thus, the objects may only be "loaned" to the collecting curator for research at the museum, and cannot be accessioned by the museum, which acts merely a borrower.

When a museum acquires an object through the marketplace, how do its obligations then change? In the United States a good-faith purchaser does not acquire clear title to stolen property. However, the rightful owner must seek restitution within a reasonable period of time after learning the identity and whereabouts of the wrongful possessor. Public opinion is coming to regard a museum as bound to an ethical duty to investigate the history of an object prior to acquisition, whether through the marketplace by good-faith purchase or by gift (even when from a good-faith purchaser). Museums cannot persuasively argue (as they once could) that it is better to acquire an object with a questionable provenance than to allow it to fall into a private collection. Good faith is coming to require investigation by the museum before acquisition.

Ethical standards and regulatory laws usually follow public demand; public demand concentrates on specific situations that need to be redressed. Thus, after years of denial, we are now properly focused on the art seized by the Nazis from the Jews. As a result, a task force assembled by the Association of Art Museum Directors issued a report containing principles and guidelines for AAMD members to follow, and the Art Dealers Association of America has issued a statement on "Nazi-looted art." In summary, the AAMD guidelines call upon art museums to "begin immediately to review the provenance of works in their collections to attempt to ascertain whether any were unlawfully confiscated during the Nazi/World War II era and never restituted"; to respond promptly to any claims by owners of or heirs to allegedly confiscated art, and "offer to resolve the matter in an equitable, appropriate and mutually agreeable manner," using the avenue of mediation to help resolve claims, when practical; and to seek as much provenance information as possible before acquiring gifts, bequests, and purchases, against the condition that "[I]f there is evidence of unlawful confiscation, and there is no evidence of restitution, the museum should not proceed to acquire the object."[5]

Speaking in the context of Nazi-looted art, a statement of the Art Dealers Association of America (ADAA) has emphasized support for the creation and use of relevant databases, and has asserted:

> ADAA members will continue to research the history of the works of art which they offer and make every effort to supply as complete and accurate a provenance as the available information permits. Like all art professionals, ADAA members know that research into provenance is not a title search, and that there are frequently gaps in a provenance for perfectly legitimate reasons. Collectors may be assured, however, that ADAA members warrant good title for every work they sell, that research into the history of each work will be professionally conducted by dealers uniquely qualified to do so because of their specialized knowledge and experience in the field.[6]

Prior to the adoption of these principles, the inadequate nature and scope of provenance research, and the failure of some institutions to adhere consistently to export and plunder treaties as well as to regulations among museums and dealers, had been clearly and repeatedly raised both professionally and publicly.[7]

Clearly, the AAMD and ADAA statements must be understood as a response to the public outcry concerning the illegal seizure of art from Jews during the Holocaust. Yet whatever their motivation, the principles and guidelines made explicit in such statements are sound, with implications for the acquisition of collections in general. For example, they are also pertinent to objects looted from pre-Columbian archaeological sites. We need to be concerned about the plunder, looting, and theft of objects from individuals and groups worldwide—and not only because the media will be.

A case in point is a series of articles that ran in the *Boston Globe* from 1997 through 1998. In addition to covering the issue of Holocaust-plundered objects at the Museum of Modern Art in New York the series also focused on Boston's own Museum of Fine Arts, which "owned" or borrowed Mayan, Malian, and Italian objects alleged to have been illegally acquired and exported from those countries. In a related report, the *Christian Science Monitor,* in a 1998 article entitled "Art World Wary of New Rules," quotes the art historian Jonathan Petropoulos as saying: "They're finally addressing the problem of Nazi art in a comprehensive manner.... With antiquities, awareness hasn't come that far. Museums and dealers are not yet prepared to engage and rectify this issue." The article goes on to state that "The issue of stolen antiquities has yet to arouse the same level of public sympathy and support" as has been generated by the question of artworks confiscated by the Nazi.[8]

A profession has the responsibility to take the lead in setting the ethical standards by which its members are governed. The museum profession should set the example for governments, private collectors, and dealers with respect to all museum collections. This includes incorporating into museum acquisition policies the sense of such international conventions as the 1970 UNESCO Convention on the Means of Prohibiting and Preventing the Illicit Import, Export and Transfer of Ownership of Cultural Property.[9] Once such policies are adopted, it is incumbent upon museums to adhere to them. For example, Harvard's

Arthur M. Sackler Museum acquired a number of Greek vase fragments alleged to have been looted and illegally exported from an Italian tomb after Harvard adopted the essence of the UNESCO convention in its acquisition policy in 1971. According to a *Boston Globe* account, the museum's policy "asks for 'reasonable assurance' that an object was not exported from its country of origin after 1971 in violation of the laws of that country." The museum took the position that "innocent until proven guilty" sufficed. The *Globe* article continued:

> But many art historians and archeologists, noting that up to 80 percent of antiquities on the market were looted in recent decades, insist on tougher standards. "Ethically, given the enormous amount of looted material on the market, we are obligated to presume these items to be guilty until they are demonstrated to be innocent, and therefore the burden of proof should be on the purveyor of the object."[10]

Recent developments in international law have called for a more active role on the part of acquirers of cultural items to ensure that the material is not of suspicious origin. An attempt has been made to improve upon the UNESCO convention with the Convention on the International Return of Stolen or Illegally Exported Objects, an initiative of the International Institute for the Unification of Private Law, or Unidroit. Current U.S. law, and the law of most other "art market" nations, puts the burden on the claimant to show that the current possessor's ownership of the item is flawed. The Unidroit convention further provides that if the possessor must return an object, an ability to establish that due diligence was exercised in acquiring the item entitles the surrendering institution or collector to "fair and reasonable compensation." In determining the right of compensation, article 4 of the convention places the burden on the possessor to show that he or she "neither knew nor ought to have known that the object was stolen" and can prove that due diligence was exercised when acquiring the object. It is important to remember that neither the UNESCO nor the Unidroit conventions are retroactive. Moreover, the United States has not yet signed or become a party to the Unidroit convention.

Even if further developments in international law have yet to be adopted by the United States, the codes of U.S. professional associations in the museum field—to which institutions and their professionals are in some sense accountable—have continued to evolve. Certainly, institutional policies should reflect the essence of such codes. The American Association of Museums ethics code, for example, enjoins museums to ensure that

> [A]cquisition, disposal, and loan activities [involving collections] are conducted in a manner that respects the protection and preservation of natural and cultural resources and discourages illicit trade in such materials. . . .
>
> The unique and special nature of human remains and funerary and sacred objects is recognized as the basis of all decisions concerning such collections.[11]

More specifically, the ethics code of the International Council of Museums stipulates that:

> A museum should not acquire, whether by purchase, gift, bequest or exchange, any object unless the governing body and responsible officer are satisfied that the museum can acquire a valid title to the specimen or object in question and that in particular it has not been acquired in, or exported from, its country of origin and/or any intermediate country in which it may have been legally owned (including the museum's own country), in violation of that country's laws.
>
> So far as biological and geological material is concerned, a museum should not acquire by any direct or indirect means any specimen that has been collected, sold or otherwise transferred in contravention of any national or international wildlife protection or natural history conservation law or treaty of the museum's own country or any other county except with the express consent of an appropriate outside legal or governmental authority.[12]

These codes imply that museums must take affirmative steps to inquire into whether they are acquiring "good title" to their acquisitions. Both the AAM and ICOM codes address the issue of biological and geological materials as well as cultural materials. This means that museums of natural history must be wary of trophy hunting as a means of adding rare and endangered species to their collections. Nowadays, special hunting permits and waivers on import bans raise red flags for museums, as evidenced by a 1999 controversy involving the Smithsonian's National Museum of Natural History.[13]

The time has come for American museums, individually and collectively, to set themselves against illicit trade, even if other countries and private individuals will not. It rings false to justify our failure to do so on the grounds that ethical conduct will deprive the American public of access to objects and specimens lost to less scrupulous museums abroad and private collectors in the United States and elsewhere.[14] Moreover, museum records and collections should be open to inspection by the appropriate representatives of claimants. The public expects museums to demonstrate leadership in ethical conduct by over-compliance, not by shaving it close.

What about collections acquired prior to present-day laws and standards of ethics? A brief summary of these issues was presented in the text of introductory label panels for a 1999 exhibit of Congolese objects at the Art Institute of Chicago. The objects exhibited came from the collection of the Royal Museum for Central Africa in Tervuren, Belgium. Speaking of the Tervuren Museum, the label read in part:

> Like other ethnographic museums of the colonial era—The British Museum, London, Musée de l'homme, Paris, Museum für Völkerkunde, Berlin, American Museum for Natural History, New York, Field Museum, Chicago—Tervuren Museum bought or acquired objects from European merchants, travelers, colonial representatives and missionaries who had obtained them in a variety of ways. Often, objects associated with ritual or political power were taken by force or coercion, others were gained by purchase, gift, or because they had been discarded from its inception. The Tervuren Museum also sent scientific missions to Central Africa, becoming the primary center for research on all aspects of the area.

> When the Lower region won independence in 1960, the Tervuren Museum forged a supportive relationship with the former colony; in the 1970s, the museum helped to return over 700 objects to the Institut des Musées Nationaux du Zaire. Today, the Tervuren Museum is renowned for its dedication to field research and

cooperative work with foreign students, scholars, institutions, particularly those from the Democratic Republic of the Congo.[15]

A rather different perspective on Tervuren's practices may be found in the pages of Adam Hochschild's recent searing indictment of King Leopold II's reign of terror and genocide in the Congo. Hochschild criticizes the exhibits in the Tervuren, noting particularly that "... in none of the museum's twenty large exhibition galleries is there the slightest hint that millions of Congolese met unnatural deaths."[16]

Looting for financial purposes dates back to tomb-robbing in ancient Egypt. As long as there is a market, there will be theft. George Stocking, a historian of anthropology and its institutions, has written:

> [M]aterial culture was, in a literal economic sense, "cultural property." The very materiality of the objects entangled them in Western economic processes of acquisition and exchange. . . . From the beginning, market processes have been potent influences on the constitution of museums as archives of material culture—the more so insofar as the objects therein have been regarded, or come to be regarded, as objects of fine art, rather than as artifact.[17]

Nor is looting for the marketplace limited to fine art, archaeology, and material culture. Curators in many fields, particularly paleontologists and meteoriticists, are disturbed by specimens going on the auction block and into private collections. In the scientific community there were mixed feelings about the $8.4 million paid by the Field Museum in acquiring "Sue," the most complete *Tyrannosaurus rex* specimen yet found, even though the specimen will be available for learning in the public domain. The fear is that a "market" for fossils and meteorites will lead to destruction, inaccessibility, and looting of specimens.

There is also growing concern about repatriation of collections acquired prior to present-day laws and standards of ethics. In the United States, Congress has adopted the Native American Graves Protection and Repatriation Act (or NAGPRA). Should other collections be returned in the absence of a U.S. statute or treaty? Regardless of whether a museum feels it has a legal or ethical duty to return objects it has held, it should at least open its records and storage areas to—and respectfully discuss the issues with—appropriate and recognized descendants of groups or individuals who created and previously possessed the objects. Such discussions should look at the circumstances, legal and otherwise, under which the museum took possession. They should also take account of the laws and traditions prevailing at the time of acquisition among the cultural groups from whom the objects were acquired. Subsequent changes in these circumstances must also be reviewed. Museum officials should anticipate that the cultural affinity groups with which they engage may bring a wide range of views to the table on both historic circumstances and desirable outcomes. Every effort should be made to reach an accommodation satisfactory to all parties. The attorney general of the state of a museum's incorporation should always be apprised of the discussions and conclusions; it is that officer's public responsibility to hold the museum to its fiduciary duties under the laws of the state of incorporation.

Such discussions could have, it must be understood, a variety of outcomes. One result could be the return of objects to the lineal descendants or culturally affiliated tribes. Alternatively, the person or group acknowledged as a legitimate representative may wish that the museum should continue to hold an object for the benefit of the other party. In such cases the terms and responsibilities of such holding should be made clear, including the museum's liability in the case of damage or theft. During the period of the museum's continued possession as a bailee, the museum should make regular reports to all parties concerned.

In a collection-based museum, deaccession is an exceedingly contentious issue—much more so than the decision to acquire. To acquire an object is to canonize it. Deaccession, by contrast, may involve not simply returning objects, but offering them for sale in the open market. Accordingly, the highest fiduciary duties found in law, and the highest ethical norms of professional conduct, obtain with respect to deaccession. Fiduciary duties are determined by the case law, and sometimes the statute law, of the state in which a museum is incorporated. The ethics code of the American Association of Museums stipulates that the proceeds from a sale of collections should be held for collection acquisitions and direct care. Whenever possible, it is desirable for deaccessioned objects to go to another museum where the objects will be conserved and remain in the public domain.

It is when issues of prior ownership and deaccession come together that the issues confronting museum professionals become truly complex. In the absence of a repatriation statute or treaty, is a museum legally permitted and ethically required to offer collections free of charge to the appropriate persons, not necessarily a museum, whose cultures and environments are represented in the collections before proceeding to public auction? Should the proceeds of a sale to third parties go to the selling museum or to the affinity group? Recognizing that museum personnel have a fiduciary duty in law to the people of the state of incorporation concerning the collections their institutions hold, should there also be at least an ethical duty on the part of museums to consult with the representatives designated by the people whose cultures and environments are represented? Such an ethical duty might require consultation with designated representatives as to accession, management, conservation, exhibition, interpretation, and deaccession of collections. Consultation takes time, and it is not always friendly. Patiently and openly conducted, it can expand knowledge and understanding among all the parties. By taking such a cooperative attitude to the implementation of NAGPRA, museums have developed positive relationships with tribes to help resolve specific issues and generate long-term associations of enduring value to both.

By advocating an open and consultative approach to collections, I am seeking better decisions rather than faster decisions. Nevertheless, I recognize the legal responsibility museums have under state laws to make timely and reasoned decisions and to be accountable for them. Failing agreement among concerned parties about the ownership and possession of collections, litigation may yet be avoided by recourse to mediation or arbitration in a manner mutually agreed upon. In deciding contentious issues reference should be made to the traditions and laws of all cultures involved. (Relevant to such considerations is article 12 of the draft UN Declaration on the Rights of Indigenous Peoples, which provides in part that "Indigenous peoples have . . . the right to the restitution of cultural, intellectual, religious and spiritual property taken without their free and informed consent or in violation of their laws, traditions, and customs.") This consideration may be complicated further by the fact that more than one claimant may come forward.

The time has come for museums to be open and conciliatory in their approach to the issues of return and repatriation. Much can be gained for all parties by openly searching for mutually agreeable solutions. There is a growing trend toward doing so by individual museums on a case-by-case basis.[18] This changing attitude, coupled with specific actions on the part of American museums, is generating new professional standards and practices. For example, the issue of "cultural patrimony" is to be taken under consideration by the Association of Art Museum Directors, which is launching a general review of its "Professional Practices in Art Museums" statement.

While it remains difficult to legislate by statute or treaty in this area, general principles of customary law are emerging from individual cases, addressing the basic issues of when restitution should take place and in what mutually supportive forms.[19] Traditionally, museums have stressed the benefits of the "movement" of objects without adequate regard for the detrimental aspects of movement from the point of view of others. Certainly, the cross-cultural transfer of the human ideas surrounding objects is regarded positively in an age of communication. However, the movement of objects that results in cultural and environmental loss, destruction, and desecration cannot be justified. Museums must realign their acquisition and retention policies to promote cultural understanding and respect for the objects and ideas of others. An ethical attitude requires that we do so. Moreover, the law allows us to do so even if it does not always mandate us to do so.[20]

One major form of positive movement is the traveling exhibit. A federal statute encourages temporary international movement of art by providing immunity from lawsuits for American museums receiving objects coming on loan. This immunity must be sought by the borrowing museum and approved by the U.S. Information Agency before it has effect. The absence of this protection is a deterrent to movement. Currently, the Museum of Modern Art is resisting an action brought by the Manhattan district attorney to prevent the return of two paintings by Egon Schiele to an Austrian foundation which had lent the paintings for an exhibit. While the Museum asserts that a special New York statute exempts arts objects loaned to New York museums from seizure, the district attorney argues that the statute does not apply to criminal investigations—in this case to determine whether the paintings had originally been confiscated by the Nazis from Jewish owners. On March 16, 1999, the Appellee Division of the New York County Supreme Court, reversing the trial division order, held that the paintings cannot be returned pending the criminal investigation. The Museum plans to appeal the decision. The policy conflict at the heart of this dispute is that between the desirability of the free flow of art (needed to encourage loans to institutions by means of traveling exhibits), and the undesirability of the free flow of stolen art in and out of New York state. As is often the case, it is easier to state legal or ethical principles than to apply them, especially when they conflict.[21] Nevertheless, such in-transit litigation deters traveling exhibits by discouraging loans and threatening costly legal fees.

WHAT AND HOW WE EXHIBIT

Museums are more than repositories; they are places where collections are interpreted for the public through exhibits and related educational programs. How museums interpret their collections changes over time with the emergence of new techniques, scholarship, and viewpoints. The extent of interpretation in American museums is rapidly expanding as museums see their mission changing from offering a passive venue for the already educated to being an active center of learning for a public of diverse educational and cultural backgrounds. In doing so, "less is more"; exhibit halls are shifting from crammed "open storage" toward an expository approach to selected objects. Reducing the number of objects on exhibit is itself

controversial—despite the fact that museums with encyclopedic collections have never simultaneously exhibited everything
because of space limitations and conservation considerations.

Seldom do museums explain to their audiences how choices
are made as to what and how we exhibit. Lonnie Bunch con-
tends that museums should be more forthcoming:

> Museums would be better served if they explained to the public
> why history museums explore social history that includes difficult
> questions of race, class, and gender, or why it is important for art
> museums to examine artists whose work challenges community
> norms and expectations. It is not enough to say that we "know
> best." . . . [M]useums can teach visitors more about points of view,
> the scholarly underpinnings of museum work, and the inherent
> fluidity of museum interpretation. As the clothing store advertise-
> ment extols, "An educated consumer is our best customer."[22]

What and how we exhibit depends primarily on the professionals within the museum—individuals with differing points of
view, admittedly affected by both their personal and professional experiences and preferences. Nevertheless, the public is
not aware of who the creators of exhibits or the authors of
explanatory texts are; it is the museum as an institution that
appears to be speaking. When an institution speaks it carries
more weight than an individual—more than an expert. The
museum profession is ever conscious of the fact that the institution essentially authenticates the objects and ideas of an
exhibit. Such institutional power of speech carries with it great
privilege and even greater responsibility to the audience.

In a university it is the professor who speaks; in a book it is
the author who speaks. In both instances we know who is
speaking. But in a museum we do not know who is speaking; the
exhibit takes on the quality of an institutional oracle. We live
in a time when institutional oracles are constantly questioned.
The time has come to unmask the museum oracle, revealing the
people who create exhibits and crediting them at exhibit en-
trances. In doing so, the museum must equally be prepared to
defend the creators of exhibits. However, both the museum
administration and exhibit authors must be prepared to live

with criticism from the profession and the public, both of which may have different views about the exhibit.

I accept the deconstruction and revision of the past by curators as essential to expanding knowledge and understanding. It is the responsibility of contemporary curators to reexamine the scholarship of their predecessors, just as those predecessors reassessed the work of their forebears. But it also follows that if the curator can deconstruct the beliefs of others, then those others—including the public—can deconstruct the work of present-day curators, whether now or in the future.

Unlike lawyers trained for the argumentative and adversarial forum, curators, like professors, generally prefer lecture to debate, especially when it comes to interaction with the museum-going public. While it may be reassuring to see students taking notes and visitors intently reading labels (if that ever happens), the scholar should keep an open mind and welcome challenge from all fronts. Moreover, in an era of pluralism there are many perspectives that need to be considered. While the scholarly community and the public respect experts, they regard neither curators nor professors as infallible.

Even as the individual authors of exhibits are revealed, we must recognize a difference between the university president and the museum director. The museum administration, most particularly the director, traditionally plays a greater role in museum exhibits than a university president or dean does in the classroom. What this means in the case of a museum is that the director historically has decided what exhibits will be done and how, often including fairly detailed decisions regarding content. That may be modified in practice in large museums; but it remains a basic assumption on the part of museum boards of directors and the general public that the museum director is, in fact as well as in theory, the ultimate exhibit decision-maker. Whoever decides the what and how of exhibits is subject to professional and public criticism and charges of censorship for including some items or interpretations, omitting others, or in other ways changing the exhibit.

Such criticism should not be dismissed as chilling and intimidating; it is the way of contemporary American cultural life. We live in a time when criticism is freely and stridently given and often through group protest and demonstrations. Whether pleasant or unpleasant, listening to and consulting with others—especially those with a different point of view—is a means of securing new knowledge and new insights that can, in turn, improve exhibits. As Harold Skramstad puts it, "the museum must be a listener as well as a talker."[23]

Museums should be affirmative in reaching out for diverse perspectives. In doing so, museums will improve the quality of exhibits and reflect the multiplicity of views present in a pluralistic democracy. Those selected to create the exhibit should include representatives of the diverse groups whose cultures and environments are reflected in the exhibit. Recognizing that within any such group there are many conflicting viewpoints, and that principal centers of the group may live a great distance from the museum, the museum needs to be resourceful in enlisting representative participation and perspectives.

Having listened, the museum staff has the ultimate responsibility to decide exhibit content. Its freedom to do so needs to be understood and defended both within and without the museum, just as a university would defend academic freedom. At the same time, the museum must exercise such freedom with integrity, never merely asserting claims of freedom as a specious defense to silence other points of view.

Intellectual freedom, however defined, is usually thought of as applying to the institution in the case of the museum, or to the individual professor in the case of the university. In both cases, the freedom at issue is institutionally created and exceeds the constitutional right of individual free speech. Intellectual freedom is essential to museum integrity. It must be resolutely supported and defended by curators, directors, and trustees as the underlying premise of the role of a museum as a "marketplace of differing ideas."[24] However, the museum's institutional freedom to challenge does not, indeed should not, preclude the freedom of others to challenge the museum.

How does all this theory work out in practice? Neither easily nor perfectly.

Museums vary greatly. As the nation's museum, the Smithsonian Institution is *sui generis*. Its audience is truly national, and thus its controversies are national. Its particular experiences and practices are always instructive and need to be considered as are those of its publicly owned kin, state and local government museums. Most American museums, however, are private non-profit organizations. Each is accountable under the laws of the state in which it is incorporated and operates. To paraphrase Tip O'Neill, most such museums are local, notwithstanding their national and international reputations. The bulk of their funding comes from local sources, as does the preponderance of their audience. These nonprofit museums are considered community resources, and they strive to be a vital part of community life. As a result, their controversies are primarily local and are directly influenced by community environments. While local environments vary markedly, sound museum policies and practices should be of value in approaching museum controversies, wherever and however they arise.

ONE LOCAL MUSEUM'S APPROACH

Starting from the premise that one learns more being critiqued than one learns doing the critiquing, I will reflect on experiences at the Field Museum, where I served as president for fifteen years, as examples of how exhibits work in local, nonprofit institutions—albeit, in this case, a local institution with a reputation extending far beyond Chicago. The exhibits described here are offered only as illustrations rather than as models—and they have, indeed, been controversial.[25]

The Field Museum's experiences occurred in the context of an overall exhibit policy and process that assumed it better to try to anticipate and deal with specific controversies in the context of previously adopted general principles than to respond by means of ad hoc reactions to particular situations. Because there is no end to the diversity of controversy that can be encountered, it is essential to address it in a manner that will both maintain the museum's integrity and recognize the value of internal and public criticism of the museum.

To understand the Field Museum's approach, it is necessary to know something of this museum's contemporary view of its mission, as well as of its role in society generally and in Chicago particularly. The institution's understanding of its purpose results from two museum-wide reexaminations of mission and methods, undertaken over a ten-year period. These were highly participatory self-studies. Basically, the museum's entire staff, and its curators in particular, were asked: What do you want to do in the future? Why? How? Notwithstanding the understandable academic suspicion of institutional review and the plurality of strongly held views, those of us involved in these reassessment efforts gained a clearer sense of where we were as an institution and where we wanted to go.

At the outset we all discovered that Dillon Ripley's comments about museums, quoted above, well described the public's view of the Field Museum; it was seen as a repository of antiquities with little relevance to contemporary life or interests. Few people knew that the museum engaged in collection-based research dealing with issues of present and future significance to environmental and cultural diversity and interconnectedness. Moreover, many of the exhibits, which together covered nearly 350,000 square feet, were old and did not incorporate the new knowledge being generated by the museum's curatorial staff and their disciplinary peers elsewhere in universities and research museums. Neither did the exhibits reflect changing attitudes about nature and human cultures. Furthermore, new exhibit processes and technologies that could expand the effectiveness of dioramas and labels, engaging the visitor's mind as an active participant rather than a passive learner, had not been comprehensively integrated.

True to its tradition, the Field Museum recommitted to its role as a center of learning for a diverse public. A museum is not just a place for the educated; it must be a place where diverse people of diverse backgrounds can learn about the natural environment and human cultures, their variety, and their interconnections. Indeed, it is this "connectedness" that is the fundamental rationale undergirding the Field Museum's overall mission. The institution has long been concerned with the connections within and across nature and cultures, and with reflecting these in its own connections with both the local community and with those whose cultures and environments are represented in the museum's collections and exhibits. In short, the museum must not stand isolated.

Since institutions tend to be inwardly driven, outwardness requires a concerted mindset and action. This is reflected throughout the museum's mission statement, which prominently includes sections on "Reaching Out," "Working With Others," and "Listening to Each Other." These sections assert, inter alia, that the museum must "work collaboratively and sensitively with the people in our locality, country, and world whose cultures and habitats are represented in our collections, research, and public programs" including "researchers and teachers who reside in the areas from which our collections come." Finally, and pretentiously, the document speaks of the Field Museum as a center of understanding and mutual respect for conflicting points of view. Thus the section entitled "Listening To Each Other" states:

> The Museum subject matter directly relates to the great issues of the present and future: environmental and cultural diversity and their interrelationships. There are differing scholarly and public viewpoints on these concerns. While the Museum does not take institutional positions on these issues, it must serve as a center of free inquiry, a marketplace for multiple points of view on these matters. In doing so it serves as a forum where relevant controversy can be aired. In this way the Museum can be a "door in the wall" of our differences and inspire greater knowledge, understanding and respect for our varied natural environments and cultural heritages.

So much for sanctimonious rhetoric. How then does "connectedness" play out in the museum's exhibits and the controversies that arise over such issues as human remains, obscenity, public disturbance, cultural interpretation, sacred objects, the making of new exhibits from old ones, or the museum's functioning as a marketplace of ideas?

Human Remains

Museums of anthropology, archaeology, and natural history have traditionally exhibited both prehistoric and historic human remains. This was true at the Field Museum. More recently, the museum has adopted a policy on the exhibition of human remains that reads, in part:

[I]n our consultations with groups having cultural affinities with the remains, we discuss whether the remains should be on public exhibit or how they should be on public exhibit. We have made the decision not to display remains where the descendant group expresses an objection to this practice. If there is no descendant group having cultural affinity, we are sensitive to the exhibit concerns of contemporary collateral descendants. In the case of human remains from foreign countries, we look to the exhibition policy of those countries and to the cultural practice of the native peoples from those countries. . . .

Museums in Illinois joined forces with the Roman Catholic Church successfully to oppose legislation that would have prohibited any public exhibition of human remains. The proposed legislation emanated from Native American opposition to the continued exhibition of prehistoric remains as the centerpiece of the Dixon Mounds historic site. As the result of the legislative debate, the state closed that portion of the site to public view.

Obscenity

The nude human figure has been represented in art, anthropological, and science museums from their inception. In the United States, nudity is not obscenity. At the same time, however, obscenity is not constitutionally protected speech. What then is obscenity? According to the United States Supreme Court in the case of *Miller* vs. *California*,[26] something is obscene only if it can be said to meet all of three tests: (1) if "the average person, applying contemporary community standards," would find that, taken as a whole, an object or image appeals to the prurient interest in sex; (2) if it depicts or describes sexual conduct in a patently offensive way; and (3) if, "taken as a whole, [it] lacks serious literary, artistic, political, or scientific value." A final determination of obscenity can only be made by judicial decision, and it is likely that a determination by a museum's professional staff that an exhibit has "serious value" would carry weight with the court.

The Field Museum's administration believed strongly that museum curators, rather than a governmental agency, should make such determinations. Thus, we declined a grant from the

National Endowment for the Arts because of an obscenity restriction that seemed clearly to provide for intervention by the NEA, a nonjudicial federal agency, in actively making judgments about museum exhibits. We felt that obscenity restrictions are properly defined and enforced with finality by the courts, not by an administrative agency of government.[27]

Notwithstanding an exhibit of serious value, a museum that holds itself out as a family or children's museum could adopt as its own policy the court-approved practices of posting a notice outside an exhibit notifying visitors that an exhibit might contain material they would find offensive, and stationing a person outside the exhibit so that minors could not enter without an adult. After internal discussion prior to the opening of an exhibit at the Field Museum, such a notice was posted at the entrance to an exhibit of contemporary art created by individuals on the museum staff, art created outside the building on their own time. Some argued in discussions that such a notice was intimidating; others contended that it expanded visitor choice.

Anthropology museums have particular problems with the issue of obscenity. Different cultures have different views at different times—views sometimes in conflict—on just what constitutes obscenity. Some cultures—past and present—are more comfortable with sexual explicitness than has historically been the case in the United States. Thus, sexually explicit objects may not be considered obscene in another culture. Contemporary times, too, bring conflicting perceptions of obscenity. Such a conflict occurred when the Field Museum received a letter from an officer of a local chapter of the National Organization for Women in another state urging us to remove a small, long-standing Native American diorama because she found it sexist, pornographic, and violent. We consulted our specially related tribal advisory group, which consisted primarily of women, and were urged not to remove the diorama on the grounds that its representation was factually accurate. The museum instead responded by placing, for several years, a "talk back" area next to the diorama, setting forth the diverse views and providing cards for visitor comments that could then be posted by the visitor.

Public Disturbance

The mere fact that an exhibit may create a public disturbance is insufficient grounds for the government to close or remove an object from an exhibit. This issue was addressed by the Federal Court of Appeals for the Seventh Circuit in *Nelson* vs. *Streeter*, a case involving the School of the Art Institute of Chicago.[28] This case centered on a show of student work not open to the public, which included a painting of the late Harold Washington, Chicago's first African-American mayor. Entitled *Mirth and Girth*, the painting showed the mayor attired in women's underwear—which outraged some students and, ultimately, many members of the public. The school stationed a security guard nearby to protect the painting from angry students. When asked by the school administration to remove the painting, the student artist refused to do so.

Once word of the painting reached the Chicago City Council, that body adopted resolutions calling for removal of the painting and demanding an apology from the Art Institute, threatening a cutoff of city funding. (Although the school and the museum are administratively separate, the board of the Art Institute governs both.) Subsequently, two separate forays to the school gallery were made by four different African-American Council members. The first two aldermen took down the painting, announcing they were doing so pursuant to the council's resolution to remove the painting. Upon their departure the painting was rehung. The second wave of aldermen also took the painting down and sought to remove it from the school. They were intercepted by the school's president, who took the painting into his office. Subsequently, the city's police superintendent ordered an officer to take the painting into police custody; there it was kept until the next evening, when it was released to the artist.

The ensuing public debate was polarized, particularly among liberals. On the one hand, the painting was viewed as racist, and the Art Institute found itself being branded as racist for allowing it to be shown. Contrariwise, others deemed the painting's removal to be censorship. The president of the board of the Art Institute issued a public apology and stated that the painting would not be further exhibited.

When the artist later sued the aldermen for violation of his civil rights, their defense centered on a claim of official immunity. Chief Judge Richard A. Posner, writing for the U.S. Court of Appeals for the Seventh Circuit, affirmed the district court's denial of the officials' immunity from suit and remanded the case back to the lower court for a "swift conclusion." In doing so, Judge Posner also rejected the aldermen's contention that their action to remove the painting was necessary to prevent public rioting. There was no "clear and present danger" justification because, he said, "There is no evidence that in creating and exhibiting *Mirth and Girth* . . . Nelson intended to provoke a riot or that the danger of a riot was great." He further stated that "First Amendment rights are not subject to the heckler's veto. The rioters are the culpable parties, not the artist whose work unintentionally provoked them to violence."[29]

Peaceful picketing and leafleting against an exhibit outside a museum are forms of protected free speech. However, it must not physically impede access to the museum. Chanting and speaking to museum visitors is not forbidden even though it may make some visitors feel uncomfortable. Aquaria are picketed by animal rights groups with sufficient frequency for the practice to become a normal part of doing business. As long as demonstrators are peaceful and do not interfere with institutional business, museum personnel would do well to consider this a logical extension of the museum's marketplace role and not act aggrieved.

Cultural Interpretation[30]

Older museums of anthropology—including the Field Museum—have invested enormous curatorial time and financial resources over the course of their histories in creating permanent exhibits that have been rendered obsolete by the passage of time. Because of the sheer physical rigidity of these exhibits and the inordinate costs and time required to change them, they cannot be readily updated. Yet not surprisingly, these antiquated exhibits have been subject to extensive criticism by anthropologists and the people whose cultures they represent. George

Stocking points out that more than physical rigidity is involved in exhibit datedness:

> [T]he meaning of the material forms preserved in museums must always be problematic. This is even more the case inasmuch as the objects viewed by museum observers are "survivals" not only of the past from which the collection wrenched them, but from those later pasts in which any given act of exhibition has placed them. Museums, in short, are institutions in which the forces of historical inertia (or "cultural lag") are profoundly, perhaps inescapably, implicated.[31]

Notwithstanding these time lags, anthropology museums are actively engaged in new approaches to cultural exhibits. The Field Museum is in the process of redoing its cultural exhibits. The manner of our doing so and the resulting exhibits have been both criticized and approved by anthropologists, affinity group members, and the general public.

It is standard Field Museum practice to include as active participants on the exhibit planning team representatives of cultures that are the focus of the exhibit. When it was decided to create a new exhibit on Africa and the Western Hemisphere diaspora from the perspective of Africans and African-Americans, the exhibit team was headed by African-Americans and included scholars from Africa as well as the United States. There was also widespread consultation in Chicago among interested groups and individuals, as well as interviews of the public at large. The costs in terms of time and money of this consultative process are considered an essential element of exhibit budgets. So, too, is the cost of the construction and public try-out of mockups of preliminary exhibit components. In this way, we learn a great deal about the effectiveness of the exhibit before it is too late (and too expensive) to make changes. Throughout the development of the Africa exhibit, the public was exposed to and queried about exhibit ideas and components.

Many views were expressed about what the Africa exhibit should be—even whether the exhibit should be. Should such an exhibit be in a natural history museum? Could the objectives of the exhibit be achieved in an institution regarded by some as historically racist? These and other views, often conflicting and sometimes forcefully expressed, informed the decision-making that followed the museum's exhibit development protocol. From consultation must be distilled a clear and coherent approach to exhibit content that can be recognized and understood by visitors. The resulting approach will, of course, be subject to criticism and debate by consultants, other experts, and the public. Indeed, the exhibit should be designed to permit the expression of that dissent, both in the present and in the future.

Since *Africa* was a collection-based exhibit, it was agreed that the exhibit would speak to the issue of how the Field Museum came to have African cultural collections in the first place. For example, there was explicit reference in the descriptive labels to the fact that some of the Benin bronzes were seized in a British punitive expedition. The focus was not only on the history of culture, however; one of the exhibit's basic purposes was to present the contemporary life of Africans and African-Americans both in Africa and in Chicago.

Pervading the exhibit was the thesis that culture and nature continually interact in generating societal and environmental change. Frustratingly, even as museums seek to present continuing cultural change in new permanent exhibits, they are inhibited in doing so. Today, as in the past, permanent exhibit-making requires investing huge amounts of time and money in fixed and static exhibit elements that inevitably become dated in content and presentation. Thus, despite extensive efforts to reflect a greater sensitivity to cultural diversity and change, modern exhibitry continues to freeze cultures in a "permanent exhibitry time warp." To overcome this, museums need to think more in terms of temporary rather than permanent exhibits. We need to find cheaper and quicker ways to exhibit in order to reflect change. As important as effective exhibit techniques are, it is still the message, not the medium, that must take precedence in exhibit-making.

Sacred Objects

As an anthropological museum, the Field Museum is a secular institution concerned with religious and spiritual beliefs. Whether and how the museum exhibits objects sacred to others depends on the perspectives of those to whom the objects are sacred. This policy applies to contemporary objects as well as older ones. We consult with the present-day affinity group most closely connected with the object. If consultation is not feasible because of distance, we look at the exhibition policy and practices of the affinity group.

Treating sacred objects with respect is an ethical matter. For some, it is unscientific to hold such a view. However, even modern science is subject to ethical standards. While it is possible to agree on general ethical principles, the application of ethics to a particular case is always debatable and never axiomatic. Respect for other points of view also makes ethical sense in how museums approach secular objects that have different meanings for different people. This is particularly true of secular objects having political, historical, or cultural iconic quality.

New Exhibits from Old Exhibits

What one generation esteems, the next deplores, and so forth *ad infinitum*. For the Field Museum, the Akeley Dioramas and Malvina Hoffman's sculptures are cases in point.[32]

The environmental dioramas of Carl and (long ignored) Delia Akeley are enduring masterpieces depicting nature's interconnections.[33] They are irreplaceable because the art of realistic taxidermic sculpture is now rare, the species included may be extinct or endangered, and the costs of diorama-making are high. These treasured dioramas of earlier times remain an invaluable teaching tool for today's environmentally oriented museum. At the Field Museum, we often augmented the area outside the diorama cases in order to help the visitor learn more from them.

Our decision to do so sprang from a number of concerns, not least the fact that a traditional hall of dioramas is often viewed by today's visitors as a dead zoo located in a dark tunnel—to be either avoided or used as a race track. By creating an environmental ambience for the entire hall, we hoped that people would be intrigued—realizing that this was a museum about nature today and in the future, as well as in the past. Moreover, we hoped to intercept uninitiated visitors who might feel themselves to be in a sea of indistinguishable dioramas. To capture the attention of visitors, a mini "field station" was created outside each diorama. The "station" was designed to help visitors focus on the message of an individual diorama by providing relevant information using labels, videos, computers, and other interactive devices. Thus, a deer diorama could be a site to explore the controversial issues associated with the overpopulation of deer in urban and suburban locales. The diorama stations also reduced the sense of visitor separation from the natural scene resulting from the glass cover needed to protect the diorama.

Anthropological dioramas pose a special challenge. They may need major revision and relabeling so that visitors are not given false or stereotypical impressions about the past or present. The perspectives of representative members of the culture need to be added along with new scholarship. Here, again, an anthropological hall should have a cultural ambience conducive to visitor learning and understanding. The walk-through diorama is a worthy complement to the sealed dioramas and exhibit cases necessary to protect research collections.

A more controversial legacy of the past arises from sculptures commissioned by museums in an era when some anthropologists were exploring whether physical differences among people were biologically significant. Now that we know the error of such an idea, the question becomes what to do with these sculptures.

In the case of the Field Museum, Malvina Hoffman, a student of Rodin, was commissioned in the 1920s to execute 104 sculptures of individuals representative of the world's people.[34] Although questions were raised then about the ability of a woman to undertake this venture, Hoffman traveled the globe sculpting from models who approximated the physical measurements the museum's anthropologists had instructed her to replicate. Instead of sculpting in wax, as she had been engaged to do, she talked the museum into allowing her to work in bronze. In 1933, concurrent with Chicago's "Century of Progress" World's Fair—held next door to the museum—many of these sculptures became a permanent exhibit in a gallery located just inside the main entrance to the museum. Entitled *The Races of Mankind*, the exhibit remained until 1968—when it was dismantled on the grounds that as an exhibit it perpetuated discredited concepts of race. A third of the sculptures were relocated in decorative positions around the museum. There was an enormous protest against the closing of the Hoffman exhibit by many regular visitors to the Museum.

What of Malvina Hoffman and her sculptures today? In the early 1980s casts of her African figures were borrowed by nearby Malcolm X College, where they are displayed in central halls under the flags of the independent nations of Africa. Hoffman's archives and some of her work have been acquired by the Getty Trust. Within the museum, her sculptures are now an important element in a museum-wide tour connected with a new cross-cultural exhibit called *Living Together: Common Concerns, Different Responses.* Artist that she was, Malvina Hoffman captured and honored the individual integrity she saw and respected in each of her models.

Contemporary Marketplace of Ideas

In what ways does the Field Museum continue to be a market-place of multiple points of view, a forum where controversy can be aired? Is it possible for a museum to serve as a forum for debate between diverse and changing points of view, one not frozen in time by the often static nature of its exhbits? Since exhibits present one or more particular points of view at a particular point in time in a fixed (and, thus, costly) format, how can we inexpensively build in opportunities for visitors to learn about and express new ideas and dissenting perspectives?

There are many ways to do so. Exhibit computer programs can be changed. Current articles from newspapers and periodi-cals can be posted on bulletin boards located in the exhibit. A visitor resource center located in the exhibit area can make available a variety of materials including books, periodicals, newspapers, photographs, maps, audio and visual tapes, CDs, and computers. These resources can be continually updated to reflect diverse perspectives.

Interpretive programs by staff and volunteers are also means of attaining these ends. Public lectures, symposia, debates, courses, performances, festivals, and films are important means of engaging the public in discourse. These should be cast as dialogues rather than monologues. Visitors should be encouraged to raise questions and state their views. In short, the public should be able to talk back to the museum on any subject the museum asks the public to consider.

The Field Museum has realized considerable success with the inclusion of "talk back" spaces in a variety of exhibits. Inexpensive to build, operate, and update, they are located next to controversial exhibit segments or at the end of an exhibit. In this way the museum can open itself to challenge, even about its basic tenets. For example, a "talk back" is prominently included in our major exhibit on evolution. These "talk backs" stimulate visitors' responses by raising specific questions for their consideration. Using index cards, visitors are able to respond to the questions, raise their own questions, and comment about the exhibit's content. The cards can then be posted on the adjacent bulletin board. It is amazing how many people respond thoughtfully and how many read the responses of others. This is a "minds-on" interactive opportunity that has the additional advantage of being inexpensive to operate, since it does not require technical staff to maintain.

In sum, if a museum is to be a marketplace of ideas, it should stimulate debate. Visitors should be heard, not just seen.

THE NATIONAL MUSEUM'S APPROACH: THE SMITHSONIAN

The exhibition controversies in which a local museum becomes engaged are felt directly within its immediate community by the museum, its staff, and its trustees. By contrast, the controversies encountered by the nation's museum are both local and national. The Smithsonian's local constituents include the members of Congress and the executive branch who speak directly and powerfully for a nationwide citizenry that expects its national museum to reflect the America it knows. However, each one of those citizens has an individual perspective on just what "America" the museum should treasure—perspectives that, taken together, are many, diverse, and conflicting.

The "exhibiting dilemmas" of the Smithsonian are well known and have been extensively reported.[35] To oversimplify, they reflect a country divided over whether the Smithsonian can, or should, celebrate the nation's past without reevaluation. We are now in a period of looking at our history from the standpoint of all of our citizens, not just from the perspective of a single group or even the majority. We are also coming to understand that no group is monolithic in its viewpoint. This is a time of inclusiveness, and our interpretation of history is no exception.

There is also a generational divide that manifests itself in the consideration of recent history. Those who lived through an era often see it in a way that can only be imagined by those who can only see it in retrospect. We need to understand the context of the times, then as well as now.

I am neither a pacifist nor a warmonger; I do not consider my views the only correct ones. However, as a citizen and a veteran of World War II—I trained as a Navy corpsman—I would like my perspectives to be represented in an exhibit on the *Enola Gay*.[36] I also believe the opinions of others on the question of America's use of nuclear force, then and now, should be heard in such an exhibit. But is that possible? Or are some issues too controversial to be presented in a national museum? Is the Smithsonian more sacred than the Congress?

When his advice on the exhibit was solicited, Mike Mansfield, then the U.S. ambassador to Japan, recommended that the Smithsonian simply display the *Enola Gay* without comment, allowing visitors to interpret the significance of the aircraft and its mission from their own varied and conflicting perspectives.[37] This would include the many visitors from Japan, our current ally and friend. But such an exhibit, an object standing alone, would not tell anyone anything more than they already knew. That, in my view, would be a fundamental error. Exhibits should be informative and stimulating. They should not be monologues. Other points of view should be acknowledged, and the visitor given an opportunity to react. One Smithsonian example that resonated with the public was the *Reminiscences* exhibit, which included the memories of a great variety of citizens about America in the years after World War II. Such an exhibit may be regarded by some as popular rather than scholarly; yet including first-person voices can serve to make exhibits accessible to visitors across a range of generations.

As a result of the *Enola Gay* controversy, on April 19, 1995, the Smithsonian cosponsored with the University of Michigan an illuminating symposium on "Presenting History: Museums in a Democratic Society." Diverse and conflicting points of view were cogently put by participants. Thereafter, on August 25, 1995, Michael Heyman, secretary of the Smithsonian, issued exhibit planning guidelines with the objectives to

· reinvigorate thinking about the processes of creating exhibitions at the Smithsonian

· establish a system for regularly reviewing exhibition planning guidelines

· identify accountability at all levels of the Institution.

Recognizing that controversy is now a way of life for museums, Secretary Heyman included in the *Guidelines* the following passage from the *Report of the Commission on the Future of the Smithsonian Institution*:

> Museums in general, and the Smithsonian in particular, are increasingly flash points in the debates that characterize our nation's transition from a society that depends for coherence on a single accepted set of values and practices to one that derives its strength and unity from a deep tolerance of diversity. This happens because museums, to fulfill their missions, must prepare exhibitions that record and illuminate this transition. This sometimes results in acrimonious and contentious debate on controversial subjects. The Smithsonian has hardly been immune. Its position is especially challenging because it is a national institution with large and complex collections and missions.

Indeed, a number of aspects of the Smithsonian's exhibit-planning guidelines reflect themes similar to those implemented at the local level. Many have already been discussed in the case of the Field Museum. A paragraph of the Smithsonian's *Guidelines* on "Accountability" reaffirms the traditional responsibility of the individual museum director to select and approve exhibits subject to the overall authority of the secretary "to approve or disapprove any Smithsonian exhibition at his discretion." The paragraph also provides:

> In general, museums are accountable for presenting information that is grounded in scholarship, but which also respects the diverse perspectives of groups and individuals. If the contents of an exhibition represent a single point of view or are aspects of an issue with multiple facets, the author must be identified.

Among "Basic Issues" enumerated in the *Guidelines* one finds:

> Advisory groups should be considered for major projects and convened at the earliest point possible. Museum staff must clearly communicate the roles of all participants and provide consultants with tangible evidence that their advice is receiving full and fair consideration.

The *Guidelines* conclude with a section on "Sensitive Issues," which provides:

> A. For each exhibition museums need to identify those who are likely to view the exhibition and those who may have concern about the exhibition topic or approach. Where desirable, museums should collect and analyze information about the experiences and expectations of visitors and others during the exhibition planning phases and through assessment of audience responses to the completed exhibition.
>
> B. Museums must establish mechanisms to identify potentially sensitive issues (i.e., those where segments of the public may disagree or where curators or other scholars may disagree). Museums should address sensitive issues by reviewing the topic and approach to determine whether changes in direction or changes in degree of emphasis or balance are appropriate. They should plan various options for handling a range of public responses, which may include identifying spokespersons for the exhibition's point of view or organizing forums to present different perspectives on the subject matter.
>
> C. When sensitive issues become apparent, exhibition staff will notify the Director who, when prudence dictates, will bring the matter to the attention of the Provost. The Office of Provost will monitor the issue, consulting with the Office of Government Relations and the Director of Communications or other senior staff, as necessary. If public debate is anticipated or if questions from the

public and news media arise about the issue, an official spokesperson should be designated and a Q&A sheet and other information materials developed for all of those who may receive inquires about it.[38]

THE INFLUENCE OF FUNDERS: WILL THE PIPER CALL THE TUNE?

Private Funders

The "Basic Issues" section of the Smithsonian's *Guidelines* document includes specific reference to exhibit funding:

> Public affairs staff should collaborate with researchers and others to understand and defend scholarship when appropriate. [Smithsonian Institution] staff raising funds for exhibitions also should consult regularly in order to ensure that conflicts do not arise between the expectations of funders and expectations of staff involved in developing exhibits.

Certainly, it is wise to keep donors aware of what museum administrators are doing with their funds. Openness and discussion on the part of the museum goes far to assure donors that institutional integrity in the exhibit process is understood to be essential in assuring public credibility. Donors—be they individuals, corporations or foundations—are also members of the institution's community, and their views are entitled to be considered.

We are, however, in a period of greater restrictions on giving. More and more donors are interested in supporting specific objectives rather than funding general operations. Foundations sometimes combine areas of focus with particular strategies for achieving focus goals. Individual donors want to see the tangible results of their giving. Increasingly, corporate support has a marketing dimension to it—understandable from their perspective, but worrisome from the museum's point of view.

What happens when conflicts between funders and staff cannot be resolved? This is when the museum is between a rock and a hard place. Institutional integrity is certainly at stake. In some cases institutional fiscal viability may be at stake as well. After friendly but forthright discussion with all concerned, followed by due consideration, institutional integrity must take precedence. After a decision is made, all responsible for the institution—directors, staff, trustees—must live with its consequences. In the short run, those consequences may be financially dire; yet in the long run they will be rewarded by community respect and increased financial support.

Government Funders

Private museums have the right to use government funds, once granted, without losing control over how and what is exhibited. But such institutions do not have a right to government funding. The 1998 Supreme Court decision in *Endowment for the Arts* vs. *Finley* makes an important distinction between the government as regulator and the government as patron in making grants to artists or private museums.[39] To oversimplify, in some situations the government may be considered as patron, which entitles it to fund its artistic preferences, "such as support for Native American art; or policy-based biases, such as decency; or aesthetic preferences or standards."[40]

I leave to constitutional-law experts the pursuit of the consequences that could flow from this regulator-patron distinction. Regardless of whether it acts as regulator or patron, the government cannot engage in viewpoint discrimination—making funding decisions simply on grounds of disagreement with the ideas expressed.[41] A case in point was another situation involving a student artist at the School of the Art Institute of Chicago. In this instance, the artist draped the American flag so that a part of it lay on the floor; visitors had to step either over or on it in order to pass. The patriotic outcry was enormous, especially from veterans' groups.

In response, a proposal was put before the board of the Chicago Park District to cut off funding to the nine museums on Park District land. This funding comes in the form of general operating support for the museums, and is generated by a special tax levy on real estate transactions that can only be used to support the museums. Together the museums argued, and the Park District's counsel concurred, that the withholding of these funds because of the school's exhibit would be unconstitutional. The institutions' argument was premised on the fact that the Circuit Court of Cook County had held that the particular exhibit constituted artistic and political expression—protected by the First Amendment to the U.S. Constitution, and article I, section 4 of the Illinois Constitution. Constitutional law, the museums asserted, does not permit a governmental agency to interfere with protected speech, either directly or indirectly, simply because of personal objection to its message from members of the public. Therefore, it would be unconstitutional for the Chicago Park District to deny funds to the museums in order to penalize them for unpopular artistic and political expression protected by the U.S. and Illinois Constitutions. Because the Park District's counsel agreed with this position, the board never adopted the proposed funding cutoff. However, in the succeeding year the Illinois General Assembly's appropriation for the State Arts Council contained a single $1.00 line-item grant for the School of the Art Institute.

MUSEUMS IN GENERAL

Can and should exhibit guidelines be established that assure institutional integrity while at the same time acknowledging and enhancing the museum's accountability to the public? Can museum professionals agree on good exhibit practices, and then publicly rally around peers who have complied with the guidelines and are under attack? Neil Harris thinks so, and cogently puts the basic issues to be addressed through guidelines:

> Museum specialists should begin to hold serious and systematic discussions about defining appropriate standards of institutional action and offering guidance about procedures of adjudication.

> And this in turn leads to the final question. Are professional staff, support staff, potential audiences, and funding sources all to be given equal voice in the discussion process? Should vetoes be extended to any of these constituencies? Is a sense of personal affront equivalent to an intellectual argument? How can multiple and sometimes divergent voices be inserted within an exhibition? Should they be included?

Coming as he does from higher education, Professor Harris proposes adapting the university peer-review model for making and reviewing recommendations concerning exhibit disputes:

> Peer review is certainly preferable to many alternatives, but who constitute the peers? Acknowledging and responding to the views of audiences and employees should not require surrendering commitments to staff and to programs . . . protest should invite response and dialogue rather than capitulation. [42]

Much would be gained if "response and dialogue" were incorporated into the exhibit process without having to be triggered only by protest. Exhibits would unquestionably be made more informative and interesting by building dialogue into the exhibit process.

In 1997 the Society for History in the Federal Government adopted exhibit standards that may be regarded as a sound basis for developing institutional exhibit policies in private as well as government museums. Recognizing the role of museums in transmitting knowledge in a diverse society, the standards emphasize that exhibits should be based on scholarship and suggest that representatives of various stakeholders participate in the exhibit-planning process. The policy admonishes museums "to be mindful of their public trust" in following its enumerated standards. The last two standards provide:

> 4. When an exhibit addresses a controversial subject, it should acknowledge the existence of competing points of view. The public should be able to see that history is a changing process of interpretation and reinterpretation formed through gathering and reviewing evidence, drawing conclusions, and presenting the conclusions in text or exhibit format.

> 5. Museum administrators should defend exhibits produced according to these standards. [43]

Indeed the entire museum profession should defend and rally to the support of museums that produce controversial exhibits pursuant to standards promoting sound scholarship as well as institutional openness and accountability. Science museums should defend art museums; children's museums should defend history museums. There is no "controversy-free museum" in this age of pluralism.

CONCLUSION

If a museum is to be a marketplace of ideas and public discourse, it will inevitably be a center of controversy. As Sinatra sang, "you can't have one without the other." Neil Harris clearly reminds us of where we have come from, and the consequences of where we are going:

> Museums . . . were treated not as places where knowledge was disputed or contested, but where it was secure. . . .

> [A controversial art exhibit of thirty years ago] signaled not only museums' willingness to become more inclusive and critical of existing establishments—or at least to call attention to paradoxes and contradictions—but a desire for greater relevance in commercial and intellectual terms. This, combined with an erosion of confidence in existing canons and the American consensus, would make museum exhibitions in the '70s and '80s more vulnerable. Anyone could become a significant critic of the museum, not merely artists and professionals. A loss of confidence in elite expertise . . . characterized this whole era, to be sure. And to some extent, the museum's increased vulnerability to popular criticism expressed this trend. But *museum exposure can also be seen as part of the price paid for increased attention and patronage. It is implausible to emphasize simultaneously social relevance and institutional connections and the need for immunity from controversy.*[44]

Recognizing this reality, museums need policies and practices enabling them to pursue their respective missions with integrity. Underlying these policies and practices must be an institutional attitude neither fearful nor disdainful of other points of view. Institutional policies must rather reflect the conviction that learning requires an open and searching mind. We learn from others, both professionals and laity. Certainly, this is now the approach of anthropologists and environmental biologists who are advancing knowledge by listening to and working with lay people in the field. Similarly, museums can learn much by listening to and working with lay people in their own communities. Particularly, museums can learn how to be more effective in their public educational role.

Museums need to be open and consultative in collecting and exhibiting. Our exhibits should allow for the expression of conflicting views. We can invite others to speak through "talk backs" and public seminars. Although a continual strain on museum staffs and boards, acknowledging the right to question over and over again is the essence of learning, scholarship, and democracy. While it is natural to be defensive in the face of challenge, we need to disagree amicably and patiently—even if others will not. Instead of being made rigid, we should be pleasantly assertive. Otherwise, we need to take Harry Truman's advice: If we can't stand the heat, we should get out of the kitchen.

Having listened and consulted, the museum must itself act as collector and speak as exhibitor. Any museum's claim to institutional freedom depends upon the museum exercising its freedom. In the end, the museum must make the final choices about what is said and done, based on its mission and professional standards. If the museum abdicates or fails to exercise the final authority to decide, it gives up any claim to deciding at all. Its claim of authority to do so rests on its institutional integrity. Institutional integrity requires principled conduct, which is sometimes unpopular in the short term. But museums are about the long term. Durability is best assured by a principled approach, which wears well through everchanging times.

Finally, and again heeding President Truman, the buck stops with the museum director. Even so, the director needs the steadfast support of courageous trustees and staff to assure the role of the museum as a center of learning about controversial issues. This requires each of us to do more than just stand our ground under fire. We must also be continuous public advocates and practitioners of the museum's mission.

In the heat of controversy, the museum's basic mission, its articles of faith, must be kept in the forefront. A museum is not an abstraction; rather, it is a group of fallible humans seeking to find and disseminate new knowledge. We are our institutions. How we act determines their future. Steve Weil wisely reminds us:

Institutions infused with faith and built on such qualities as respect, caring, and decency must inevitably strengthen and bring to the fore those very same qualities in people who work with and for them.[45]

ENDNOTES

[1]Sidney Dillon Ripley, *The Sacred Grove* (New York: Simon and Schuster, 1969), 24–25.

[2]Ibid., 38.

[3]"Museums for the New Millennium: A Symposium for the Museum Community," report of a symposium held 5–7 September 1996, Center for Museum Studies, Smithsonian Institution, in association with the American Association of Museums (Washington, D.C.: Center for Museum Studies, Smithsonian Institution), 36, 38.

[4]Willard Boyd, "Wanted: An Effective Director," *Curator* 38 (3) (1995): 171, 175.

[5]"Report of the AAMD Task Force on the Spoliation of Art during the Nazi/World War II Era (1933–1945)," AAMD press release, 4 June 1998. See also *Professional Practices in Art Museums* (New York: AAMD, 1992), section 18 of which provides: "The Director must not knowingly acquire or allow to be recommended for acquisition any object that has been stolen, removed in contravention of treaties and international conventions to which the United States is a signatory, or illegally imported into the United States."

[6]"A Statement by the Art Dealers Association of America on Nazi-Looted Art" (press release, n.d.), 2–3.

[7]See Hector Felciano, *The Lost Museum* (New York: Basic Books, 1998); Peter Watson, *Sotheby's: The Inside Story* (London: Bloomsbury, 1998); and "Big Auction Houses Take Closer Look at Issue of Ethics," *Christian Science Monitor*, 10 February 1998, 11.

[8]Gail Chaddock, "Art World Wary of New Rules," *Christian Science Monitor*, 10 February 1998, 11.

[9]See Franklin Feldman and Stephen Weil, *Art Works: Law, Policy, Practice* (New York: Practicing Law Institute, 1974), 528 ff. for the text of the UNESCO Convention; and ibid., 627–636, for policy statements of the Field Museum, University of Pennsylvania, and Harvard University.

[10]Walter Robinson and John Yemma, "Harvard Museum Acquisitions Shock Scholars," *Boston Globe*, 16 January 1998. See also "Harvard University Accused of Acquiring Looted Antiquities," *Chronicle of Higher Education*, 30 January 1998, A6.

[11]American Association of Museums, *Code of Ethics for Museums* (Washington: American Association of Museums, 1994), 8. See also the AAM "Statement

on Cultural Property" (19 January 1999) stating that the AAM "has aggressively promoted the objectives" of the UNESCO Convention. The statement also reports that AAM requires in its accreditation program and promotes as part of good collections management that:

· Each institution should have a policy in place which addresses the legal, ethical, and managerial practices to deal with questions raised about the legal ownership of items on exhibition, whether owned by the museum or on loan, and

· Institutions also have the responsibility to the public to insure that claims of lawful ownership are rightful and fact-based, so that the public is assured that if the object leaves the public trust, it does so appropriately.

[12]International Council of Museums (ICOM), "Code of Professional Ethics," at 3.2 ("Acquisition of Illicit Materials"), 1996.

[13]Tim Golden, "Big-Game Hunter's Gift Riles Smithsonian," *New York Times*, 17 March 1999, A14. As to biological collections, see Field Museum policy: Feldman and Weil, *Art Works: Law, Policy, Practice*, 627.

[14]The contrary position was taken by the American Association of Dealers in Antiquities, Oriental and Primitive Art in *United States* vs. *McClain*, 545 F2d 988, 991 (1977).

[15]See also *Masterpieces from Central Africa: The Tervuren Museum*, ed. Gustaaf Verswijver (New York: Prestel, 1996), 7–12.

[16]Adam Hochschild, *King Leopold's Ghost* (Boston: Houghton Mifflin, 1998), 293.

[17]George Stocking, *History of Anthropology*, vol. 1, *Essays on Museums and Material Culture* (Madison: University of Wisconsin Press, 1983), 5–6.

[18]See Walter Robinson, "Question of Ownership Taints MFA Painting," *Boston Globe*, 25 February 1999, A1, A12 (describing the Museum of Fine Arts' cooperation in returning a painting to the Netherlands); Judith Dobrzynski, "Ancient Sculpture, Once Stolen, Surrendered to India," *New York Times*, 24 February 1999, B1, B5 (describing the return of objects by the Asia Society, the J. Paul Getty Museum, and the Denver Art Museum).

[19]P. J. O'Keefe and Lyndel Prott, *Law and the Cultural Heritage*, vol. 3 (Abingdon: Professional Books, 1984), chap. 16.

[20]Ibid., chap. 1. See also Norman Palmer, *The Recovery of Stolen Art* (London: Kluwer Law International, 1998); Jeanette Greenfield, *The Return of Cultural Treasures*, 2d ed. (Cambridge: Cambridge University Press, 1996).

[21]*People of the State of New York* vs. *Museum of Modern Art*, 688 N.Y.S. 2d. 3 (App. Div., First Dept. 1999). This decision reversed the decision of a lower state court, *In the Matter of the Museum of Modern Art*, 177 Misc. 2d 985 (N.Y. County 1998).

[22]Lonnie G. Bunch, "Fighting the Good Fight: Museums in an Age of Uncertainty," *Museum News* (March/April 1995): 35.

[23]"Museums for the New Millennium," 39. See generally American Association of Museums, *Excellence and Equity: Education and the Public Dimension of*

Museums (Washington, D.C.: American Association of Museums, 1992); Nina Archabal, in *Museums and Sustainable Communities: Summit of the Museums of the Americas*, ed. Donald Garfield, Alvaro Madrigal, and Oscar Navarro (Washington: American Association of Museums, 1998), 18; Robert Archibald, "Narratives for A New Century," *Museum News* 33 (November/December 1998); Danielle Rice, "Modern Art: Making People Mad," *Museum News* 53 (May/June 1997); Donald Garfield, "The Next Thing Now: Designing the 21st-Century Museum," *Museum News* 34 (January/February 1996); Robert Macdonald, "Museums and Controversy: What Can We Handle?" *Curator* 39 (3) (September 1996): 167; Perry Ottenberg, "Value Conflict in Exhibitions: A Psychiatric Perspective," *Curator* 12 (1) (March 1996); Edward Linenthal, "Can Museums Achieve a Balance Between Memory and History," *Chronicle of Higher Education*, sec. 2, 10 February 1995; Ivan Karp and Steven Lavine, "Partners in Crisis," *Museum News* 44 (May/June 1993); Hilton Kramer, "The Assault on the Museums," *The New Criterion* 13 (March 1991).

[24]Amy Hendersen and Adrienne Kaeppler, *Exhibiting Dilemmas* (Washington, D.C.: Smithsonian Institution Press, 1997), 152–155.

[25]William Honan, "Say Goodbye to the Stuffed Elephants," *New York Times Magazine*, 14 January 1990, 35; Adrienne Kaeppler, "Traveling the Pacific, Exhibit Review," *American Anthropologist* 93 (1991): 269–270; John Terrell, "Disneyland and the Future of Museum Anthropology," *American Anthropologist* 93 (1991): 149–153; David Standish, "What Was Wrong With Dull?" *Chicago Tribune Magazine*, 7 December 1997, 22.

[26]413 US 15, 24–25 (1973). As to nudity in museums see Harriet Fowler, "Fear and Loathing in Lexington," *Museum News* 52 (November/December 1996).

[27]See Kathleen Sullivan, *Artistic Freedom, Public Funding and the Constitution* (New York: W. W. Norton, 1991); and Stephen Benedict, ed., *Public Money and the Muse* (New York: W. W. Norton, 1991), 80–95.

[28]*Nelson* vs. *Streeter*, 16 F3d 145 (7th Cir 1994).

[29]Ibid., 150.

[30]The literature on cultural interpretation is vast. See, generally, Henderson and Kaeppler, eds., *Exhibiting Dilemmas*; Richard Kurin, *Reflections of a Culture Broker* (Washington, D.C.: Smithsonian Institution Press, 1997); Dan Monroe et al., *Gifts of the Spirit: Works by Nineteenth-Century and Contemporary Native American Artists* (Salem, Mass.: Peabody Essex Museum, 1996); Edward Linenthal, *Preserving Memory: The Struggle to Create America's Holocaust Museum* (New York: Viking, 1995); Susan Vogel, Mary Roberts, and Chris Müller, *Exhibition-ism: Museums and African Art* (New York: Museum for African Art, 1994); Michael Ames, *Cannibal Tours and Glass Boxes* (Vancouver: UBC Press, 1992); Maresa Tucker et al., *Different Voices: A Social, Cultural, and Historical Framework for Change in the American Art Museum* (New York: Association of Art Museum Directors, 1992); Ivan Karp, Christine Kreamer, and Steven Lavine, *Museums and Communities:, The Politics of Public Culture* (Washington, D.C.: Smithsonian Institution Press, 1992); Ivan Karp and Steven Lavine, *Exhibiting Cultures: The Poetics and Politics of Museum Display* (Washington, D.C.: Smithsonian Institution

Press, 1991); George MacDonald and Stephan Alsford, *A Museum for the Global Village* (Hull: Canadian Museum of Civilization, 1989); and Franklin Feldman, Stephen Weil, and Susan Duke Biederman, *Art Law*, vol. I (Boston: Little, Brown, 1986), chap. 1. See also Enid Schildkrout, "Ambiguous Messages and Ironic Twists: *Into the Heart of Africa* and *The Other Museum*," *Museum Anthropology* 15 (2) (1991): 16; J. Cuyler Young, Jr., "Into the Heart of Africa: A Director's Perspective," *Curator* 36 (3) (1993): 174.

[31]Stocking, *History of Anthropology*, 4.

[32]Michael Anderson, "Book Review," *Curator* 37 (1994): 214; Sandy Bauers, "As Museums Look to the Future, They Discover Dioramas Aren't a Dead Issue," *Chicago Tribune* ("Tempo" section), 14 November 1996. See also Karen Wonders, *Habitat Dioramas* (Uppsala: Acta Universitatis Upsaliersis, 1993).

[33]Elizabeth Olds, *Women of the Four Winds* (Boston: Houghton Mifflin, 1985), 71ff.

[34]Malvina Hoffman, *Heads and Tales* (New York: Charles Scribner's Sons, 1936).

[35]The phrase is from the title of the work of Hendersen and Kaeppler, *Exhibiting Dilemmas*. See also Kurin, *Reflections of a Culture Broker*; Steven Lubar, "Exhibiting Memories," *Museum News* 60 (July/August 1996); and Matthew Hoffman, "Guilt Tripping at The Smithsonian," *Washington Times*, 15 October 1992, G1; 16 October 1982, F1.

[36]Martin Harwit, "An Exhibit Denied: Lobbying the History of *Enola Gay*," *Copernicus* (1996): 148–149. See also John Correll, "The Activists and the *Enola Gay*," *Air Force Magazine*, 18 September 1995; Mike Wallace, "The Battle of the *Enola Gay*," *Museum News* 40 (July/August 1995).

[37]Harwit, "An Exhibit Denied," 152.

[38]Smithsonian Directive 603, "Exhibit Planning Guidelines" (25 August 1995).

[39]*Endowment for the Arts* vs. *Finley*, 118 Supt. Ct. 2168 (1998).

[40]Randall Bezanson, "The Government Speech Forum: Forbes and Finley and Government Speech Selection Judgments," *Iowa Law Review* 83 (5) (1999).

[41]Sullivan, *Artistic Freedom*. See also Susan O'Donnell, "Red Flags in Phoenix," *Museum News* 11 (July/August 1996).

[42]Neil Harris, "Dreaming By Committee," *Museum News* (March/April 1996): 69, 70.

[43]Society for History in the Federal Government, "Exhibit Standards," adopted by the SHFG Executive Council, 8 January 1997.

[44]Neil Harris, "Exhibiting Controversy," *Museum News* (September/October 1995): 37, 57 (emphasis added).

[45]Stephen Weil, *A Cabinet of Curiosities* (Washington, D.C.: Smithsonian Institution Press, 1995), 264.

Stephen E. Weil

From Being *about* Something to Being *for* Somebody: The Ongoing Transformation of the American Museum

A T THE END OF WORLD WAR II, the American museum[1]—notwithstanding the ringing educational rhetoric with which it was originally established and occasionally maintained—had become primarily engaged in what my Washington colleague Barbara Franco once called the "salvage and warehouse business."[2] It took as its basic tasks to gather, preserve, and study the record of human and natural history. To the extent that some further benefit might be generated by providing the public with physical and intellectual access to the collections and information thus accumulated, that was simply a plus.

Fifty years later, caught up in the confluence of two powerful currents—one flowing throughout the worldwide museum community, the other specific to the United States—the American museum is being substantially reshaped. In place of an establishment-like institution focused primarily inward on the growth, care, and study of its collection, what is emerging instead is a more entrepreneurial institution that—if my own vision of its ultimate form should prove correct—will have shifted its principal focus outward to concentrate on providing a variety of primarily educational services to the public, and will measure its success in that effort by the overarching criterion of whether

Stephen E. Weil is emeritus senior scholar at the Center for Museum Studies at the Smithsonian Institution in Washington, D.C.

it is actually able to provide those services in a demonstrably effective way.

This prognostication makes no distinction between museums and museum-like institutions in terms of their funding sources, scale, or discipline. It applies equally to a large statewide historical society, a campus-based natural history museum, and a small private art gallery. The situation of the so-called private museum requires particular mention. Even the most ostensibly private of American museums—through the combined effects of its own tax exemption and the charitable contribution deductions claimed by its donors—receives a substantial measure of public support. Given the nature of that support, such private museums must inevitably be expected not only to provide a level of public service comparable to that required of so-called public institutions but also to maintain the standards of accountability and transparency appropriate to such public institutions.

Among workers in the field, the response to this ongoing change in the museum's focus has been mixed. Some number— a minority, certainly—view it with distress. They argue that the museum—if not at the height of its salvage and warehouse days, then not long thereafter—was already a mature, fully evolved, and inherently good organization in no compelling need of further change. Particularly troublesome, in their view, would be to tamper with the centrality of the collection—even to entertain the notion that the collection might no longer serve as the museum's raison d'être but merely as one of its resources.

Another and far larger group of museum workers—including several contributors to this issue of *Dædalus*—is sympathetic to the museum's evolution from a collection-based organization to a more educationally focused one but nevertheless tends to retreat from making institutional effectiveness so exclusive a test of institutional failure or success. Characterizing the museum as analogous in some measure to the university, they argue that the traditional museum activities of preservation (which may include collecting), interpretation (which may include exhibiting), and—above all—scholarly inquiry are not merely instrumental steps toward an ultimately external outcome but are activities that should also be valued in their own right—as ends as well as means. From that moderate position, they nevertheless share with this author the vision of an emerging new museum model—a transformed and redirected institution that can, through its public-service orientation, use its very special competencies in dealing with objects to contribute positively to the quality of individual human lives and to enhance the well-being of human communities. Acknowledgedly vague as those purposes may at first appear, so multifarious are the potential outcomes of which this emerging museum is capable that to be any more specific than "quality of life" or "communal well-being" would be unnecessarily exclusive.

Finally, at the other extreme, are those museum workers who question whether the museum truly *is* an inherently good organization (or whether it has any inherent qualities at all) and whether the traditional museum activities of preservation, interpretation, and scholarship have any real value in a museum context apart from their capacity to contribute to an outcome external to the museum itself. Rejecting any analogy with a university, they argue that museum work might better be understood instead as a basically value-neutral technology and the museum itself as neither more nor less than a highly adaptable instrument that can be employed for a wide range of purposes.

This essay considers the American museum from this last point of view, both examining the currents that now press against it as well as suggesting several possibly unanticipated consequences that may well follow in the wake of those currents. It is based on the twin premises that, first, those pressures now reshaping the museum will continue unabated for the foreseeable future, and, second, that in yielding to those pressures nothing innate or vital to the museum will be lost or even compromised. As Adele Z. Silver of the Cleveland Museum of Art wisely observed some twenty years ago: ". . . museums are inventions of men [*sic*], not inevitable, eternal, ideal, nor divine. They exist for the things we put in them, and they change as each generation chooses how to see and use those things."[3]

I

In a reflection on the recent history of museums written for the fiftieth-anniversary issue of the UNESCO magazine *Museum*

International, Kenneth Hudson—perhaps the museum community's most astute observer—wrote:

> . . . the most fundamental change that has affected museums during the [past] half-century . . . is the now almost universal conviction that they exist in order to serve the public. The old-style museum felt itself under no such obligation. It existed, it had a building, it had collections and a staff to look after them. It was reasonably adequately financed, and its visitors, usually not numerous, came to look, to wonder and to admire what was set before them. They were in no sense partners in the enterprise. The museum's prime responsibility was to its collections, not its visitors.[4]

Among the several factors to which Hudson points in seeking to account for this change is the enormous increase during the postwar period in both the number and the magnitude of museums. By his count, at least three-quarters of the world's currently active museums were established after 1945. In no way has the level of direct governmental assistance to these museums kept pace with that growth. In some countries it has remained stagnant; in others—the United States, for one—its vigorous growth in the 1960s and 1970s has been followed by an actual decline. The result, almost worldwide, has been the same: to change the mix in the sources of support for museums with a decrease in the proportion coming directly from governmental sources and a corresponding increase in the proportion that must be found elsewhere.

It seems clear, at the most elementary level, that the greater the degree to which a museum must rely for some portion of its support on "box office"—not merely entrance fees but also the related income streams to be derived from shop sales and other auxiliary activities—the greater will be its focus on making itself attractive to visitors. Likewise, the greater the extent to which a museum might seek corporate funding—most particularly funding for its program activities—the more important it will be that the museum can assure prospective sponsors that its programs will attract a wide audience. Under such circumstances, it should hardly be surprising that museums are increasingly conscious of what might be of interest to the public. The consequence is that museums almost everywhere have, in essence, shifted from a "selling" mode to a "marketing" one. In the selling mode, their efforts had been concentrated on convincing the public to "buy" their traditional offerings. In the marketing mode, their starting point instead is the public's own needs and interests, and their efforts are concentrated on first trying to discover and then attempting to satisfy those public needs and interests.

Hudson argues, however—and correctly, I think—that something more profound than mere box-office appeal is involved in this change of focus. He suggests that the museum's growing preoccupation with its audience may be attributable as well to the tremendous increase of professionalism within the museum community during the postwar years. The impact of that development—and, as a principal consequence, the equally tremendous growth in the scale and influence of a great variety of professional associations—should not be underestimated. The policy positions taken by those professional associations—and the insistent repetition of those policies over time—have played a particularly compelling part in shaping the mind-set and expectations of both new practitioners in the field and the larger public beyond. As the sociologists Walter W. Powell and Rebecca Friedkin point out in their analysis of the sources of change in public-service organizations, beyond such changes in focus as may be attributable to changes in the sources of an organization's support—for museums, the box-office factor—institutional change may frequently represent "a response to shifts in the ideology, professional standards, and cultural norms of the field or sector in which an organization is situated."[5]

That would appear to be the case for the museum. A broad range of national and local professional organizations have played important ideological roles in reshaping the American museum. Earliest among these was the Washington-based American Association of Museums (AAM), founded in 1906 as something of a parallel to the United Kingdom's Museums Association, which dates back to 1889. Narrower in focus but also with considerable impact have been the more recently established Association of Science-Technology Centers (ASTC) and the Association of Youth Museums (AYM). Of perhaps lesser consequence for the American museum—but of enormous influence elsewhere—has been the International Council of Museums (ICOM). More or less descended from the International Museums Office founded under the auspices of the League of Nations in 1927, ICOM was established in 1946 as a UNESCO-affiliated Non-Governmental Organization and is headquartered in Paris.

The publications and program activities of these associations amply document the degree to which, over the past several decades, they have changed their emphasis from collections and collections' care to public service. Within the AAM, for example, that shift can be directly attributed to the growing influence that museum educators have exercised over the association's public-policy positions. That influence can be traced on an ascending curve beginning in June of 1973 when a group of prominent museum educators threatened to secede from the organization. In June of 1976—as a gesture of conciliation—a change in the AAM's constitution granted a committee of educators together with other disciplinary groups a role in the association's governance. With the publication of *Museums for a New Century* in 1984, education was declared to be a "primary" purpose of museums.[6] This upward curve reached its zenith in May of 1991 when the association's governing board adopted the educator-prepared position paper *Excellence and Equity* as an official statement of the association's policy.[7] Woven throughout *Excellence and Equity* are the linked propositions that a commitment to public service is "central to every museum's activities" and that "education—in the broadest sense of that word—[is] at the heart of their public service role."[8]

A similar shift of focus can be traced in the AAM's program of institutional accreditation, which was first proposed in 1968 and which became operational in 1971. In its earliest phase, accreditation was primarily concerned with how an institution cared for its collection and maintained its facilities. With the passage of time, the scope of accreditation has steadily broadened to consider not only the institutional care of collections but also, as importantly, the programmatic use of those collections. Consider the contrast between the types of concern expressed in the AAM's first accreditation handbook of 1970 and in its most recent one, published in 1997. In the 1970 publication, among the positive traits that might support a museum's accreditation were the avoidance of "crude or amateurish" exhibits, evidence that exhibit cases were dust- and vermin-proof, and a showing that the exhibits themselves were "selected to serve [some] purpose and not just [as] 'visible storage.'"[9] Regarding special exhibitions, it suggested that the better practice was to offer exhibitions that appealed to the interest of the general public and not simply to that of an "antiquarian or dilettante" audience. In the AAM's 1997 publication, the emphasis shifted entirely. Suggested areas of inquiry include whether the "museum effectively involves its audiences in developing public programs and exhibitions," whether it "effectively identifies and knows the characteristics of its existing and potential audiences," and whether it "effectively evaluates its programs and exhibitions" in terms of their audience impact.[10]

Contrasting quotations from two other AAM publications may suggest how far the rhetoric—if not yet all of the operational practices—of the museum community has evolved during this period. Those responsible for the 1968 *Belmont Report*—a mostly forgotten document that was once thought (wrongly, in the event) to offer an irrefutable argument for the increased federal funding of American museums—were certainly aware that "education" would prove the most likely heading under which such increased funding could be justified.[11] They nevertheless seemed reluctant to relinquish entirely the kind of old-fashioned satisfaction ("pleasure and delight") that museum collections were traditionally thought to provide. "Art museums," they explained,

> . . . aim to provide the esthetic [*sic*] and emotional pleasure which great works of art offer. This is a primary purpose of an art museum. It is assumed that a majority of the people who come regularly to art museums come to be delighted, not to be taught, or preached at, or "improved" except by the works of art themselves. An art museum, especially, is—or ought to be—a place where one goes to get refreshed.[12]

Never adequately explained in the *Belmont Report* was why so much refreshment (particularly in the case of the art museum where that refreshment was disproportionately consumed by the more affluent members of society) should properly be provided at public rather than private expense.

The escalation in rhetoric is suggestive. Over three decades, what the museum might be envisioned as offering to the public has grown from mere refreshment (the museum as carbonated beverage) to education (the museum as a site for informal learning) to nothing short of communal empowerment (the museum as an instrument for social change). Describing the growth of museums in rural Brazilian communities seeking to discover their roots and preserve a unique history, Maria de Lourdes Horta wrote in a 1997 AAM publication:

> A museum without walls and without objects, a true virtual museum, is being born in some of those communities, which look in wonder to their own process of self-discovery and recognition. . . . For the moment, in my country, [museums] are being used in a new way, as tools for self-expression, self-recognition, and representation; as spaces of power negotiation among social forces; and as strategies for empowering people so that they are more able to decide their own destiny.[13]

ICOM, like the AAM, has put an increasing emphasis on the active public-service role of museums. Going still further, however, it has advanced toward a view—similar to that from Brazil—that museums can play a particularly powerful role in bringing about social change. To some extent, that conviction has grown almost in tandem with the number of developing countries included within its membership base. Given that fact, as well as its ongoing relationship with UNESCO, ICOM's current emphasis on social activism must be understood as more than simply a passing phase. It clearly permeates virtually every aspect of ICOM, beginning even with its membership requirements. Unlike the AAM, which continues to use a more traditional approach that defines museums primarily in terms of their activities—to present essentially educational programs that use and interpret objects for the public—ICOM's statutes were amended in 1974 to redefine eligible museums as those that have among their characteristics the *purpose* of serving (in an earlier iteration) "the community" or (in ICOM's current definition) "society and . . . its development."[14]

Among the clearest articulations of ICOM's evolving position was a resolution adopted by the membership at its ninth General Conference in 1971. Rejecting as "questionable" what it called the "traditional concept of the museum" with its emphasis "merely" on the possession of objects of cultural and natural heritage, the conference urged museums to undertake a complete reassessment of the needs of their publics in order that they, the museums, could "more firmly establish their educational and cultural role in the service of mankind." Rather than prescribing any monolithic approach to this task, individual museums were urged to develop programs that addressed the "particular social environment[s] in which they operated."[15]

At a meeting held in San José, Costa Rica, in April of 1998, organized by the AAM in collaboration with a number of ICOM's national and other committees—what is referred to as the first summit of the museums of the Americas—the proposition that museums might play a useful role in social development was taken still a step further. By way of a three-tiered finding that amounted, in effect, to a syllogism, the 150 delegates representing 33 Western countries took the position that the museum was not merely a potential or desirable instrument for sustainable social advancement but, in effect, an essential one. The logic of that position went as follows:

> First, sustainable development is a process for improving the quality of life in the present and the future, promoting a balance between environment, economic growth, equity and cultural diversity, and requires the participation and empowerment of all individuals; second, culture is the basis of sustainable development; and third (and, in effect, *ergo*), museums are essential in the protection and diffusion of our cultural and natural heritage.[16]

This is the first of the two currents that are today pushing the American museum out of the salvage, warehouse, and soda-pop business and toward a new line of work. It is powered both by economic necessity—the box-office factor—and by the museum field's changing ideology as transmitted not only through such major professional associations as the AAM, ASTC, AYM, and ICOM but through countless smaller ones as well. It is coupled with the reality that for many of the more recently founded museums in newly populous parts of this country it will never be possible—whether because of scarcity-driven market prices, international treaties and export/import controls, or endangered species and similar legislation—to amass the kinds of in-depth and universal collections that were built many years ago by the longer-established institutions. For those older museums, public service may nevertheless be their more viable future. For younger ones, though, with neither important collections now nor any great prospect of ever acquiring these, public service may be their only future.

II

The second current pushing against the American museum is a local one. Its source is in the not-for-profit or so-called third sector of this country's economy, the organizational domain to which a majority of its museums belong and by which all of them are profoundly influenced. Comprised of well over one million organizations—museums account for less than 1 percent of these—and generally estimated to include something on the order of 7 percent of the nation's wealth, jobs, and economic activity, the third sector itself is in the midst of a profound change as to how it evaluates the relative funding worthiness of its constituent organizations. Increasingly, the principal emphasis of such evaluations is being put on organizational performance, on the kinds of results that an organization can actually achieve.

The genesis of this change may be found in the long-simmering sense that the managers of both governmental agencies and third-sector organizations—lacking in common the reality checks of a competitive marketplace as well as the operational discipline required to demonstrate consistent profitability—have rarely been required to apply their resources with the same effectiveness and efficiency that would be demanded of them in a for-profit context.[17] In the case of federal government agencies, the Congress's desire to assure greater effectiveness has now culminated in the Government Performance and Results Act (GPRA), which was passed with strong bipartisan support in 1993 and which will become fully effective in 2000. GPRA requires every federal agency to establish—preferably in objective, quantifiable, and measurable terms—specific performance goals for each of its programs and then to report annually to the Congress on its success in meeting those goals. For the third sector, where nothing so draconian as GPRA has yet to be proposed, this new emphasis on organizational performance nevertheless constitutes a sharp break with past practice.

Two recent events can be singled out as having further accelerated this growing emphasis on performance. One was the development of the "social-enterprise" model of third-sector organizations by Professor J. Gregory Dees at Harvard Business School.[18] The other was the development and advocacy by the United Way of outcome-based evaluation as the appropriate means by which to evaluate the effectiveness of the health and human-service agencies to which it provides funds.[19]

The impact of Dees's social-enterprise model can best be understood by considering some of the ways in which third-sector organizations have previously been viewed. As recently as the end of World War II—a time when museums were still in their establishment stage and when survival (as contrasted with accomplishment) was widely accepted as a perfectly reasonable indicator of institutional success—the three adjectives most commonly used to describe such organizations were "philanthropic," "benevolent," and "charitable." Remarkably, none of these referred either to what those organizations actually did or to what impact they might hope or expect to make on some target audience. Their reference instead was to the high-minded motives of the individuals responsible for their establishment and support: philanthropic (from the Greek for a lover of humankind), benevolent (from the Latin for somebody wishing to do well), and charitable (from the Latin also: *caritas*, or with loving care). In the years since, those adjectives have largely been replaced by the terms "nonprofit" and "not-for-profit," notwithstanding the repeated criticism that the third sector is far too large and its work far too important to define it so negatively in terms of what it is not instead of positively in terms of what it is.[20]

What is particularly striking about Dees's social-enterprise model is the way in which it cuts through earlier approaches to the evaluation of these third-sector institutions to concentrate directly on what might variously be called organizational outcomes, impacts, or results. In the long run, says Dees, it is those outcomes that matter—not good will, not an accumulation of resources, not good process, and not even highly acclaimed programs, but actual outcomes, impacts, and results. In essence, those are the organization's bottom line. Thus envisioned, the social enterprise can be seen as at least partially parallel to the commercial enterprise—like it in having the achievement of a bottom line as its ultimate operational objective, yet nevertheless wholly different from it because of the way in which that bottom line is defined. The commercial enterprise pursues a quantifiable economic outcome; the social enterprise pursues a social outcome that may or may not be quantifiable but that, in any event, must certainly be ascertainable.

Dees points to a second important difference between the commercial enterprise and the social enterprise. He calls this the "social method." Whereas the commercial enterprise must rely on "explicit economic exchange relationships, contracts, and arm's-length bargains" in order to obtain resources and to distribute its product, the social enterprise operates in a different environment. At the input end, it may, to some degree, rely on the voluntary contribution of funds, goods, and/or labor. At the output end, it typically provides its services to the public either without any charge or at a price below the actual cost of producing those services. Those differences aside, however, in the social-enterprise model—just as in the commercial-enterprise one—the ability to achieve an intended bottom line is what distinguishes organizational success from organizational failure.

For the American museum, this is a fresh challenge. To the extent that it has ever accepted that its performance might be legitimately subject to some overall and even possibly comparative evaluation, its "worst case" scenario was that such an evaluation would, like the AAM's accreditation program, be wholly internal. What constitutes a good museum? At one time, it might have been defined in terms of the loyalty and generosity of its benefactors. At some later date, "good" might have referred to the magnitude of its resources and the excellence of its staff: a fine collection, a highly regarded and well-credentialed group of curators, an appropriately large endowment, and a substantial building. Among government-related museums, a good museum might be one that adhered to the best practices and highest professional standards in the field, one that did things "by the book." Or, and this was particularly the case during the heyday of the National Endowments for the Arts and the Humanities with their emphasis on program funding, it might be a museum whose exhibition and other programs were considered exemplary by knowledgeable colleagues who worked in peer organizations. What now seems so extraordinary—at least in retrospect—is that not one of those approaches took into the slightest account the museum's external impact on either its visitors or its community.

Curiously, a rigorous bottom-line evaluation with its primary weight on just such considerations would not really eliminate any of those other inner-directed approaches. It would simply incorporate and supersede them. For a museum to achieve a solid bottom-line result on any consistent basis, it would still need the ongoing support of generous donors; it would still need a solid spectrum of tangible and intangible resources; it would still need to establish and adhere to sound working practices; and it would still need to produce high-quality programming. In the social-enterprise model, those are all necessary but not—either in themselves or in combination—sufficient. The museum that aspires to be successful must still manage to combine those elements with whatever else may be necessary in order to render the specific public service that it itself has identified (both for itself and its supporters) as its own particular bottom line.

And what, for museums, might such a bottom line be? Here, I think, the museum community can find useful guidance in the evaluation model that the United Way of America formally adopted in June of 1995. Prior to that time, the United Way had centered its evaluation process around the programs of its applicant health and human-service agencies. What it determined in 1995 was that it would henceforth concentrate instead on the results of those programs, i.e., on the identifiable outcomes or impacts that those agencies were actually able to achieve through those programs.

The key concept in the United Way's newly adopted approach is "difference." To qualify for funding, the United Way's applicant agencies are called upon to demonstrate their ability to make a positive difference in the quality of individual or communal lives. A 1996 United Way program manual spells out what some of those differences might be. They are benefits or changes for individuals or populations that may be attributable to their participation in a program.

> [They] may relate to behavior, skills, knowledge, attitudes, values, condition, status, or other attributes. They are what participants know, think, or can do; or how they behave; or what their condition is, that is different following the program.[21]

There are, I think, few people working in the museum field today who doubt for a moment that museums can meet just such a standard. Museums are quintessentially places that have the potency to change what people may know or think or feel, to affect what attitudes they may adopt or display, to influence what values they form. As Harold Skramstad, president emeritus of Henry Ford Museum & Greenfield Village and an author in this issue of *Dædalus*, asked in 1996 at the Smithsonian's 150th Anniversary Symposium in Washington, unless museums *can* do those things—unless museums can and do play some role relative to the real problems of real people's lives—then what is the point?

In a sense, given the considerable funding that they receive both directly and indirectly from a variety of public sources, American museums have no other choice but to embrace such a role. To repeat an observation I made during a 1997 conference:

> If our museums are *not* being operated with the ultimate goal of improving the quality of people's lives, on what [other] basis might we possibly ask for public support? Not, certainly, on the grounds that we need museums in order that museum professionals might have an opportunity to develop their skills and advance their careers, or so that those of us who enjoy museum work will have a place in which to do it. Not certainly on the grounds that they

provide elegant venues for openings, receptions and other glamorous social events. Nor is it likely that we could successfully argue that museums . . . deserve to be supported simply as an established tradition, as a kind of ongoing habit, long after any good reasons to do so have ceased to be relevant or have long been forgotten.[22]

With the ongoing spread of outcome-based evaluation, however, two cautions seem in order. First, museums need to observe a certain modesty as they identify their bottom lines, lest they overstate what they can actually accomplish. Grand proclamations such as those made at the first summit of the museums of America may be important in highlighting the museum field's overall capability to contribute importantly toward social development. Nevertheless, the individual museum that declares "denting the universe" to be its bottom line may only be setting itself up for failure unless and until it can produce a perceptibly dented universe to demonstrate its accomplishment. Museum workers need to remind themselves more forcefully than they generally do that museums can wonderfully enhance and enrich individual lives, even change them, and make communities better places in which to live. Only rarely, however—and, even then, more often than not in synergy with other institutions—do they truly dent the universe.

The second caution is that museums must take care to assure that the need to assess the effectiveness of their public programs does not distort or dumb down the contents of those programs to include only what may have a verifiable or demonstrable outcome and exclude everything else. The problem is parallel to that faced by the nation's school systems with respect to nationally standardized tests. For all its promise, outcome-based evaluation—like any system—requires a wise and moderate application. Taken to an extreme, it can damage the very institutions that it was designed to benefit.

As part of the worldwide museum community, the American museum is under pressure to make public service its principal concern. Because it is also part of the American not-for-profit sector, the nature of the public service it will be expected to provide can be defined in more specific terms—it is to be through demonstrably effective programs that make a positive difference in the quality of individual and communal lives.

Recast in marketing terms, the demand is that the American museum provide some verifiable added value to the lives of those it serves in exchange for their continued support. Recast in blunter terms, the museum is being told that to earn its keep requires that it be something more important than just an orderly warehouse or popular soda fountain.

III

Traditional wisdom holds that an organization can never change just one thing. So finely balanced are most organizations that change to any one element will ultimately require compensating and sometimes wholly unanticipated changes to many others. As the focus of the worldwide museum community continues to shift from the care and study of collections to the delivery of a public service, I want to examine at least two other aspects of American museums that may be considered ripe for compensating changes. One is the way that they are divided along disciplinary lines by the types of collections they hold—most typically art, history, and science. The other is the way they are staffed and how museum workers are trained. In both these respects, the overwhelming majority of American museums and museum-training programs continue to operate as if World War II had only just ended and as if collections were still at the center of the museum's concerns.

With regard to the division of museums by discipline, let me start with an anecdote. During a visit to British Columbia in 1997, I learned of an exhibition mounted earlier that year by the Nanaimo District Museum on Vancouver Island. Entitled *Gone to the Dogs*, the exhibition not only traced the history of dogs in the community back to its pre-European roots but also took into account the various ways in which dogs—"as companions and coworkers"—continued to relate to the community today: from tracking predators for the Royal Canadian Mounted Police to acting as "seeing eyes" for the visually handicapped to serving as pets. In a Doggy Hall of Fame, local residents were invited to post photographs of favorite dogs together with brief typed statements as to why they thought them special. A free film series—*Dog Day Afternoons*—presented feature films about dogs. Supplementary programs addressed local dog-related businesses such as pet grooming and veterinary services and highlighted the work of the SPCA.[23] By all accounts, the exhibition was an enormous success. It brought many first-time visitors to the museum, its popularity required the museum to transfer the exhibition to another local venue and extend the closing date, and, above all, it appeared to have left behind the palpable sense of a public enriched by its recognition of a common bond. In the end, the exhibition proved not to have been so much about dogs as it was about the shared concerns and interconnectedness of a community.

Almost as striking as the novelty of that exhibition, however, was the recognition of how few communities in the United States might ever hope—notwithstanding the ease with which it might be replicated—to see a similar exhibition in their own local museums. The mission of the Nanaimo District Museum is defined by geography, not by discipline. It was established to serve the City of Nanaimo and its surrounding district. In seeking to illuminate that region's cultural heritage and link that heritage to its present-day development, no restrictions limit the range of materials that the museum can employ to illustrate such links. In the United States, the overwhelming number of museums are confined to specific disciplines. In the 1989 National Museum Survey—the most recent broad-based statistical information available—only 8.6 percent of American museums classified themselves as general museums not tied to a particular discipline.[24] If children's museums—which are generally multidisciplinary—are counted as well, the total is still barely above 15 percent.

For the remaining 85 percent of American museums, to present an exhibition such as *Gone to the Dogs* would generally be out of the question as beyond their disciplinary boundaries. When collections were at the center of a museum's focus, that kind of disciplinary exclusivity might have made a certain sense. From a managerial perspective, at least, it limited the number of such narrowly trained specialists as discipline-specific curators and conservators who had to be kept on staff. With the refocus of the museum on its public-service function, however, strong arguments can be advanced for releasing the museum from this disciplinary straightjacket—most particularly in communities that have only a single museum or, at best, two. Why should those museums not try to broaden their disciplinary scope? Whatever staffing problems that might entail could readily be dealt with through collaboration with local colleges, universities, and research institutions, by outsourcing, or through the use of consultants. In the words by which James Smithson described his expectations of the institution that was to bear his name—that it be for "the increase and diffusion of knowledge"[25]—the public-service oriented museum might well conclude that, rather than pursue both these goals with equal vigor, it would make better sense to emphasize "diffusion"— where the museum's unique competencies lie—and to leave the "increase" part to possibly more competent academic institutions with which it could closely collaborate.

Easing the disciplinary boundaries of museums would not be as radical a step as it might first appear. A separation into disciplines was never inherent to the museum as an institutional form. In tracing its origin back to those sixteenth- and seventeenth-century cabinets of curiosities from which it sprang, it seems clear that such a separation was a later development. The Tradescant collection, for example—ultimately to become the founding collection for the Ashmolean Museum at Oxford—comfortably combined both natural history specimens and what its first catalog of 1656 called "Artificialls"—objects that ranged from works of art, weapons, and coins to ethnographic materials and Egyptian and Roman antiquities.[26] Many continental European *wunderkammers* were similar. In the United States, the first museums—such as the one Charles Willson Peale opened in Philadelphia in 1786—held equally eclectic collections. Peale's Museum included not only portraits of American Revolutionary War military heroes but also fossils, shells, models of machinery, and wax figures of North American natives.[27] Throughout this century, the case for multidisciplinary museums has been advanced by museum practitioners as diverse in their views as John Cotton Dana in the first quarter of this century and by the proponents of the ecomuseum in more recent years.[28]

There is, moreover, ample room within contemporary museum practice to envision museums organized along other than disciplinary lines. One immediate example, of course, is the children's museum. In her 1992 survey of children's museums across the United States, Joanne Cleaver credits Michael Spock and his staff—with their revivification of the Boston Children's Museum starting in 1961—for having pioneered the idea that "the museum was for somebody rather than about something."[29] An alternative institutional form—a museum that *is* about something, but nevertheless is nondisciplinary—is the community or neighborhood museum. One well-established type is the *heimat*— or "homeland"—museum, a local institution that first began to appear throughout Germany during the latter part of the nineteenth century and which, after some twists and turns, still survives today.[30]

Although *heimat* museums were intended originally to document rural life and popular culture, particularly in their pre-industrialized forms, the potential role of these museums in education and community development was recognized by the turn of the century. Thereafter, under the Nazi regime, it was only a short step from education to propaganda. The *heimat* museums were employed to disseminate a pseudoscientifically based message of Aryan superiority and to preach a nationalist gospel of blood and soil. Notwithstanding that dark episode, there is nevertheless something remarkably prescient of current museological thinking in these 1936 observations by a German curator writing about a *heimat*-like museum in Cologne:

> The *heimatmuseum* must not be a kingdom of the dead, a cemetery. It is made for the living; it is to the living that it must belong, and they must feel at ease there. . . . [T]he museum must help them to see the present in the mirror of the past, and the past in the mirror of the present . . . and, if it fails in that task, it becomes no more than a lifeless collection of objects.[31]

In the contrasting attitudes that German museum workers take toward its postwar continuation, the *heimat* museum can be seen as providing a litmus test by which to separate those who still believe in the primacy of collections from those who now see the museum primarily in terms of public service. Some

German colleagues dismiss the contemporary *heimat* museum as beyond the boundaries of the field because, in addition to holding objects, it also serves as an active cultural and social center. For exactly that same reason, other German colleagues consider it to be an especially valuable and viable kind of museum. Outside of Germany, the *heimat* concept has taken on a life of its own. With its emphasis on everyday life and ordinary objects, for example, the Museum of London—which opened in 1976, and which Kenneth Hudson has acknowledged to be "one of the finest city-biography museums in the world"[32]— might simply be seen as the *heimat* museum writ large.

With regard to neighborhood museums, perhaps the best-known model in the United States is the Anacostia Neighborhood Museum, opened by the Smithsonian Institution in 1967. As an institutional type, the neighborhood museum was described by the late John R. Kinard, Anacostia's founding director:

> [It] encompasses the life of the people of the neighborhood—people who are vitally concerned about who they are, where they came from, what they have accomplished, their values and their most pressing needs. Through the various media of its exhibits the museum reflects the priorities already determined by neighborhood people and other community agencies and is, thereby, able to present the issues that demand attention.[33]

Just as few American museums might have had the flexibility to mount the Nanaimo Museum's *Gone to the Dogs*, few might have had the inclination to undertake so bold and neighborhood-specific an exhibition as *The Rat: Man's Invited Affliction*—an early Anacostia project generated by local children and the concern they expressed about the problem of rat infestation in their neighborhood.

Kinard later wrote that it was the *Rat* exhibition that convinced him and his staff that the museum could no longer afford to deal only with life in the past. Its exhibitions, he said, "must have relevance to present-day problems that affect the quality of life here and now. . . ."[34] That conviction notwithstanding, the museum's focus on its immediate neighborhood was eventually to change. Scarcely more than a decade after the founding of the museum, Anacostia's Board of Trustees adopted a new mission statement pursuant to which it was to offer a more generalized—but still multidisciplinary—program dealing with African-American history, art, and culture.[35] In essence, it was now to be a community rather than a neighborhood museum with the understanding that the community it served was to be a national one. In 1987, two years before Kinard's death, the Anacostia Museum officially dropped the description "neighborhood" from its name and moved from its first site in a converted movie theater to a new purpose-built facility in a nearby park. In recent years, with additional space at its disposal, its name was changed again—this time to the Anacostia Museum and Center for African American History and Culture.

In general, neighborhood museums—following the original Anacostia Model—have primarily been considered in connection with economically depressed inner-city or similar locations. There appears to be no reason, though, why their use should be so limited. One possible sign of the wider application of the neighborhood museum concept—particularly in its concentration on contemporary issues of genuine concern to its constituents—is the remarkable metamorphosis that has occurred over the past several years at the Strong Museum in Rochester, N.Y. Founded as a salvage and warehouse museum almost by default—Margaret Woodbury Strong, its patroness, left it more than three hundred thousand objects after her death in 1969, nearly twenty-seven thousand of them dolls—the museum, several decades into its life and after extensive and even painful consultation with its community, determined to change its original focus and to become instead a museum that had special appeal to local families.

From its previous emphasis on life in the northeast prior to 1940—a concentration supported well by Mrs. Strong's collection—it has turned instead to what its director calls "history that informs civic discourse about contemporary issues."[36] Since 1992, the topics examined by its exhibition program have included the Cold War, AIDS, bereavement, racism, drug abuse, and health care. Most recently, it has entered into joint ventures with the Children's Television Workshop for an exhibition built around *Sesame Street* and with the Rochester public library system to integrate a branch library into the museum.

Some observers argue that museums can only achieve this kind of organizational breadth through the sacrifice of the depth with which they were previously able to address a narrower range of subjects. Others—my Smithsonian colleague Robert D. Sullivan, for one—respond that, whether or not museums are or ever were the most appropriate places for learning in depth, the reality is that an emerging electronic information environment is rapidly reshaping how information is distributed and that breadth-based learning, as typified by the Internet's capacity to provide infinitely branched linkages, will be its hallmark. "In the same way," Sullivan says,

> that the printed word as a medium of diffusion encouraged linear, sequential, and vertical ways of thinking, the Internet encourages non-linear, non-sequential, horizontal ways of thinking and connecting knowledge. The instantaneous horizontal connectivity of the Internet collapses time and space and evaporates and/or challenges all efforts by information and knowledge rich institutions to remain isolated, fragmented, walled chambers.[37]

The abandonment by the American museum—certainly a "knowledge-rich" institution—of its old scavenger/warehouse business would seem fully synchronous with such a change. All the same, though, many in the American museum community—and not merely the moderates of whom I spoke earlier—would be very reluctant to see museums lose their capacity to deal with knowledge in depth as well as breadth.

IV

The second unintended consequence of the American museum's shift in its central focus away from the care and study of its collections involves the way museums are staffed and how museum workers are trained. Here, we enter uncharted territory. One thing, however, seems clear: tomorrow's museums cannot be operated with yesterday's skills. While museums will still require the expertise of the discipline-centered specialists who today hold many of their senior positions, the successful operation of public-service museums will require that those specialists at least share these positions with museum workers of a very different orientation and expertise, museum workers who will bring to their institutions a new combination of skills and attitudes.

Along these lines, Leslie Bedford—for many years with the Boston Children's Museum and more recently associated with the Museum Leadership Education Program at the Bank Street School in New York—has recently proposed the establishment of a training institute that would prepare museum workers for careers in public programming.[38] A thoroughly trained public programmer would, in her view, be a "creative generalist" who combines a variety of specialties now found scattered both inside and outside the museum. These would include an ability to work directly with community members to assess the ways in which the museum might appropriately meet their needs, a practical knowledge of how to establish productive collaborations with other community organizations, both for-profit and not-for-profit, a solid understanding of how best to use all the myriad means—exhibitions, lectures, films, concerts, programs of formal education, and more—through which the museum may interact with the community, and a thorough knowledge of how to make appropriate use of audience research and various forms of program evaluation.

Going beyond Bedford's proposal, the fourth of these skills— knowing how to make appropriate use of audience research and various forms of program evaluation—ought to be in the curricula of museum-training programs at every level. In some instances, its current neglect—particularly in the case of management training—may in part be due to the tangency of such programs with graduate schools of business. In the for-profit sphere, where at least short-term success or failure can be determined from financial and other periodic reports, evaluation simply does not perform the same critical function of measuring effectiveness and distinguishing success from failure that it does among governmental agencies and not-for-profit organizations.

Critical to understand here is the changing standard of not-for-profit accountability. As effectiveness becomes more firmly established throughout the third sector as the overarching criterion of institutional success, accountability will eventually boil down to a single hard-nosed question: is this institution demonstrably using the resources entrusted to it to achieve what it said it intended to achieve when it requested and was given those resources? In contradistinction to what he calls "negative accountability"—being able to show that no financial improprieties have occurred and that all of an institution's funds can properly be accounted for—Peter Swords of the Nonprofit Coordinating Committee of New York has referred to this enhanced standard as "positive accountability": being able to show that the resources entrusted to an institution were in demonstrable fact used to accomplish its intended purpose.[39] In such an environment, an organization without the capacity to monitor its outcomes on a regular and credible basis—unable, that is, to render a positive account of its activities—may no longer be fundable. Nor will meeting such a requirement simply be a matter of appropriate staffing. It will also be a matter of budget. Monitoring program impacts is costly, but it will no more be a dispensable frill tomorrow than filing tax returns or tending to workplace safety are today.

For museums particularly, the work that needs to be done here is daunting. In many instances it may start with something so basic as getting a museum's leadership to articulate just what it is that it hopes or expects its institution to accomplish. That so many museums continue today to be so unfocused about their purpose—avoiding any reference to outcomes at all and/or mistakenly defining them in terms of organizationally controllable outputs—is only the beginning of the problem. Compounding it further is, first, that the range of potential museum outcomes—educational, experiential, recreational, and social—is so extraordinarily wide and, second, that the achievement of those outcomes may be far more difficult to ascertain than are the frequently quantifiable results that can be achieved by health and human-service agencies.

On occasion, museums may provide anecdotally recoverable and even life-transforming "Oh Wow!!" experiences.[40] Most often, however, the impact of museums on their communities—on their visitors and nonvisitors alike—is subtle, indirect, frequently cumulative over time, and often intertwined with the impact of such other sources of formal and informal educational experiences as schools, religious bodies, and various social and affinity groups. Museums must not only educate themselves as to how their impact can be captured and described; they must also educate those to whom they are accountable as to what may and may not be possible in rendering their accounts. In no way, however, do these complexities make evaluation any less essential. On the contrary; because the value that the museum can add to a community's well-being may not be nearly so self-evident as that provided by an emergency room or a children's shelter, credible evaluation will be all the more critical to the museum's survival.

At the level of institutional leadership, the most important new skill of all will be the ability to envision how the community's ongoing and/or emerging needs in all their dimensions—physical, psychological, economic, and social—might potentially be served by the museum's very particular competencies. Given its tremendous technical facility in assembling, displaying, and interpreting objects—and given moreover the enormous power that the well-interpreted display of those objects may have to affect what and how people think or know or feel—what can the museum contribute? Can it be a successful advocate for environmentally sound public policies? In what ways might it help the community to achieve or maintain social stability? In what ways might it energize and release the imaginative power of its individual citizens? Can it serve as a site for strengthening family and/or other personal ties? Can it trigger the desire of individuals for further education or training, inspire them toward proficiency in the creative arts or the sciences?

For the newly reshaped American museum fully to achieve its public-service objectives, though, even those new skills may not be sufficient. Needed as well may be some attitudinal changes—two in particular. First, museum workers generally must learn to relax their expectations as to why the public visits their institutions and what it may take away from those visits. Exhibition curators, for example, may sometimes imagine a far greater congruence than is really the case between the intensity with which they have prepared an exhibition and the interest that the general public may take in the educational content of that exhibition. The public is not a monolith. It comes to museums for many different reasons and it gets many different things out of that experience.

In *Speak to My Heart*, an exhibition opened by the Anacostia Museum and Center for African American History and Culture in 1998, a label text described the community role of the contemporary African-American church as being, among other things, "A safe place to be . . . a haven from the stressful workaday world, a place for personal growth and community nurture, and an outlet for the development and use of natural talents." How pertinent might such a description be to the museum? Is the museum only important as a place in which to receive the authorized curatorial word, or might it have some other legitimate uses as well?[41] That so many different visitors may choose to use the museum in so many different ways should not matter. That it is so potentially open-textured as a destination, so adaptable to a variety of public uses should not—at least in the emerging and visitor-centered museum—be regarded as a defect. Rather, it should be understood as one of its greater glories.

The other attitude in need of change involves the museum's relationship to the community. The emerging public-service-oriented museum must see itself not as a cause but as an instrument. In some considerable measure, the cost of maintaining that instrument is paid by the community: by direct community support, by the community's forbearance from collecting real estate, water, sewer, and other local taxes, by the considerable portion of every private tax-deductible contribution that constitutes an indirect public subsidy from the community. For that reason alone, it might be argued, the community is legitimately entitled to have some choice—not the only choice, but *some* choice—in determining just how that instrument is to be used.

In the emerging museum, responsiveness to the community—not an indiscriminate responsiveness, certainly, but a responsiveness consistent with the museum's public-service obligations and with the professional standards of its field—must be understood not as a surrender but, quite literally, as a fulfillment. The opportunity to be of profound service—the opportunity that museums truly have to use their competencies in collecting, preserving, studying, and interpreting objects to enrich the quality of individual lives and to enhance their community's well-being—must certainly outdazzle any satisfactions that the old salvage, warehouse, or soda-pop business could ever have possibly offered.

ENDNOTES

[1] Notwithstanding that museums throughout all of the Americas might appropriately be so designated, the phrases "American museum" and "American museums" as used in this essay are intended to refer solely to museums in the United States.

[2] Barbara Franco is director of The Historical Society of Washington, D.C. Her observation was made in conversation with the author, June 1998.

[3] Barbara Y. Newsom and Adele Z. Silver, eds., *The Art Museum as Educator: A Collection of Studies as Guides to Practice and Policy* (Berkeley: University of California Press, 1978), 13.

[4] Kenneth Hudson, "The Museum Refuses to Stand Still," *Museum International* 197 (1998): 43.

[5] Walter W. Powell and Rebecca Friedkin, "Organizational Change in Nonprofit Organizations," in Walter W. Powell, ed., *The Nonprofit Sector: A Research Handbook* (New Haven: Yale University Press, 1987), 181.

[6] American Association of Museums, *Museums for a New Century: A Report of the Commission on Museums for a New Century* (Washington, D.C.: American Association of Museums, 1984).

[7] American Association of Museums, *Excellence and Equity: Education and the Public Dimension of Museums* (Washington, D.C.: American Association of Museums, 1992).

[8] Ibid., 7.

[9] American Association of Museums, *Museum Accreditation: A Report to the Profession* (Washington, D.C.: American Association of Museums, 1970).

[10] American Association of Museums, *A Higher Standard: The Museum Accreditation Handbook* (Washington, D.C.: American Association of Museums, 1997).

[11] American Association of Museums, *America's Museums: The Belmont Report* (Washington, D.C.: American Association of Museums, 1968).

[12] Ibid., 2.

[13]From a presentation made during the Smithsonian Institution's 150th anniversary symposium, Washington, D.C., 5–7 September 1996. The full text appears in *Museums for the New Millennium: A Symposium for the Museum Community* (Washington, D.C.: Center for Museum Studies, Smithsonian Institution, and American Association of Museums, 1997). The quoted passage is reprinted in Ibid., 107–108.

[14]ICOM Statutes, sec. II, art. 3.

[15]*ICOM News* 71 (September 1971): 47.

[16]Taken from the May 1998 interim report to the American Association of Museums' Board of Directors and the International Council of Museums' Executive Committee on the summit meeting of the museums of the Americas on the theme "Museums and Sustainable Communities," San José, Costa Rica, 15–18 April 1998.

[17]See, for example, Judge Richard A. Posner's observation in *United Cancer Council* vs. *Commissioner of Internal Revenue*, 165 F3d 1173 (7th Cir 1999): "Charitable organizations are plagued by incentive problems. Nobody owns the rights to the profits and therefore no one has the spur to efficient performance that the lure of profits creates."

[18]J. Gregory Dees's views can be found in two published Harvard Business School "notes": *Social Enterprise: Private Initiatives for the Common Good*, N9–395–116 (30 November 1994) and *Structuring Social-Purpose Ventures: From Philanthropy to Commerce*, N9–396–343 (15 April 1996).

[19]For a basic description of the United Way's approach, see *Measuring Program Outcomes: A Practical Approach* (Arlington, Va.: United Way of America, 1996).

[20]Nancy R. Axlerod, the former president of the National Center for Nonprofit Boards, suggested that these negative descriptions of third-sector organizations were no less inappropriate than that offered by the father who, on being asked the gender of his three children, responded that "two were boys and one was not."

[21]United Way, *Measuring Program Outcomes: A Practical Approach*, 2.

[22]Stephen E. Weil, keynote address to the annual meeting of the Mid-Atlantic Association of Museums, Rochester, N.Y., 13 November 1997.

[23]Information about *Gone to the Dogs* and about the Nanaimo District Museum generally was kindly supplied by Debra Bodner, the museum's director/curator.

[24]All figures are from the Data Report for the 1989 National Museum Survey, American Association of Museums, Washington, D.C., 1992.

[25]In his 1826 will through which the Smithsonian Institution was ultimately to be established, Smithson specifically mandated that it be ". . . for the increase and diffusion of knowledge among men."

[26]Arthur MacGregor, "The Cabinet of Curiosities in Seventeenth-Century Britain," in Oliver Impey and Arthur MacGregor, eds., *The Origins of Museums:*

The Cabinet of Curiosities in Sixteenth- and Seventeenth-Century Europe (Oxford: Clarendon Press and Oxford University Press, 1985), 147–158.

²⁷Germain Bazin, *The Museum Age* (New York: Universe Books, 1967), 242.

²⁸The writings of Dana (1856–1929)—beyond question this country's most original thinker about museums—have long been largely out of print. That situation should be remedied in October of 1999, when a generous selection of those writings is scheduled to be published jointly by the Newark Museum and the American Association of Museums. For a brief overview of his life, see the chapter "John Cotton Dana and The Newark Museum: The Museum of Community Service," in Edward P. Alexander, *Museum Masters: Their Museums and their Influence* (Nashville: The American Association for State and Local History, 1983). A selected bibliography of Dana's museum-related writings was published in *The Newark Museum Quarterly* (Spring/Summer 1979): 58. For a description of the ecomuseum movement, see Nancy J. Fuller, "The Museum as a Vehicle for Community Empowerment: The Ak-Chin Indian Community Ecomuseum Project," in Ivan Karp, Christine Mullin Kreamer, and Steven D. Lavine, eds., *Museums and Community: The Politics of Public Culture* (Washington, D.C.: Smithsonian Institution Press, 1992), 327–365.

²⁹Joanne Cleaver, *Doing Children's Museums* (Charlotte, Vt.: Williamson Publishing, 1992), 9.

³⁰For a brief history, see Andrea Hauenschild, "'*Heimatmuseen*' and New Museology," a paper delivered at the Third International Workshop on New Museology, Toten, Norway, 14–19 September 1986.

³¹Quoted in Alfredo Crus-Ramirez, "The *Heimat* Museum: A Perverted Forerunner," *Museum* 48 (1985): 242–244.

³²Kenneth Hudson, *The Good Museums Guide: The Best Museums and Art Galleries in the British Isles* (London: The Macmillan Press, 1980), 102–103.

³³John R. Kinard and Esther Nighbert, "The Anacostia Neighborhood Museum, Smithsonian Institution, Washington, D.C.," *Museum* XXIV (2) (1972): 203.

³⁴Ibid., 105.

³⁵Zora Martin-Felton and Gail S. Lowe, *A Different Drummer: John Kinard and the Anacostia Museum 1967–1989* (Washington, D.C.: The Anacostia Museum, 1993), 37.

³⁶Scott G. Eberle and G. Rollie Adams, "Making Room for Big Bird," *History News* 51 (4) (Autumn 1996): 23–26.

³⁷Robert D. Sullivan is the associate director for public programs at the Smithsonian's National Museum of Natural History. The quoted language comes from "The Object in Question: Museums Caught in the Net," an unpublished essay presented at the annual meeting of the Visitor Studies Association, Washington, D.C., 7 August 1998.

³⁸Letter to the author, 14 December 1997.

[39]Peter Swords discusses this in "Form 990 as a Tool for Nonprofit Accountability," delivered at the "Governance of Nonprofit Organizations: Standards and Enforcement" conference, New York University School of Law, National Center on Philanthropy and the Law, 30–31 October 1997.

[40]For a report of one such experience together with an argument that such experiences should be given greater weight in visitor studies, see Anna M. Kindler, "Aesthetic Development and Learning in Art Museums: A Challenge to Enjoy," *Journal of Museum Education* 22 (2 and 3) (1998): 12–15.

[41]I am grateful to Camilla Boodle, a London-based museum consultant, for her suggestion that visitors may find a museum rewarding without necessarily accepting its authority. Conversation with the author, August 1998.

John H. Falk

Museums as Institutions for Personal Learning

I
T HAS LONG BEEN RECOGNIZED, but rarely publicly acknowledged, that most people learn much if not most of what they know outside of the formal education system. As Patricia Albjerg Graham recently wrote in *Dædalus*, "Scholars ranging from the late James S. Coleman and Lawrence A. Cremin to Christopher Jencks have quite properly reminded us of the limited role that schools play in children's education."[1] A vast educational infrastructure exists to support public learning, both inside and outside the workplace. Leisure opportunities for learning are particularly rich. Museums, along with print and broadcast media, community-based organizations, trade book publishing, and (more recently) the Internet, play a vital role in facilitating public learning. Despite years of public educational efforts, the important role museums in particular play in helping the public learn has never been fully understood nor appreciated. The reasons for this are many. However, at the risk of oversimplification, I would suggest that the root of the problem lies in the museum community's historic inability to document the educational impact it has on its visitors.

LEARNING IN MUSEUMS

Millions of people visit museums every year, and the vast majority, if not all, learn as a consequence of these visits. The failure of museums to document this learning stems from the

John H. Falk is director of the Institute for Learning Innovation in Annapolis, Maryland.

assumptions, and the approaches to assessing learning, of an earlier generation of museum professionals and researchers, rather than from any lack of learning on the part of the public. Given that learning is such a common concept in our society, it would seem reasonably straightforward to document. However, as a vast scholarly literature (including numerous issues of this journal) has made clear, learning is *common,* but definitely not *straightforward*—particularly if one is trying to understand and document the type of free-choice learning that occurs in places like museums.

Over the years, providing compelling evidence for museum-based learning has proved challenging. The overwhelming majority of earlier investigations of museum learning were predicated on historical, primarily behaviorist, views of learning. In this traditional view, what Jeremy Roschelle calls the absorption-transmission model,[2] individuals were assessed to determine whether they learned *specific, predetermined* information, much as someone would test learning in a traditional classroom. Only recently have museum-learning investigators appreciated the problems with this model. Although well-thought-out exhibitions and programs can facilitate visitor learning of predetermined topics, the inherent complexity and choice afforded by the museum environment, coupled with the widely varying prior experiences and knowledge levels of museum visitors, yields a far greater range of possible learning outcomes than can be accommodated by the assessment strategies created for the older absorption-transmission model. In addition, also as suggested by Roschelle, people in museums rarely spend time reflecting upon or synthesizing their experiences. As a consequence, significant conceptual change is unlikely to occur within a single visit. It may take days, weeks, or months for the experience to be sufficiently integrated with prior knowledge for learning to be noticeable even to the learner himself, let alone measurable. Finally, most learning, but certainly most learning that occurs in museums, has more to do with consolidation and reinforcement of previously understood ideas than with the creation of totally new knowledge structures. This means, as science-center director Tom Krakauer recently quipped, that museums teach the public "what they almost already know."[3]

Thus, an investigation of museum learning must encompass a respect for what individuals bring to the museum in terms of prior knowledge, experience, and interest; an eye to focusing on what visitors actually see, do, say, and think about during their experience; and a sense of time that takes into account what happens subsequently in visitors' lives. If these criteria can be met, then evidence of learning could meaningfully be sought—and could reasonably be expected to emerge.

Utilizing this "search image," I will present below a sampling of studies that, in my opinion, provide evidence for the kind of learning that occurs in museums. Examples will be presented for the general public visiting an exhibition and for schoolchildren on field trips. The studies were done by a range of investigators, using a diversity of methodologies, in a variety of institutions including a history museum, a zoo, a science center, and an art gallery. Space permits only a sampling of results, but my hope is that it will be indicative of both the range and the character of museum-facilitated learning.

A Regional History Center

The first example is an assessment of visitor learning from the *Points in Time* exhibition at the Senator John Heinz Pittsburgh Regional History Center, an exhibition that presents a rich, lively depiction of western Pennsylvania's history utilizing a number of artifacts, photographs, period rooms and spaces, live theater, and multimedia components.[4] Researchers were asked to determine what visitors experienced and learned while visiting the exhibition. Over one hundred face-to-face interviews were conducted with visitors as they exited the exhibition. Questions focused on the many elements of the exhibition, their usefulness and significance, what visitors learned from them, overall thoughts and opinions, expectations, highlights, and main messages.

Visitors said that they appreciated the opportunities provided throughout the exhibition to learn in different ways and to engage many of their senses. The use of multimedia technologies served to animate the exhibition and make it seem more current. The artifacts and photographs made the greatest impact on visitors; all of the visitors used these items to learn about the region's history, and their comments demonstrated that these items had helped them to visualize the different people who had lived in the region in the past. In particular, period rooms and recreated spaces were an excellent way to display the items and photographs and to communicate their uses within an appropriate context. The majority of visitors were from the local area, and their comments showed clearly that the exhibition evoked memories and extended understanding of a way of life, now almost gone and nearly forgotten:

> I'm amazed how close, if you stop and think. It's the same kind of life we live today, living in the city. [Especially with] the one with the clothesline between the houses, the one where they were cleaning the clothes with the washboard. (Woman in her fifties)

> I liked stuff I could remember, like the kitchen and living room from the mid-1900s. (Woman in her forties)

> I used it to see about coal mining in McKeesport, my hometown. . . . (Man in his thirties)

> I always knew it was a dangerous job, coal mining, when I grew up, because that was big in my area [West Virginia]. Here, it was steel. I didn't realize how dangerous that was, but it was really clear in the exhibit. (Woman in her twenties)

> I used to work in J and L steelworks. The exhibit was excellent because it was so real, especially the washroom at the steel mill. It brought home my youth. For my wife, it was the kitchen. . . . (Man in his sixties)

> [The best part was] the rooms, like the steelworkers' room, you hear the voiceovers and think about what life might have been like. (Man in his forties)

> I loved the insides of the different churches, the synagogues, the school. I didn't have an opportunity as a child to enter those places. Growing up Roman Catholic, God forbid you ever stepped foot in another's place of worship. (Woman in her seventies, who lived her entire life in Pittsburgh)

> I've lived here since '85. I went to school here. [The exhibition] gave me a better idea of the communities. I know they are very divided. We have Polish Hill and stuff, and now I saw how they were settled and it gave me a better idea. I was surprised Indians

settled here. I didn't know the Hill District was settled by Italians as well as African-Americans; I thought it was just African-Americans. I was surprised. (Woman in her twenties)[5]

Visitors not only enjoyed *Points in Time*; they were later able, in their own ways, to describe something that they had learned. Although the learning described was nearly always very personal, most visitors either mentioned empathizing with others' experiences (such as those visitors who said they had thought about what it felt like to live in other times) or relayed some fact or detail about a specific topic of interest. Because this exhibition was so experiential, allowing visitors to visualize and think concretely about living in the past, reference to such experiences was the primary way that visitors expressed their learning from *Points in Time*. Though few visitors said, "I learned what a suburban house looked like in the 1950s," probably all visitors could now describe a 1950s suburban home better than they could before visiting. The *Points in Time* experience was about reconfirming, expanding, and visualizing time periods in Pittsburgh's regional history. As a result, visitors left the exhibition with an enriched understanding of the human experience in Pittsburgh's past.

A Traveling Exhibition

Several years ago, with support from the U.S. Centers for Disease Control, a consortium of prominent American science museums developed a traveling exhibition on Acquired Immune Deficiency Syndrome, entitled *What About AIDS?* By all measures this exhibition was a successful learning experience for virtually all visitors.[6] Although not every visitor walked out of the exhibition knowing one, predetermined, specific new fact or concept about AIDS, the exhibition afforded each visitor the opportunity to learn at least one new thing that was personally relevant to him or her. Not only did visitors find the exhibition exceedingly accessible in a number of ways, with information presented from a variety of different perspectives and at a variety of different points within the exhibition, but observational data collected during the assessment of the exhibition revealed that visitors readily took advantage of the choices offered.

In-depth, open-ended interviews with people after they completed their visit to *What About AIDS?* revealed just how personally constructed each visitor's learning was:

> They [in the exhibit] were talking about coming in contact with people who have AIDS and they were saying that you are more . . . of a threat to them then they are to you. You know, because the virus, uh, something about how the viruses can't be treated with antibiotics, but bacteria can. I saw that on one of the things, and I said, that's very interesting because everyone is so scared of the person with AIDS, but the person with AIDS should be scared of you.

> I like the beginning to the end, the history of what started, where it started, and where it's gone through until now.

> It made you aware, it made you really realize that it can happen to anybody, you know. And I think it also puts, for people who don't know it, the three main things how you can get it.[7]

As might have been predicted, few people evinced a radically new view of the epidemic. Most people made statements such as, "I learned a few new things, but mostly the exhibit helped me better understand stuff that I already knew." However, the benefits of the AIDS exhibit extended far beyond the brief time visitors were within it. Three months after seeing the exhibition, people said:

> I found myself still thinking about some of things in the exhibit even weeks later. For example, I hate to say it, but the dice exhibit [which interactively related the probability of getting AIDS] really made me think about who I go out with these days.

> Just the other day, I saw this piece on TV about AIDS and I was able to understand what they were talking about, the immune system and all, because of that exhibit.[8]

A Zoo

A study at the National Zoo in Washington attempted to determine the impact of the zoo's *Think Tank* exhibition on visitors.[9] The *Think Tank* exhibition includes live animals, demonstrations, and a myriad of individual interactive exhibit elements all designed to engage visitors in a deeper understanding of animal thinking, in particular the use of tools, language, and social behavior.

Several hundred visitors to the exhibition were surveyed both before and immediately after their visit. Immediately after their visit, a majority of the visitors were found to have a better understanding of animal thinking behavior. For example, when visitors were asked to give examples of such behavior before experiencing the exhibition, their answers were vague and generally inaccurate. After the exhibition experience, the most frequent response was something about tool use or social behavior, both intended learning outcomes. Visitors also had a significantly improved respect for animals and their capabilities after the experience.

Thirteen months later, 150 of these visitors were contacted by telephone and resurveyed. The evidence for learning in this group of visitors remained essentially unchanged, even after more than one year had elapsed. Examples of the responses included:

> It was another addition to the information I already know about animals. . . . Brain size isn't what really matters; it just matters what type of thinking it does.

> I got a more realistic approach of their everyday living as opposed to what I see on TV.

Not only was there evidence for learning from the exhibition, but half of the visitors in the call-back group reported that the exhibition had influenced their behavior relative to animals. Some individuals said that the zoo experience prompted them to watch relevant television shows; others said they were inspired to read books on the subject; and still others said the exhibition caused them to engage in conversations on the topic of animal learning with friends and family. Approximately half the interviewees claimed to have thought about the exhibition in the ensuing thirteen months, and as many reported recommending the exhibition to others.

A Science Center

In February of 1998 the California Museum of Science and Industry reopened as the California Science Center, featuring two brand-new major exhibitions—*World of Life* and *Creative World*. Both of these exhibitions were designed to fulfill very specific conceptual goals. In the case of the *World of Life*, the exhibition was designed to communicate a single overall message that all living things share many characteristics and that these shared characteristics can be grouped under five basic life processes—the need to acquire and eliminate food, the ability to process energy, the ability to respond to the environment, the need for self-protection and defense, and the need to reproduce. A comprehensive evaluation was conducted to determine how successfully this information was conveyed.[10]

Several hundred visitors to the exhibition were tracked, observed, and interviewed. Both prior and subsequent to their visit to *World of Life*, visitors were asked a series of questions related to their understanding of life processes and the relationship of humans to other life forms. Not surprisingly, many visitors entered the exhibition aware of many of the life processes all living systems share. In particular, a majority of visitors entered the exhibition aware of the similarities between humans and other organisms in the areas of food intake and digestion, reproduction, and circulation/supply network functions. After completing their visit, visitors of all ages were able to demonstrate a significantly greater understanding of the multiple life processes that all living systems share. Statistically significant increases were seen in visitors' comprehension of four of the five life processes described in the exhibition; only the area of circulation/supply network showed no significant increase in visitors' comprehension as a function of visiting the museum. Not only did the quantity of responses increase after viewing the exhibition; also changing from pre-visit to post-visit was the quality of the vast majority of visitors' responses, several examples of which are presented below:

Pre: "We all have babies, eat, breathe."
Post: "We all reproduce, digest food, expend energy."—Male, thirteen years old

Pre: "We need to eat, and we have eyes, ears, and nose."
Post: ". . . take in energy and have similar senses."—Male, eight years old

Pre: "Reproduction and digestion."

Post: "Passing on genetic material through reproduction; digestion, elimination of waste, defending."—Female, thirty-five
years old

Pre: "We are all similar in the things we do to stay alive."

Post: "Similar chemical and biological processes like reproduction
and other intercellular processes."—Male, forty-five
years old

Pre: "We all eat, run, walk, have arms and babies."

Post: "All living things see, have brains and nerves, defend, reproduce."—Female, ten years old[11]

Particularly notable was the increase in the length and richness
of children's explanations. Most children's pre-visit descriptions were short and simplistic; post-visit explanations were
consistently longer and more sophisticated. The exhibition successfully fulfilled its overarching goal of facilitating the public's
understanding of the similarities and interrelatedness of all
living organisms.

School Visit to an Art Gallery

In the spring of 1993 the National Gallery of Art initiated a
multiple-visit program for fifth- and sixth-grade students from
Washington, D.C., inner-city elementary schools. The program,
called *Art Around the Corner* (AAC), reflected the gallery's
desire to increase involvement with Washington's schools, to
include the gallery's collections in the public-school curriculum,
and to enhance students' art-related enjoyment and learning.
The lessons introduced students to the sensory, technical, and
expressive properties of art, and culminated in "Docent for a
Day," in which each student chose a work of art on display at
the gallery to present to his or her family and friends.

Over a several-year period, investigators assessed the impact
of this program on student participants. Interviews were conducted with equal numbers of program graduates and nonprogram
graduates (matched by age, gender, academic ability, race/
ethnicity, and socioeconomic background) in each of the first
three years of the assessment. Students were asked open-ended
questions relating to their relationships with art museums and

works of art and were shown a number of reproductions, which they were asked to discuss.[12] Findings from this series of studies suggested that not only did participation in the program impart positive attitudes in graduates toward both art museums and art in general, but relative to controls, *Art Around the Corner* graduates expressed a genuine appreciation and love for works of art and demonstrated enhanced abilities to articulate their responses toward art.

A subsequent study attempted to complement these primarily qualitative findings with a quantitative study exploring the long-term impact of the program on a larger number of graduates.[13] This study was designed to determine the extent to which the *Art Around the Corner* program produced a lasting effect on students' knowledge of, and attitudes toward, both works of art and art museums. With the cooperation of the District of Columbia Public Schools, students who had participated in *Art Around the Corner* from one to three years previously were identified and located in twenty classes across grades 7, 8, and 9. Students who had not participated in the program were also included in the sample as a control group for comparison purposes. Students were shown a reproduction of Edward Hopper's *Cape Cod Evening* and asked to respond with a written interpretation. In addition to the written component, a subset of both *Art Around the Corner* participants and control students was selected from the larger sample and given an opportunity to talk about art in a small informal group discussion. Results revealed that although there was no difference between students in their interest in or appreciation of art, the *Art Around the Corner* program did have a lasting impact on participating students. *Art Around the Corner* graduates, as compared with control students, provided significantly more richness, detail, and depth in their description of paintings and were able to support their descriptions using vocabulary they had learned in the program. This was true in both the written and focus-group forums. As compared to the unsupported, simplistic, and adjective-free descriptions offered by the control group, *Art Around the Corner* graduates gave such responses as:

I see a brown and white collie and two dreary-looking people standing in front of a classic-looking country house outside beside the dark woods. (Female, grade 8)

[I see] a chubby woman with a blue-green dress [and] a red-necked man with a white undershirt and black pants sitting underneath trees that look dark and shadowy. (Male, grade 8)

I see sadness . . . because the artist used a color that makes the trees look dead and the back is full of darkness in the forest. (Male, grade 9)

The trees [are] at an angle because of the wind blowing, and the green and white grass [is at an angle] too. (Male, grade 9)[14]

There were no significant differences between students as a function of grade level. In other words, the impact of the program was equally expressed in students graduating one, two, or three years previously.

School Field Trip to a Science Center

The final example is a recently completed dissertation study at Queensland University of Technology, which looked in detail at the learning experiences of a few people rather than the more general learning of many.[15] In-depth case studies were developed for five students, documenting their understandings of electricity and magnetism prior to a visit to the Queensland Sciencentre in Australia. Prior to the visit each of the students created a concept map detailing what he or she knew about the topics, and an in-depth interview was conducted, utilizing the map as a discussion point. Students then visited the science center and were interviewed again in an in-depth manner shortly after the visit; once again their maps were used as a probing tool, and students could modify their maps and make a new one. After participating in post-visit activities back in the classroom, designed to reinforce and extend the museum experience, students were again interviewed at length, again using their own concept maps as a probing device.

All five students showed evidence of changes in their understanding of magnetism and electricity resulting from their science-center experience and subsequent classroom-based activities. The learning observed varied in its form. In some instances it was a subtle change; much of it involved recontextualizing or strengthening something that a child already knew; and, in a few cases, the experience fostered personal theory-building. These variations in learning seemed to depend in part upon what the student brought to the experience in terms of prior knowledge and experience, but also reflected each student's personal approach to learning. Interestingly, even among the theory-builders, each student's knowledge developed in ways that were at times consistent with current canons of science, and at other times in ways that entrenched or developed new alternative conceptions. Regardless of the scientific acceptability of each student's knowledge, his or her understandings were changed and developed as a consequence of the science center visit.

The other fascinating aspect of learning that this study elucidated is that each student's knowledge was clearly constructed and developed from a rich variety of related learning experiences, including interacting with parents and other people in enrichment and extracurricular activities and in more informal interactions at home; reading books; watching television programs; playing with and disassembling electric and motor-driven toys; and participating in school and museum-based experiences. In one case, information had been gained from a book a child had at home and was based on conducting a scientific experiment at home, facilitated by his mother. In fact, all of the students indicated having talked about their museum experience to people, primarily their parents, after the field trip. In many cases, the experiences had been followed up at home by doing an experiment or reading further. The science-center experience served both to reinforce prior experiences and to stimulate subsequent experiences.

Summary

The museum-learning studies presented here, picked from among a hundred or more recent assessments of museum learning, demonstrate consistent evidence of learning in museums. The examples chosen are neither the best nor necessarily even the most compelling, but they admirably illustrate the range and depth of learning that occurs as a consequence of visiting a museum, whether as a casual visitor or as part of an organized school field trip. Results of the visitor research at the Senator John Heinz Pittsburgh Regional History Center reinforce how powerful the museum context can be in providing evocative experiences for visitors, enabling disparate individuals to comprehend and envision historical periods. Studies of the AIDS traveling exhibit reveal how important choice is as a component of museum learning. The exhibition provided visitors with numerous opportunities to self-select which aspect of the topic most closely fit their personal learning needs and interests—and, given that choice, the public was able to advance their own learning agenda. The studies at the National Zoo and National Gallery of Art demonstrate the ability of even brief museum-based learning experiences to have a long-lasting impact on visitors' knowledge and attitudes. The California Science Center example illustrates that, contrary to popular belief, museums not only enhance visitor attitudes and interest but have the capacity to facilitate the learning of a wide range of complex concepts. Finally, the in-depth investigation of the impact of a visit to the Queensland Sciencentre on a small group of children reinforced the continuous, cumulative nature of learning whereby experiences at the museum were combined with classes at school, outside reading, television watching, and conversations with family and friends to build scientific knowledge and understanding.

In contrast to an earlier generation of learning studies that showed that museums only occasionally facilitated learning, the research presented here strongly supports the premise that museum learning experiences facilitate some degree of learning in virtually all participants and significant learning in the majority of visitors. As long as the "search image" for learning was reasonable and the assessment tools appropriate to the task, museums were found to support rich and consistent learning—learning that persisted over long periods of time, learning that included both cognitive and affective dimensions. Yet even though abundant evidence now exists that visitors learn in all kinds of museums—including history, science, and art museums, zoos, and aquariums—questions about the educational value of museums still remain.

THE EDUCATIONAL ROLE OF MUSEUMS
IN A KNOWLEDGE ECONOMY

Unfortunately, there are many within the larger educational community who continue to question the real value of museums, raising questions that no amount of study will answer. In large part these doubts stem from a view of museums as primarily elitist institutions serving only a small fraction of the public, in particular the better educated and more affluent sectors of the community. In this view, museums are nice but much like an expensive dessert, a pleasing frill for a privileged few. Historically this characterization may have been true, but times are changing. Thirty years ago only about one in ten Americans went to museums with any regularity. By ten to fifteen years ago that number had increased to nearly one in four. Today, two out of every five Americans visit a museum at least once a year.[16] The rate of museum-going appears likely to continue to increase, with the result that sometime early in the next century a majority of Americans will visit some kind of museum at least once a year. Museum-going is currently one of the most popular out-of-home leisure activities in America. Once almost exclusively the preserve of the wealthy and well-educated, museums today serve an increasingly diverse audience.

Providing additional support for these changes, research on general public leisure values conducted in the late 1970s found that 14 percent of the general public possessed a strongly held interest in and concern for learning as a fundamental goal of leisure.[17] This group was much more likely than the other 86 percent of the public to consist of frequent museum-goers (three or more visits per year); and, not surprisingly, they were also considerably better educated and more affluent than the average citizen. However, when similar data was collected in the early 1990s it was found that fully 45 percent of the public held these same values.[18] This group of individuals, representing nearly half of the public, was not disproportionately made up of frequent museum-goers, nor were these people the most affluent and well educated. In fact, the percentage of the public fitting these descriptions had not changed appreciably. What has shifted are both the underlying leisure values of the American public and the number of individuals visiting museums infrequently. As I have argued elsewhere, these changes are all part of a larger trend, the evolution of America from an industrial to a knowledge-based society.[19] This is a trend that is not only changing the way Americans work, but is also affecting the way they play.

Museums, in part responding to these trends and in part helping to shape them, are working harder than ever at attracting and retaining a broad public interest in learning-oriented leisure experiences. Evidence from a wide range of sources suggests that museums are currently achieving success in these endeavors. No longer exclusively the domain of the elite, all museums find themselves catering to a growing base of potential visitors as Americans of all backgrounds and educational levels seek more meaningful leisure experiences.[20] Significant investments have been made by museums to engage historically underrepresented publics, and, although not uniformly successful, most museums currently attract a significantly more representative sampling of their communities than ever before. This trend, too, is likely to continue into the twenty-first century with the very real prospect that museums will become ever more accepted as broadly welcoming, widely representative public-education institutions.

In conclusion, museums are rapidly moving toward becoming ever more significant institutions for education. This is true both by virtue of the diversity of individuals they serve and because of the quality of educational experiences they offer. Museums represent significant community learning resources, particularly for facilitating free-choice learning—that is, learning that occurs in an individual's free time and that is motivated by choice rather than necessity. As free-choice learning comes to represent an ever-greater percentage of the total learning an individual does in his or her lifetime, museums promise to become ever more important and ever more accepted as vital links within the educational infrastructure of the community.

ACKNOWLEDGMENTS

Much of the material for this essay derives from a forthcoming book by Lynn Dierking and me. I am deeply indebted to Dr. Dierking for her substantial intellectual contributions to this essay. I would also like to thank the other contributors to this issue and the editors of this volume for their thoughts and suggestions.

ENDNOTES

[1]Patricia Albjerg Graham, "Educational Dilemmas for Americans," *Dædalus* 127 (1) (Winter 1998): 233.

[2]Jeremy Roschelle, "Learning in Interactive Environments: Prior Knowledge and New Experience," in *Public Institutions for Personal Learning*, ed. John Falk and Lynn Dierking (Washington, D.C.: American Association of Museums, 1995).

[3]Tom H. Krakauer, "Yes, Kids are Having Fun, But . . . Are They Learning Science?" *Scientific American Explorations* 2 (1) (Winter 1999): 7.

[4]Courtney Abrams, Dale R. Jones, and John H. Falk, "Summative Evaluation of *Points in Time* at the Senator John Heinz Pittsburgh Regional History Center," technical report, Institute for Learning Innovation, Annapolis, Md., 1997.

[5]Ibid.

[6]Dana G. Holland and John H. Falk, What About AIDS *Traveling Exhibition: Summative Evaluation* (Annapolis, Md.: Science Learning, Inc., 1994).

[7]Ibid.

[8]Ibid.

[9]Stacey Bielick and David Karns, *Still Thinking about Thinking: A 1997 Telephone Follow-up Study of Visitors to the* Think Tank *Exhibition at the National Zoological Park* (Washington, D.C.: Smithsonian Institution, Institutional Studies Office, 1998).

[10]John H. Falk and Rinoti Amin, "*World of Life*: Summative Evaluation," technical report, Institute for Learning Innovation, Annapolis, Md., 1998.

[11]Ibid.

[12]Courtney Abrams and John H. Falk, "*Art Around the Corner*: Year Two Evaluation Report," technical report, Science Learning, Inc., Annapolis, Md., 1996; Courtney Abrams and John H. Falk, "*Art Around the Corner* Evaluation Pilot Testing," technical report, Science Learning, Inc., Annapolis, Md., 1995; and Courtney Abrams, John H. Falk, and Marianna Adams, "*Art Around the Corner*: Year Three Evaluation Report," technical report, Science Learning, Inc., Annapolis, Md., 1997.

[13]Jessica Luke, Marianna Adams, and John H. Falk, "*Art Around the Corner*: A Longitudinal Investigation of Effectiveness," technical report, Institute for Learning Innovation, Annapolis, Md., 1998.

[14]Ibid.

[15]David Anderson, "Understanding the Impact of Post-visit Activities on Students' Knowledge Construction of Electricity and Magnetism as a Result of a Visit to an Interactive Science Centre," unpublished doctoral dissertation, Queensland University of Technology, Brisbane, Australia.

[16]This trend has been documented in a number of recent studies, including American Association of Museums, *Data Report: From the 1989 National Museum Survey* (Washington, D.C.: American Association of Museums, 1992); John Crothers Pollock, Peter Finn, Elizabeth A. Garfield, Adam Snyder, and Arthur G. Pfenning, *Where Does the Time Go?* (New York: Newspaper Enterprise Association, 1983); John P. Robinson, Carol Keegan, Terry Hanford, and Timothy A. Triplett, *Public Participation in the Arts: Final Report on the 1982 Survey* (Washington, D.C.: National Endowment for the Arts, 1985); John P. Robinson, Carol Keegan, Marsha Karth, and Timothy A. Triplett, *Survey of Public Participation in the Arts: 1985 Volume 1 Project Report* (Washington, D.C.: National Endowment for the Arts, 1987); John P. Robinson, Mones Hawley, and Chris Holleyman, *Arts Participation in America: 1982–1992*, NEA Research Division, Report #27 (Washington, D.C.: National Endowment for the Arts, 1993); and U.S. Bureau of the Census, *Statistical Abstract of the United States, 1995*, 115th ed. (Washington, D.C.: U.S. Government Printing Office, 1995).

[17]Marilyn G. Hood, "Staying Away: Why People Choose Not to Visit Museums," *Museum News* 61 (4) (April 1983): 50–57.

[18]John H. Falk, *Leisure Decisions Influencing African-American Use of Museums* (Washington, D.C.: American Association of Museums, 1993).

[19]John H. Falk, "Visitors: Toward a Better Understanding of Why People Go To Museums," *Museum News* 77 (2) (1998): 38–43.

[20]B. Joseph Pine II and James H. Gilmore, *The Experience Economy: Work is Theatre & Every Business a Stage* (Boston: Harvard Business School Press, 1999).

With dismal regularity, we return to efforts to improve K-12 education. These efforts usually fail because education is conceived narrowly as schooling. Yet, improvements to schools do not necessarily correspond to an improvement in the education of children. Whether or not children will learn does not depend primarily on what happens in school, but on the experiences, habits, values, and ideas they acquire from the environment in which they live.

Another limitation of schools is that they concern themselves almost exclusively with the development of cognitive skills, or the passing along of factual knowledge and—at best—critical thinking abilities. Knowledge of facts and how to interpret them will not result in an educated population unless some wisdom—or the goals and priorities that justify the use of knowledge—is also acquired. Thus, instead of concentrating exclusively on schools as the sites for change, we must take into account the broader processes involved in formative education.

Formative education (i.e., what Germans call *Bildung*) is the result of a continuous process of interaction between individuals and the environment. Children are formed by their experiences with parents, teachers, peers, and even strangers on the street, and by the sport teams they play for, the shopping malls they frequent, the songs they hear, and the shows they watch. The citizens of the next century will be a product of these various social forces. Schools, while certainly important, contribute only a relatively modest fraction to the education of the young.

Mihaly Csikszentmihalyi

From "Education for the Twenty-First Century"
Dædalus 124 (4) (Fall 1995)

Emlyn H. Koster

In Search of Relevance: Science Centers as Innovators in the Evolution of Museums

MUSEUMS IN NEW CONTEXTS

O NE OF THE MOST WIDELY READ recent publications of the American Association of Museums (AAM) dealt with the role museums play in public education, and framed this evocative question:

> How can museums—as multi-dimensional, socially responsible institutions with a tremendous capacity for bringing knowledge to the public and enriching all facets of the human experience—help to nurture a humane citizenry equipped to make informed choices in a democracy and to address the challenges and opportunities of an increasingly global society?[1]

In 1997, when the AAM charted its current strategic agenda, the first of five main goals was to help museums anticipate and respond to changing community needs.[2] One year later, in a parallel move, the International Council of Museums (ICOM) identified as two of its strategic objectives the need for the museum profession to adapt to changing global situations, and the need to support museums as institutions of social and cultural development.[3]

The subject of how museums have increased their societal context has attracted much commentary by the news media in recent years. While national museums have been criticized by some as bland, and major art museums have been challenged to

Emlyn H. Koster is president and chief executive officer of Liberty Science Center, Jersey City, New Jersey.

present the prevailing historical circumstances to the collection they display, not all accounts have been so critical.[4] For example, one Canadian newspaper was hyperbolic in its praise, saying:

> The museums of the world . . . are not only archives of what past civilizations have accomplished, but the foundations from which the future of humankind's cultural accomplishments will rise.[5]

More recently, the *New York Times* issued a special section on museums with the arresting headline "Culture's Power Houses."[6]

It looms as a fundamental task before museum professionals to identify the when, where, how, and why of innovation that advances these new purposes. This essay develops a position that *science centers*, a relatively new kind of museum, have capitalized on their opportunity to be innovative in a search for greater relevance. The essential claim is that science centers are a relatively flexible type of museum, having shown repeatedly over a relatively short history an ability to be highly responsive to community needs. The essay accordingly explores what it means for a museum to be relevant, and the kind of steps science centers have taken, and may continue to take, with a view to assuring their relevance to the communities they serve.

Implicit in this essay is the view that museums need new performance measures. That is, the number of visitors who choose to come to a museum is only a first-order indication of the public's assessment of the museum's relevance to their needs, of its overall value to society.[7] Museums cannot rest on laurels of popularity. Modern society abounds with examples of activities that enjoy high popularity, yet are of questionable societal benefit when viewed in the longer term. As enduring institutions in society, museums urgently need to become both popular and useful.

Museums are often regarded as repositories of a nation's culture. As such, science centers have had something of a challenge finding acceptance as "cultural" institutions. Yet "culture" refers to society's common experiences and identity. That the performing arts, art museums, and history museums address significant aspects of culture is readily accepted. Indeed in many quarters, the arts encompass the public's sense of culture. But it would be well to expand this view such that our scientific research and technological heritage, as well as the philosophy that shapes the present and prospective impact of science and technology on individuals and societies, are seen as equally integral dimensions of culture.[8] Certainly from the standpoint of creativity, it is fair to state that accomplishments in science and technology rank with other fields of human endeavor, such as literature, music and the arts.[9]

SCIENCE MUSEUMS AND SCIENCE CENTERS

The first science museums opened well over a century ago. In the United States, the Franklin Institute opened in Philadelphia in 1824; earlier in this century, Chicago's Museum of Science and Industry opened in 1926, and the Henry Ford Museum and Greenfield Village in Dearborn, Michigan, in 1929. In Europe, early influential institutions include London's Science Museum and the Deutsches Museum in Munich. With large collections of industrial artifacts and often sizeable endowments, they opened their doors to a public intrigued by science and new technologies. The experience they offered to visitors was mainly one of viewing scientific and industrial artifacts, models, and whole machines, some kept in working order. There were also live demonstrations of scientific principles, most commonly of electricity, and some simulated experiences, such as a coal mine. Industrial and technological developments tended to be portrayed as positive advancements with no attention to the possibility of adverse environmental impacts. Early world's fairs and expositions were similar in content and emphasis.[10]

The late 1960s saw a different style of science museum—known as a science-technology center, or simply science center—appear on the museum scene.[11] In 1969, perhaps not coincidentally the same year that America's astronauts first walked on the moon, the first two science centers opened their doors: the Exploratorium in San Francisco and the Ontario Science Center in Toronto.

Three decades later, practically every major city in the United States has a science center.[12] The Association of Science–Technology Centers (ASTC), based in Washington, D.C., reports that there are nationally some three hundred museums describing themselves as science centers with a total annual visitation of 115 million—more than the live spectatorship at professional sporting events in this country. According to the National Science Foundation, 60 percent of the American adult public visited a science museum, zoo or aquarium in the past year.[13] Moreover, 700,000 families have joined the membership programs of science centers across the U.S., most of whom participate in a cooperative arrangement of free reciprocal visits.

With a shared mission to open the public's mind to science and technology—especially young minds, in ways complementary to their formal education—the hallmark of science centers became the interactive exhibit. Different halls covered an array of science and technology themes with topics and treatments ranging from highly entertaining to quite contemplative. Science centers also brought about a blurring of boundaries with other non-museum institutions. Elements of zoos, aquaria, botanical gardens, and even art galleries and history museums were freely incorporated. Scheduled live demonstrations for visitors, large numbers of floor staff and volunteers, educational materials for school classes, and professional-development services for teachers all became popular additional features of science centers. Most science centers charged admission and their search for funding became quite entrepreneurial. Demonstrations went on the road as traveling outreach programs, and science centers started to help one another by co-designing touring exhibitions. The now popular overnight camp-in programs in American museums were first introduced by a science center.

People are drawn in massive numbers to visit museums because they provide an enjoyable social outing, a chance to engage in diversionary activities, sensory stimulation, new perspectives, and the opportunity to connect with the world beyond the sphere of their everyday lives.[14] Schools, whose field excursions typically make up a major part of museum attendance, are now finding that science centers are paying much greater attention to their educational needs.

THE EVOLUTION OF SCIENCE CENTERS

Despite their tremendous popularity and growth over the past thirty years, science centers have not been without philosophical and operational difficulties.

Interactive exhibits that fail to work as intended are a frustration to visitors and create an image problem for science centers. New institutions—beset by large opening crowds and the inexperience of some staff—commonly encounter this problem, and otherwise positive news coverage often comments on it. However, as the whole field of science centers has matured and shared its expertise, exhibit-monitoring systems have improved, more robust design techniques have been developed, and visitor communications have become more thoughtful. Interactive exhibits, which had been on a trend of increasing complexity, have lately been getting more straightforward. Computers, for example, were never designed for vigorous use in busy public settings: physical damage and rebooting of software were recurring problems. Nowadays, museums have access to a much larger, more sophisticated menu of multimedia approaches. Interactive exhibit maintenance no longer is, nor needs to be, a problem on the scale it once was.

Another difficulty that developed was widespread reproduction of exhibits from one institution to another. Until quite recently, this stymied creativity and innovation in science-center exhibitry. The "cookie-cutter science center," a commonly heard phrase in museum circles, was all too apt in many instances. An easy route to supplying a new science center with exhibits, this approach unfortunately thwarted the potential to be relevant to local community needs. It also led to a degree of exhibit duplication abroad as U.S. and Canadian science centers, along with the many design firms they spawned, acted on the sales potential represented by many new institutions elsewhere in the world.

In hindsight, another difficulty has been posed by the science center's attraction of grant funds on the premise that such investments would lead directly to improved student performance. Science centers succeed in being places to inspire insight and motivate learning.[15] But they are only one resource, ideally a frequently used one, in lifelong journeys of learning. While serving as the Exploratorium's founding director, Frank Oppenheimer made his oft-quoted statement that no one ever fails a science center. Science centers do not test the knowledge of their visitors, who in any event often come in intergenerational groups. The National Science Teachers Association has further noted that the informal, participatory environment of a science center is especially well suited to learners of mixed-language backgrounds and varied learning styles.[16] For some students, a visit to a science center will spark a career choice in science and technology. But more information is needed on the relationship between science-center experiences and learning. Tracking surveys of museum visitors have long been needed. In the science center field, several long-term studies to quantify the community impact of these institutions are now getting underway.

Science centers have also encountered an image problem as places only for children. A predominantly young audience and high noise level, compared to more traditional types of museums, made it initially difficult for science centers to be accepted as worthwhile places. However, the fast-growing popularity of interactivity in museum exhibitions and the surging popularity of science centers in urban redevelopment plans led to their fairly quick acceptance by the mainstream museum community. In their enthusiastic entry to the arena of lifelong learning, science centers have started to design programs specifically for adults and, in the latest move, for grandparents with grandchildren as well.

A more recent difficulty has loomed as a result of the rapid growth of themed entertainment centers.[17] Science centers reacting to this niche competition have experienced some troubling drift in pursuing their missions. Negative developments have included the overt coverage of science fiction; a tendency toward sensationalism in marketing messages; addition of purely entertainment experiences; avoidance of sensitive issues; and retrofitting of educational objectives on experiences that lacked this intention while being developed. More recently, there have been some discernible shifts away from this unfortunate trend among science centers. An increasing orientation to local and regional issues in science and technology is one indicator. Another is a growing resistance to show large-format films lacking scientific integrity.[18] On the positive side, the competition has reminded science centers that their visitors' experiences need to be fundamentally enjoyable and engaging with high service levels.

THE FLEXIBILITY OF SCIENCE CENTERS

Several reasons may be cited to support the assertion that science centers are the most flexible sort of museum in terms of being able to increase their institutional relevance to community needs. Acting together, these differences add up to make a substantially different climate for such institutions.

Perhaps the most fundamental reason is that science centers typically lack a permanent collection—and, if there is one, it in no way resembles the scale and purpose of the collections typically held by history museums or art galleries. A large collection is a mission-defining characteristic for these museums, their raison d'être. It is manifested in large space allocations, information cataloguing-and-retrieval systems, and organizational and budgetary priorities that support the conservators and curators who study, and add to, collections. Quite often, collections are also a focal point of external interest because of high-profile donation policies.

By contrast, a science center, in its purest form, maintains a changing collection of participatory exhibit experiences, fabricated from parts. Whereas a static object from a collection of artifacts or specimens needs interpretative text to explain its significance, a science center exhibit is expressly designed to be publicly useable with direct educational aims. Typically in a science center that has opened within the last decade or so, any artifacts permanently held are generally on display, sometimes as institutional icons. Examples are whole machines (sometimes used for working demonstrations), recreations of famous laboratories, and collections of widely available artifacts, such as typewriters or televisions, which children can disassemble as a learning exercise. In a science center's mission statement, one does not typically find any reference to collections, curatorial research, or the interpretation of a collection.

Progressive museums are more audience- and experience-focused than collection-focused.[19] Being comparatively young institutions with an entrepreneurial bent, science centers are able to change their content and focus with relative ease. Because science centers focus on presenting the rapidly changing world of science and technology—and find support for this mission from research and development industries—there is also an external stimulus encouraging a significant degree of flexibility. Aspects of the environment, health, or invention, for example, can be flexibly responded to by multimedia exhibitions in ways that are profoundly different from what would invariably be the constraining potential of a static collection.

The entrepreneurial spirit and increasingly business-styled operation of science centers have their roots, arguably, in the bottom-line pressures that come with a high dependence on earned revenue.[20] Science centers, being latecomers to the museum scene and without collections in the traditional sense, have generally lacked the cachet that attracts large cash gifts from wealthy trustees, outside donors, or bequests. Being newer has also meant that endowments and interest income are typically much smaller and have slower growth. The situation for state- and federally-operated science museums with collection mandates is quite different; they receive public operating subsidies and are commonly prohibited from generating earned revenue. Among publicly sponsored science centers in the United States, those of the state of California and city of St. Louis are notable rarities in terms of there being a direct government interest in assuring universal access, signified by the fact that neither institution charges a regular public admission fee. Neither is prevented from receiving private-sector contributions.

Another contributing factor to the adaptability of science centers is the often different career path of their directors. In collection-based museums, senior curators traditionally rise to the rank of director, either at their original institution or another. College and university presidencies have lately been another source for their directorships. In science centers, partly because of their rapid growth in numbers and a lack of tradition, CEOs have a much wider variety of backgrounds. These include NASA's astronaut program, public-service agencies, government departments, broadcasting, industry marketing, university-based research, and other nonprofit organizations. With this diverse array of backgrounds have flowed new perspectives—another reason why science centers have had an accelerated ability to change and take on new aims.

MUSEUMS BECOMING RELEVANT

At a symposium in 1996 marking the sesquicentennial of the Smithsonian Institution, Harold Skramstad noted:

> The mission statement of most museums that goes "our mission is to collect, preserve and interpret (fill in the blank)" will no longer do. Such statements do not answer the vital question of "so what?" Increasingly, the mission statement of a museum, its essential statement of value-added, is going to have to contain not only a concise statement of what the museum does, but a description of the outcome of its actions and a sense of the value that this outcome has in the larger work of the community.[21]

Striking a similar chord, Donald Duckworth, of Honolulu's Bishop Museum, commented in 1993 that the museum's

> ...introverted focus has engendered the belief that artifactual collections are the "reason for being" of museums, rather than a tool through which we gain and disseminate knowledge. This orientation toward "things" rather than "societal needs" is why many museums, and the science pursued in them, have acquired an image as out of touch, musty store-houses of relics of a dead past, of interest to, and only intended to serve, a social or intellectual elite.[22]

Nowadays in the museum field, one often hears the word *relevance*. At the 1998 and 1999 gatherings of the Museum Management Institute (MMI) held at the University of California at Berkeley, I asked the class for synonyms of this word. *In touch, useful, inclusive, valuable, meaningful, symbiotic, pertinent,* and *worthwhile* were the responses. Next, my request for antonyms was met with *distant, marginal, unrelated, exclusive, elitist, remote, arcane,* and *self-absorbed.* I then shared the dictionary definition of relevance; "relating to the matter(s) at hand." The responses I received make clear that societal and community needs are the matters at hand for the museum. This MMI class then identified the major internal and external drivers why museums are now sensing a need to increase their relevance (such as funding, equity, opportunity, need, accountability) as well as the major factors that seem to hold them back (chief among which were various internal interests and traditional priorities).

Another way of expressing societal and community needs is to speak in terms of the *common good*. This stands as a clear opposite to *self-interest*. How a museum shifts its values, mission and practices toward the common good ranks as a major challenge. Richard Barrett has described this switch in paradigms as an evolutionary step in the social consciousness of business organizations.[23] Along parallel lines, Greg Parston has offered insight on the attributes of progressive leadership:

> The leaders of tomorrow's socially responsible businesses will coach and educate others in their organization to contribute to a social result that is bigger than themselves and bigger than their organizations. . . . And they will work with people outside their organizations to form new partnerships and new dialogues focused on social results. In this role, the leaders of tomorrow's organizations will be social activists. . .establishing and clarifying the social agenda of their organizations.[24]

Arguably, symptoms of self-interest in museums include acquisition of preserved specimens of endangered species, curatorial research divorced from any public interest, cultural exhibitions insensitive to aboriginal rights, keeping of artifacts that should be repatriated, or a lack of action to broaden attendance to be more inclusive of the whole community. At the other end of the spectrum, encouraging symptoms of a philosophy aimed at the common good include designing of multilayered experiences through exhibitions and programs aimed at visitors of all ages and backgrounds, high hospitality standards for visitors; partnering with other community organizations for greater quality-of-life improvements, innovative marketing aimed at access for disadvantaged neighborhoods, full service to persons with disabilities; and hiring practices that embrace diversity. Recent conference themes for America's museums reflect a desirable trend, as even a brief review shows: "Museums and Sustainable Communities," "Catalysts for Social Change," "Coming of Age in the Twenty-First Century," and "Reinventing the Museum—Relevance and Renewal."

That many museums are now seeing themselves anew as an important player in a number of external contexts is indicative of a powerful paradigm shift. In today's wide spectrum of museum philosophies, the two end states seem to be 1) a curator-driven, collection-based museum with a passive stance on public programs, and 2) an audience-driven, educationally-active museum that positions itself as a relevant community resource. In arriving at either of these two states, museums, like any other type of organization, visualize a desired result and then decide how best to attain that goal. Stephen Covey usefully distinguishes between *effectiveness* and *efficiency* by noting that while the former involves doing the right things, the latter involves doing things right.[25] Framing the right things to do requires both *mission* and *vision*, in that mission describes an organization's basic raison d'être and vision anticipates an achievable future scenario in which a given mission achieves greater impact. *Strategy* refers to the best pathway for doing things right—that is, for advancing mission-driven performance to achieve the vision.

Different socioeconomic conditions from country to country and region to region appropriately lead to variation in museum mission-vision-strategy statements. In a recently industrialized nation, oppressive conditions of environmental pollution and poor human health might lead a science center to have a strongly issues-orientated mandate. On the other hand, a science center in a developed country with a major tourism industry ought to offer experiences that are mindful of many different expectations. Calcutta, India and Orlando, Florida stand as examples of these extremes.

SCIENCE CENTERS AND SOCIAL RESPONSIBILITY

Science centers are about practical aspects of today's world and, therefore, have been connected from their origins with regional communities by way of educational partnerships. This outwardly directed philosophy has, in turn, led science centers generally to be the first to delve more deeply into addressing how a greater concern for social responsibility makes necessary new ways of thinking about, exhibiting, and interpreting the museum's presentation of its subject. The Association of Science–Technology Centers, for example, has hosted CEO forums around this topic. There is, indeed, a broad palette of possibilities shaping how science museums of various types can increase their social relevance.

Science museums with collections of scientific and industrial artifacts can forge a deeper understanding, for example, of the research, prototyping, and patent-protection process. They can also inquire into the lives and times of famous scientists and inventors. The world does not know enough about Nobel laureates in terms of their service to humankind or their philosophical outlook. So far, this opportunity has been mainly answered by occasional touring blockbuster exhibitions on the engineering achievements of Leonardo da Vinci and of the early Chinese.

Natural history museums can apply the evidence of past global change in the context of modern environmental and ecological changes. Given the current weight of evidence pointing to global warming with a human cause and to the clearly harmful human impact on natural biodiversity and habitats, this is a major, even urgent role for natural history museums to play. In many of the major institutions of this sort—the American Museum of Natural History in New York City being a notable example—such efforts are already underway.

For their part, science centers are increasingly positioning themselves as socially valuable resources for information about science and technology and its social implications, with their organizational strengths directed at particular community needs. The latter may take the form of new subjects to cover, new audiences to serve, new partners with which to develop alliances, new multimedia approaches for greater impact—and, ideally, all of these.

Science centers can also do a better job at orienting their visitors to the way science and technology unfold in the world. Developments in science and technology that make the headlines do not result from the sort of science-as-discrete-subject most adults learned at school. Instead it is the product of multi-disciplinary packages of science and technology, and their engagement with human affairs.[26] Science centers can reflect this reality through more holistic interpretations and better briefings at entrance and exit on what the institution is aiming to achieve for its visitors. It is still commonplace for science centers to brand themselves as simply places for having fun. Being mindful of the greater overall aims of such experiences—for education, for informed public discussion—is a critical dimension of the science center's social responsibility.

Science centers have a particular opportunity to capitalize on the public's need to function in a technologically advanced world in which science-technology-society issues are interwoven.[27] The lifelong interest of all citizens in personal and community health are properly regarded as a primary focus of science center attention. The pressures of a rapidly expanding human population in the twenty-first century will likely also increase attention to a broadening array of environmental matters. Ecotourism is already the fastest growing segment of tourism, itself the world's largest industry.[28] Science centers also have the opportunity, as yet almost entirely untapped, to empower people to be active commentators on the science and technology issues surrounding them. Imagine how our public-policy debates might change on a host of issues if the views of the more than one hundred million annual visitors to science centers across the United States could somehow be surveyed and shared with the news media and government authorities.

Planning for visitor experiences needs to consider the inside and outside of the facility, both physically and electronically, as one total experience appropriate to the twenty-first century. There is also a growing recognition that the science center does not need to have all the answers on a given subject in order to present an illuminating experience to the public. It seems eminently preferable to open minds by offering partial insights than it is to fill minds with an authoritative account—or to fail entirely to address a subject.

A science center's inherent appeal to children is also worthy of greater attention. Research in developmental psychology has demonstrated that we are born with innate scientific talents—observing, sorting, experimenting, trial and error, discovery, and so forth. Clearly, these modes of learning are well challenged by the interactive, inquiry-based learning style of science centers, compared to the vision-based environments of other museum types. The growth of interactive science-focused museums specifically for children, as well as of specific areas for young children within larger museums, are an appropriate and promising response to these developmental realities. The Indianapolis Children's Museum and the Cité des Enfants within the world's largest science museum in Paris are leading examples. The growth of the Association of Youth Museums (AYM) in the United States is an additional and significant indicator of these trends. An exciting new opportunity exists for science centers to serve and attract preschool children—while at the same time examining early childhood development with a view to sustaining children's interest in science through their years in school.

Other social needs to which science centers are making an increasing contribution include the school-to-work transition, lifelong learning, and career retooling. In the economic arena, science centers are growing players in urban renaissance projects, in promotion of environmental stewardship, and as tourism destinations.

THE CONTRIBUTIONS OF SCIENCE CENTERS

Science centers have now existed for three decades, a period long enough to allow an assessment of their contribution to the broader museum field. It is important in doing so to begin by reflecting on why science centers evolved in the first place.

The closing decades of the twentieth century have seen an exponential pace in scientific and technological developments. These have profoundly affected how we live, work, communicate and manage information, travel, care for ourselves and the environment, or fight wars; what we eat, drink, and wear; and where and how we explore. Science centers have arguably filled a void in the museum scene by profiling many of these subject areas for the public. Some have also given rise to single-subject museum projects, focusing on such topics as computers (Boston) and news-media technology (Arlington, Virginia). In a parallel fashion, surely the nationwide growth in the popularity of aquaria reflects a public interest in today's oceans and rivers on par with our long-standing fascination with animals and plants that have made zoos and botanical gardens major out-door attractions for more than a century. For their part, war museums and aviation museums have had much new material to add to their collections and interpretations because of tech-nological advances. The National Air and Space Museum, part of the Smithsonian Institution, shares with the Louvre in Paris the distinction of being one of the world's two most visited museums; each have an annual attendance in the range of seven to ten million visitors.

At a more detailed level, the contributions of science centers to the museum field have been notable in three areas. First, the definition of what constitutes a museum has expanded to in-clude institutions that do not possess a large collection of ob-jects. Holding a collection had been *the* defining characteristic of museums; the basic questions to ask of such institutions were what they acquired, researched, displayed, and became known for. The now widespread acceptance of the science center into a broader definition of museums has been a major adaptation for the field.

The science center's methodology—one initially described as hands-on and now increasingly multi-sensory and multimedia in nature—has been an important innovation in the museum field.[29] The public's impression of the museum had been mostly one of a quiet place with large numbers of static objects on display, often behind glass and only with brief identification labels. Science center experiences stand in sharp contrast to this traditional museum atmosphere. They are characteristically active and noisy places due to dynamic interaction of visitors and exhibits, invited participation on stage with live demon-strations, and line-ups for hourly shows in giant-screen the-aters. Some aspects of the science-center methodology have been adapted, it seems increasingly, by other museum types. The consciously theatrical atmosphere of certain science-center layouts seems to have been a forerunner to the recently popular line of thinking that museums should see themselves as in the business of creating memorable experiences.

Finally, science centers have forged many new productive connections with primary and secondary education. While museums have always been a major destination for school field trips, science centers have adopted a strong service mentality. This includes such measures as aligning exhibit and program materials for classes with state and national curriculum-content standards; generating pre- and post-visit materials for teachers to prepare and debrief their students; organizing teacher-training sessions to help in field-trip management; hosting teacher sabbaticals and summer institutes; creating customized classroom and studio facilities included in new facility designs; developing mobile programs that can be taken to schools; and facilitating video conferencing with schools from exhibit floors. Certainly, science centers had the advantage of an inherent appeal to young minds, and therefore became attractive field-trip choices for science teachers. For other museum types, it has taken a long time indeed to describe themselves freely as explicitly educational places, or for their education departments to become well integrated within the museum's whole organizational structure.[30]

LOOKING AHEAD

Current patterns of change suggest that an emerging set of seven attributes will largely define the next generation of science centers.

· A mission centering on integrated interpretations of science-technology-society issues focused more on today and tomorrow than on yesterday, and entertaining multiple points of view.

· A dedication to providing access and outreach to visitors and users of all ages, learning styles, and backgrounds;

· A unifying institutional theme that helps to create context and connections for visitors, that fosters a unique experience for them, and that facilitates brand identity for the organization in its marketplace.

· Adoption of the full menu of available multimedia to create engaging experiences in attractive and contextual settings.
· Developing topical multidimensional experiences that will serve to make the science center regarded as a worthwhile lifelong resource to many invested stakeholders.
· Establishing numerous partnerships with other like-minded organizations that make possible combining resources for greater collective impact.
· Serving as a neutral ground for airing of society's most vexing issues related to science and technology.

A personal anecdote may serve, by way of conclusion, to show just how it is that science centers can both communicate, and model, a responsibility to act in a manner mindful of long-term global interests.[31] I vividly remember visiting London's Natural History Museum while growing up in England, and being fascinated by the cased specimens of taxidermic wildlife from around the world. Later, while conducting doctoral research in geology at a university in Canada, I visited the London Zoo for what turned out to be the last time. Armed then with more critical thinking skills, I concluded that its caged specimens of wildlife from around the world were not far removed from their ancestors who, a century or so before, had been killed and preserved for the Natural History Museum a few miles away. Much more recently I sat with an audience viewing an IMAX film at a science center, which explored the annual cycle of wildlife in Africa's Serengeti. With only the camera having invaded the ecosystem, and with many of its inhabitants on the brink of extinction, I felt better about the potentially helpful role of museums in society. The film experience made me think again, for example, of all the lions who had been abruptly removed from their habitat, dead or alive, to the hundreds of museums and zoos around the world.

Increasing the museum's sensitivity to its social impact, and the ongoing search for yet greater relevance to community needs, is an intellectually satisfying area of work. More importantly, perhaps, this work can also be financially rewarding for the museum. A mission of relevancy to the community attracts external funding from corporations, foundations, and individuals who also want to help make positive differences in the world. The challenge facing the museum field, both in science centers and elsewhere, is to create compelling experiences on subjects of importance in ways that increasingly attract society to view museums as engaging resources for lifelong learning.

ENDNOTES

[1] American Association of Museums, *Excellence and Equity—Education and the Public Dimension of Museums* (Washington, D.C.: American Association of Museums, 1992), 8.

[2] American Association of Museums, "Strategic Agenda, FY 1998–2000: A Report to the Membership," *Museum News* (September/October 1997).

[3] International Council of Museums, "Program Highlights for ICOM Activities for 1999, 2000 and 2001," *ICOM News* 51 (Special Issue) (1998): 26–27.

[4] S. Riley, "Why are Our Museums so Bland?", *Ottawa Citizen*, 7 December 1996 D1-D2.; Nancy Keats, "Why Are Museums So Clueless?" *Wall Street Journal*, 9 April 1999, W1-W16.

[5] J. B. Mays, "Are Blockbusters a Bust?" *Globe and Mail*, 17 May 1997; E1-E2.

[6] Herbert Muschamp, "Culture's Power Houses: The Museum Becomes An Engine of Urban Redesign," *New York Times*, 21 April 1999; G1-G6.

[7] Emlyn H. Koster, "Our Community Relevance," *Technology Museum Review* (journal of the National Science and Technology Museum, Taiwan) 2 (3) (May 1998): 94–108.

[8] See John Durant and John Gregory, *Science and Culture in Europe* (London: Science Museum, 1993).

[9] Bernard Schiele, Michel Amyot and Claude Benoit, "Introduction," in *When Science Becomes Culture*, ed. Bernard Schiele (Ottawa, Ontario: University of Ottawa Press, 1994), 1–11.

[10] Alfred Heller, *World's Fairs and the End of Progress–An Insider's View* (Corte Madera, Calif.: World's Fair Inc., 1999), 11.

[11] See Victor J. Danilov, *Science and Technology Centers* (Cambridge, Mass.: MIT Press, 1982).

[12] Association of Science–Technology Centers, *ASTC Directory 1998–99* (Washington, D.C.: ASTC, 1998).

[13] Association of Science–Technology Centers, "Science Centers in the United States–Fact Sheet," in *Yearbook of Science Center Statistics* (Washington, D.C.: ASTC, 1999).

[14]Neil Kotler and Philip Kotler, *Museum Strategy and Marketing* (San Francisco, Calif.: Jossey-Bass Publishers, 1998), 35.

[15]See Institute of Museum and Library Services, *True Needs, True Partners—Survey Highlights* (Washington, D.C.: Institute of Museum and Library Services, National Endowment for the Humanities, 1998).

[16]See National Science Teachers Association, "Informal Science Education—A NSTA Position Statement" (approved by the NSTA board of directors in January of 1998); <http://www.nsta.org/handbook/informaleducation.htm>.

[17]Ann Mintz, "That's Edutainment!" *Museum News* (November/December 1994): 33–35.

[18]Emlyn H. Koster, "Edutainment—To Be or Not to Be?" *The Big Frame* (Spring 1999): 96.

[19]Neil Kotler, "Delivering Experience: Marketing the Museum's Full Range of Assets," *Museum News* (May/June 1999): 30–61.

[20]Victoria Newhouse, "As a Life Preserver, Popularity May Not Be Enough," *New York Times*, 7 March 1999, 40, 48.

[21]Smithsonian Institution, *Museums for the New Millennium: A Symposium for the Museum Community* (proceedings of a conference held in commemoration of the Smithsonian's 150th anniversary, 5–7 September 1996) (Washington, D.C.: Center for Museum Studies/American Association of Museums, 1997), 38.

[22]W. Donald Duckworth, "Museum-Based Science for a New Century," in *Research Within the Museums: Aspirations and Realities* (proceedings of an international symposium held at the National Museum of Natural Science, Taichung, Taiwan, 13–14 December 1993) (Taichung: National Museum of Natural Science, 1994), 13–19.

[23]See Richard Barrett, *Liberating the Corporate Soul: Building a Visionary Organization* (Boston: Butterworth Heinemann, 1998).

[24]Greg Parston, "Producing Social Results," in *The Organization of the Future*, ed. Frances Hesselbein, Marshall Goldsmith, and Richard Beckhard (San Francisco, Calif.: Jossey-Bass Publishers, 1997), 341–348.

[25]Stephen R. Covey, *The Seven Habits of Highly Effective People: Powerful Lessons in Personal Change* (New York: Simon & Schuster Inc., 1990), 101–102.

[26]See Paul Kennedy, *Preparing for the Twenty-First Century* (New York and Toronto: Harper Collins Publishers, 1993).

[27]See James Trefil and Robert M. Hazen, *The Sciences: An Integrated Approach* (New York: John Wiley & Sons, 1995).

[28]See, for example, Erlet Cater and Gwen Lowman, eds., *Ecotourism–A Sustainable Option?* (New York: John Wiley & Sons, 1994).

[29]Tim Caulton, *Hands-On Exhibitions: Managing Interactive Museums and Science Centers* (London and New York: Routledge, 1998), vii.

[30]See *Evaluation and Museum Education: New Trends*, ed. Colette Dufresne-Tassé for the Committee for Education and Cultural Action, International Council of Museums (Quebec: AGMV Marquis Imprimeur, 1998).

[31]Emlyn H. Koster, "The Human Journey and the Evolving Museum" (Fiftieth anniversary address to the Geological Association of Canada), *Geoscience Canada* 24 (2) (1997): 73–76.

Susanna Sirefman

Formed and Forming:
Contemporary Museum Architecture

T HE VERY NOTION OF A MUSEUM embodies physicality. The
word itself implies a built structure, where the activities
on offer revolve around human motion through articulated space. The experiential narrative that a museum embodies is inseparable from its physical condition—its architecture.
Architecture represents the museum's public image, defines the
institution's relationship to its setting, and constructs the framework of the visitors' experience.

No other building typology represents such intricate complexities or a multiplicity of functions as does that of the museum. Cultural repository, dynamic civic space, popular entertainment center, tool for urban revitalization—much is asked of
contemporary museum architecture. A striking paradox of past
achievements and future possibilities, museum architecture—
unlike art, or a great collection—never stands alone. Architecture is intrinsically part of something greater: a cultural ambition, a corporate ideal, a climactic condition, a historical setting, a topology, a geography. By virtue of being within the
public realm, museum architecture is laden with social, political, and moral issues.

A museum building has a lengthy laundry list of technical
tasks to fulfill: security and storage; crowd control and circulation for staff and visitor; fire detection and prevention; micro-
climates and specialized systems; lighting, heating, ventilation,
air conditioning, plumbing, electricity, and communications for

---

Susanna Sirefman is adjunct associate professor of architecture at City College of New York.

various different spaces. Very often fully half of the building housing these necessary internal mechanisms is not visible to the public. As for its public persona, the building must accommodate the objects on display, integrating a flexible interior with a meaningful exterior. Site, scale, space, and place-making are all integral aspects of the process. The ideal museum building cultivates both anticipation and memory while relating to its location and community.

Universally associated with cultural myths and rituals,[1] museum architecture does not only serve as a tangible container of lore; it itself possesses mythical attributes. Both myth and architecture are narrative metaphors for social construction, defining boundaries for human interaction with other humans and nature.[2] Posturban museum architecture revolves around fresh rituals and contemporary myths—those of site, fragmentation, scale, technology, programmatic flexibility, and cross-cultural connection.[3]

This essay, not intended as a comprehensive survey, looks at issues currently surrounding contemporary museum architecture in North America. These issues are addressed by way of conceptual snapshots taken at varying distances starting with an airborne panoramic view, zooming in closer and closer until focusing on the objects on display.[4]

SITE

A building that aspires to cultural significance is one that takes risks, engages the public, and seriously explores a structure's role as a part of the city and social context rather than merely functioning as a box. Posturban museum architecture cannot simply be a container; it must have content of its own. As a building in and of itself, the architecture need not compete with the art or artifacts on display; in fact, it can enhance the exhibition experience. These two needs—container and architectural presence—are not mutually exclusive; a museum can at once be a significant edifice and be sympathetic to its required functions. It is analogous to a reversible jacket; the inside is equal to the outside and vice versa. Reflector and projector, the successful contemporary posturban museum should demonstrate a strong symbiotic relationship not only with its contents, but with its context—the city.

Much discussion of new museum architecture currently revolves around the most recent revolutionary museum building, the Guggenheim Museum Bilbao. This new building has raised the bar of museum design on many levels. Architects, architectural critics, artists, and tourists are all enamored of the new Guggenheim. Fantastical descriptions abound. The architect, Frank Gehry, is being compared to Frank Lloyd Wright, his museum design lauded as a ground-breaking new category of architecture. For all its practical drawbacks (notably, vast size and exorbitant cost), this is a remarkable structure and a hugely successful icon for the city of Bilbao. Part of a larger urban revitalization scheme for reclaiming the waterfront and reformulating Bilbao's cultural and tourism infrastructure, the new building serves as a tangible symbol of the city, the crown jewel of the Basque capital's urban and economic renewal.

Treating the city itself as a museum, Gehry has designed a sensuous, inhabitable sculpture. A significant landmark, the building serves as a powerful cultural nexus. The city of Bilbao becomes a collective interior, the museum being part of a greater whole, bringing to life Walter Benjamin's seductive observations of the parallel between city and apartment:

> The collective is an eternally alert, eternally moving being that witnesses, experiences, perceives and devises as much between the house walls outside as individuals within the protection of their own walls.[5]

The impact of the museum is not just confined to the individual's experience of cultural exchange inside but extends to the institution's urbanistic reach.

Rather ironically, this romantic exterior embodies an American ideology—liberty, expansiveness, rugged individualism. Yet this building was realized as an exported commodity.[6] Gehry is exploring unknown territory, a fresh approach to architecture, a sort of artful manifest destiny. Jettisoning a clear architectural precedent or a pedantic approach (there is much reference to both Wright and Gaudi, as well as the surrounding architectural context), Gehry has made a step in the direction of redefining our notion of a museum's civic presence. Unafraid to use a local material in an innovative way (titanium cladding), not intimidated to play with scale in relationship to art, this building is an effort, whether successful or not, to move museum architecture forward. Perhaps this is fitting in a country ruled by a dictatorship for thirty-six years, only returning to democracy in 1975. After all, "it is a truism that all cities are shaped by politics."[7] Architectural historian Victoria Newhouse calls our attention to precedent, likening the circumstances surrounding Bilbao's genesis to that of

> ...one of the first and most influential purpose-built museums: Altes Museum in Berlin (1830) by Karl Freidrich Schinkel, early nineteenth-century Germany's leading architect. Both museums arose from the need for a new civic image to mark the end of political and economic turmoil: the Napoleonic Wars in Prussia, Basque terrorism and industrial decline in Bilbao. Both were part of a new beginning, entailing urban renewal for a historic city where a museum is the major feature of a newly developed area: in Berlin a filled-in canal, in Bilbao the obsolete port facilities. And both raised the issue of container versus content.[8]

Winning a large museum commission is perceived as an instant claim to fame for most architects. A recognizable, innovative edifice becomes a useful marketing tool for the commissioning institution. As North American museums depend upon individual and corporate patrons, admissions, gift-shop income, and rental fees to survive, the building itself has become a marketable product. Architecture is most certainly not an arena immune to the cult of celebrity; the Bilbao Guggenheim is further proof of the financial pull of a signature building by a signature architect. In brash retail-entertainment terms, the Guggenheim has successfully "branded" itself through progressive architecture. The museum building has become an integral part of what the museum has to offer; it is the ultimate object on display.

The obvious worry is that—much like the world of fashion advertising, which relies on sexy sensationalism to sell—the Bilbao Guggenheim has raised the desire for voluptuous architecture. Some fear that "pornographic architecture"—seductively inventive form minus meaningful substance—will proliferate.[9] But such a worry is senseless; the mediocre knock-off is inevitable, and there is so much architecture lacking substance already. Bad imitations will follow; so will equally inspired work. The Bilbao Guggenheim has raised public consciousness, renewing a global interest in architecture.

The museum has been employed as a tool for urban revitalization by many North American cities. Philadelphia, Kansas City, San Francisco, and Baltimore have all anchored their master plans for new cultural districts with museums. We have imported internationally celebrated architects for several of our larger public museums, yet a building such as the Bilbao Guggenheim could not and did not happen here first. By way of comparison, two recent disappointments come to mind: the Museum of Contemporary Art (MCA) in Chicago (1996) and the San Francisco Museum of Modern Art (1995).

Chicago's MCA, designed by the German architect Josef P. Kleihues, is essentially an elaborate though understated container. Kleihues, a self-titled poetic rationalist, has created a visually hostile, formal classical exterior. A rather pompous, grandiose staircase, inspired by the propylaeum of the Acropolis, leads the visitor up to the entry. The perception is a throwback to nineteenth-century museums, a grand staircase elevating art into a highbrow plane, yet the MCA is most definitely a populist museum. The steps at the Metropolitan Museum of Art in New York are a fabulous meeting place, resting spot, and people-watching perch. The vista from the steps at the MCA is not nearly as enticing nor are the steps themselves. At the Bilbao Guggenheim, Gehry deliberately sends the visitor (if arriving via the riverside) on a journey around the building, up a set of stairs, and then down into the small lobby, disregarding any suggestion of a grand entranceway. Inventing his own architectural language, Gehry forces the viewer to be engaged with the building's animation, creating a sense of excitement and curiosity. What better way to enter a museum than with senses aroused and anticipation high? No longer merely a container, the architecture itself is loaded with content.[10]

Chicago's MCA, an intellectual building that is driven by a sophisticated interplay between transparency and containment, never fully engages with its surroundings—the city of Chicago. Situated in a deliciously posturban canyon, smack between two public parks and surrounded by vast vertical landmarks, the infrastructure for this dialogue between transparency and containment could and should have been exploited, creating a meaningful civic place. The San Francisco Museum of Modern Art has an equally pugnacious exterior and has become a favorite target for architectural criticism. Much of the pointed commentary is spot-on, likening the museum exterior to a Mesopotamian ziggurat, an armory, or a shopping mall.[11] This heavy, cumbersome form, with next to no visible fenestration, is defiantly determined to ignore its location. Situated in the middle of a city center, the museum seems to be cut off from its adjacent cultural district, completely unrelated to its surrounding context. Visually analogous to Lego blocks on steroids, the museum has a massive presence that makes an identifiable picture postcard, but neither architecturally nor urbanistically enhances its neighborhood.

The idea of museum as "substitute cathedral"[12] is not a new one. The North American museum was characteristically an architectural pastiche of a European palace. Historically interpreted in a multitude of ways, the museum-as-enlightenment-palace idea can today achieve architectural expression only as a metaphor—not as a literal form. Formal church references—a dome in the form of a truncated cylinder, pulpit configurations, crosses—are straightforward translations of church architecture that fail as museum architecture. Mario Botta has created in San Francisco a grand entrance space that leads nowhere, celebrates nothing—and, most importantly, is divorced from the display of the art.

In 1959 Frank Lloyd Wright changed museum architecture forever by creating in the Fifth Avenue Guggenheim a new building typology. Wright was interested in programmatic contextuality, and the form of the Guggenheim—a circular concrete building designed around a seven-story spiral ramp—was generated by a desire to create an egalitarian way of viewing art. This new museum of new art, where the innovative interior was visible on the exterior, immediately became an icon. James Stirling's Staatsgalerie New Building (1983) in

Stuttgart, and in Paris the radical Centre National D'Art et de Culture Georges Pompidou and I. M. Pei's pyramid at the Louvre (1989), highlighted the economic power of building an architectural spectacle. These museums are now popular tourist destinations, as much for the architecture as for the art.

It is interesting to note that one of the most architecturally significant museum buildings of the last thirty years—the above-mentioned Pompidou, designed by Renzo Piano and Richard Rogers and built in 1977—was also part of a large, government-driven urban revitalization scheme. In an effort to democratize the museum experience, eliminating a visual barrier between inside and outside, the building's exterior is transparent, animated by the external circulation system. Providing an important voyeuristic moment in Paris, the Pompidou attracts a large number of visitors just for the sensational views from the transparent exterior escalators.[13] What a marvelous way to celebrate both contents and container, inside and outside.

FRAGMENTATION

The rapid growth of our museum culture is not confined to new buildings; additions, adaptive reuse, and renovations are frequent solutions to growing collections and expansion pressures. This has created the cracking of the museum district or the museum mile. In our denser cities, museums devoted to either art or artifacts can be found dotted across the cityscape—sometimes highly visible, sometimes completely hidden. Certainly in Manhattan, posturban spatial configuration is about insertion, fragmentation, and assemblage. The new museum in New York, as a built cultural convention, has been physically integrated into the fabric of the city. Today's peripatetic culture vulture can find a museum in practically any part of town.

The relatively recent (1992) addition to Frank Lloyd Wright's seminal Fifth Avenue Guggenheim building, in conjunction with the downtown SoHo Guggenheim, represents the physical layering (both horizontally and vertically) of one institution within the city. Many architects, critics, and locals felt that the existing building was a piece of art in itself, precluding the possibility of an addition: one would not paint something new onto a

Raphael; why add to the Guggenheim? Yet buildings are not art, and the programmatic life of a building requires the capacity to reconfigure, renovate, and—if absolutely necessary—expand. Expansion, in general, has become a rather contentious issue. In many if not all cases, the notion "bigger is better," as applied to the art museum, seems puzzling. Forcing the issue of scale has very real architectural, spatial, and experiential implications exacerbating the museum's need for flexibility. Will private contemplation and reverie still be possible? How does one prevent the large museum from resembling an airport, where "flow management" and security are the foremost priorities?[14]

In the constant chase for money and status, museums across the nation are striving to grow. Directly correlated to a booming economy, museum expansion offers much-coveted community recognition for its donors.[15] The reverse, permanence and stasis within a museum or a collection, would be a more valuable asset. Temporality in both collection and building inhibit intimacy between artwork and space, as well as between artwork and viewer.

Functional and organic, buildings are participants in, not merely witnesses to, the passage of time. This is the position taken by the architects Gwathmey Siegel, responsible for the Guggenheim addition: "Architecture is not static, nor is it perception. We believe in the idea of the addition as much as in its realization."[16] The resulting ten-story limestone annex to the east of the original edifice has considerably transformed the original building. What used to be a freestanding sculptural object now resembles a three-dimensional abstraction of a cubist painting, its volume part of a greater composition.[17] One's experience of the interior is now skewed as the effect of the enclosed spiral is diluted by adjacent rectilinear galleries. Good or bad, this is part of the life cycle of a building.

The nearby Whitney Museum of American Art was also the focus of much public upset in 1985 when a proposed (and never realized) Michael Graves addition seemed to suggest swallowing up Marcel Breuer's masterpiece in a postmodern skin. The expansion ultimately built, designed by a different architect—Richard Gluckman (and completed in 1998)—barely addresses the Breuer building and is only noticeable to those visitors who were intimate with the pre-expansion museum.

Adding to the city by making a new building that is indistinguishable from its neighbors, creating invisible architecture, is a far more insidious design approach. A dramatic missed opportunity to contribute a bold architectural timepiece to New York is exemplified by the 1993 addition to Manhattan's Jewish Museum (designed by Kevin Roche). A nearly imperceptible 30,000-square-foot addition was built, expanding the existing location, the historic Warburg Mansion on Fifth Avenue (built in 1908 by the architect C. P. H. Gilbert), and linked to a later building and courtyard. The addition was designed in the same style and to the same height as the existing fancified beaux-arts mansion, such that it is impossible to distinguish the new from the old. The resulting seven-story museum appears to be a Gilbert design. It seems as if by powers of magic the mansion was pulled, stretched, and tweaked into expanding itself. Where is the architecture in this?

The Guggenheim's horizontal expansion in 1992 to a downtown site was the first step in a worldwide satellite scheme. The current Guggenheim philosophy of the "one museum with discontiguous galleries," although much derided, offers a rich laboratory for architectural experimentation.[18] Intended to provide the Guggenheim a presence within the wider context of the city, the scale of the expansion instead suggests a position perilously close to that of a commercial chain of stores. (Detractors refer to the museum branches as McGuggenheims.) Thankfully, the Guggenheim offers a differing product downtown than uptown. Housed in the shell of a cast-iron commercial structure dating back to 1882, the museum is an insertion (designed by Japanese architect Arato Isozaki), a skin-tight fit into an existing building, adopting the minimalist "white cube" vernacular of the surrounding neighborhood art galleries. The ornate, beautifully detailed facade was left virtually intact; but inside, the building's original function—housing manufacturers and wholesalers of clothing—has been erased, forfeiting any historical link.

The birth of the public museum in Europe revolved around the conversion of existing buildings, palaces, and stately homes into public galleries.[19] One of the first civic museums, the Louvre Palace, was converted after the French Revolution. The current twist, for at least the last twenty-five to thirty years, is for museums to inhabit not domestic buildings but industrial edifices: railroad stations, power stations, public schools, abandoned government structures. This is not just an American phenomenon; some of the largest museums in Europe have been created within unlikely sites. The Musée d'Orsay in Paris is a museum implanted in a glorious turn-of-the-century train station designed by Victor Laloux. The Gare d'Orsay was converted into galleries devoted to art of the nineteenth century in the early 1980s by the architect Gae Aulenti. Train stations have been utilized as museums in the United States as well; in fact, the second-largest train station in America—Union Station in Kansas City—is now "Science City," an interactive science museum.

These "graftings" typify how cities and their architecture are continually evolving through an intricately entwined layering of culture, politics, and history. The George Gustav Heye Center of the National Museum of the American Indian characterizes these spatial and temporal stratifications. A more resonant location could not have been chosen for a celebratory venue of the American Indian. The disparate juxtaposition between program and building is wonderfully ironic. It is bizarre and remarkable that such an imposing, politically incorrect capitalist monument is now the haven for Native American artifacts. The result is an extraordinary example of lateral and literal potency in architectural narrative.

It was at the southern tip of Manhattan—then Fort Amsterdam, now Bowling Green—that Peter Minuit negotiated the phantom "purchase" of Manhattan Island from the Indians in 1626, supposedly trading jewelry worth twenty-four dollars for ownership of the island. Government House was constructed on the site in 1790 (after a statue of George III was demolished by a crowd in 1776), serving first as George Washington's executive residence, then as a tavern, and finally, in 1799, as a customs house. The splendid beaux-arts edifice that now occupies the site, designed by Cass Gilbert in 1907, is lavishly decorated. Tagged "a Great Temple to Commerce" by the *New York*

Times shortly after its completion, the architecture was clearly intended to impress visiting foreigners as well as Americans.[20] Abandoned in the 1970s, the Customs House was slowly deteriorating. Today the Heye Museum has been inserted into the two lower floors of the Customs House, sharing the building with bankruptcy court and federal government offices.

Four large sculptures by Daniel Chester French (1850–1931), set on massive pedestals, flank the entrance. The four seated female figures represent America, Asia, Europe, and Africa. America sits proudly on her throne, a sheaf of Indian corn in her lap. Her foot rests on the ruins of the head of the Aztec deity Quetzalcoatl. A Native American wearing full headdress crouches behind her, unmistakably depicted as a second-class citizen. This antiquated, prejudiced work symbolizes the victory of America over the continent's indigenous civilizations. The hooded Africa is asleep; Asia represents the conquest and superiority of Christianity over paganism; and, of course, Europe proclaims the eternal moral superiority of its culture, traditions, and judicial system. How ironically symbolic that today the interior of this building is dedicated to celebrating the culture of the Native American.

SCALE

Within the United States the smaller art museum—very often the university museum—has reached a higher degree of architectural success. There is a direct correlation between scale and the design process. The pithy maxim "too many cooks spoil the broth" certainly holds true for making buildings. There is such a vast array of forces involved throughout the process of erecting any building that architects are fond of referring to architecture as a performance art. Complex motives inform the conception, design, and construction of a museum, as well as the exquisite layering of activities that a museum contains. Unfortunately, the building process for our city museums involves so many layers of participants—directors, donors, trustees, zoning boards, community boards—that no matter how marvelous the initial design might have been it is bound to end up distorted and diluted. Hence the smaller the project and the fewer the players, the greater is the chance for success.[21]

The Kimball Art Museum (1972) in Fort Worth, Texas, designed by Louis Kahn, is often upheld as a seminal art-showing building. This delightful edifice was conceived around a permanent exhibition, had one client and no board to satisfy, and (most importantly) is nearly of a domestic scale. Kahn's preoccupation of the moment, that of the individual skylit room, was eminently suitable for this small-scale scheme. Both Kahn and his clients wanted a museum with a homey quality, making the museum visit relaxed and comfortable rather than overwhelming and exhausting.[22] The fixed program and single-story layout enabled Kahn to create the extraordinary cycloidal vaulted skylights that fill the galleries with natural light.

The more recent darlings of the North American art world are the Cy Twombly Gallery in Houston, Texas, and its neighbor, the Menil Collection, both designed by Renzo Piano (in 1987 and 1995 respectively). The Menil was constructed for a rotating exhibit, only 10 percent of the client's private collection to be shown at one time.[23] (The architect was privy to the entire collection during the design process, however.) Like the Kimball, the building is certainly at a human scale. The Twombly Gallery, conceived and developed with much input from the artist and following a program of permanent exhibition, allowed for an ideal, tight, design process. A building that is only 9,000 square feet, the plan is based upon a nine-square grid, each room being a perfect square. Piano's exploration of natural light, an obsession building upon Kahn's work, continued at the Twombly Gallery—culminating in a spectacular, quite complex ceiling system.

Two larger projects—the Wexner Center for the Arts and the Frederick R. Weisman Art Museum—represent museums with unusual architectural ambitions for the United States. Both buildings were commissioned by state universities and represent an excitingly liberal attitude. The Wexner (1989), located at Ohio State University in Columbus, Ohio, and designed by Peter Eisenman, is a rather self-conscious building. Designed with the intention of displaying installation art created on campus, the building is programmatically rigid, but it is an important architectural feat. The Weisman, designed by Frank Gehry (1993), a commission of the University of Minnesota, is an early experimental version of his Bilbao Guggenheim—a much watered-down version. Whether one loves or hates, agrees or disagrees with these museum buildings, it is critical that they and more like them exist. Progressive architecture, just like progressive art, needs an assured place in our culture.

Occupying a tiny pie-shaped slice of lower Manhattan is a minuscule museum that illustrates the complexity of the relationship between art and architecture. The Storefront for Art and Architecture (1993) straddles that fine line, standing both as a work of art and a functional space.[24] Displayed as an object, the building itself was the exhibit in its initial two months of existence. A design collaboration between architect Steven Holl and artist Vito Acconci, the building was clearly intended to maximize public interaction. Quite literally just a storefront, the concrete-board facade is composed of irregular, rectilinear plates that fit together as if a jigsaw puzzle. In the warm weather these plates revolve from either a horizontal or a vertical pivot point and can be adjusted by the public into varying states of openness. Engaging the passerby, physically blurring the boundaries between street and building, the small space and its surroundings merge. Inside and outside begin to become one and the same; city, museum building, visitor, observer, and passerby all become objects of display.

The Dia Center for the Arts has unfolded this notion of reciprocity by placing artworks throughout existing spaces in Manhattan and the United States. These include two permanent Manhattan sites, containing work by Walter De Maria: *The New York Earth Room* (1997) and *The Broken Kilometer* (1979). The consumption of contemporary art therefore becomes a rambling journey, suggestive of alternative ways to contemplate art. Since the mid-seventeenth century there have been movements promoting alternative viewing spaces, a kind of museum underground, termed "the anti-museum" by Douglas Davis.[25] From the dissident founding of the Royal Academy of Arts in London in 1768 to the Impressionist's Société des Artistes Indépendants, the Dada movement, Flux, and the 1960s Situationists, anti-establishment sentiment has flourished. Davis classifies the neutral, stripped-down warehouses popular in the 1980s as a continuance of these "anti-museums."

The Dia, champion of the museum as neutral canvas, planned its original site (completed in 1987) as one of the first reductive conversions in Manhattan. The project's architect, Richard Gluckman, feels strongly that it is the art that should dominate the space, placing himself in a supporting role. Describing himself as "an expediter for the artist, not a collaborator," Gluckman feels compelled to "create a backdrop, make the most of a beautiful existing space, looking at the structure of the building as a three-dimensional grid: width, breadth, and length."[26] This deceptively simple approach, designing viewing space without visual noise, is quite powerful when manipulated in such a facile fashion on such an intimate scale. The relentless "white cube" can become oppressive in a larger museum setting. The Rooftop Urban Park Project at the Dia is largely occupied by Dan Graham's glass and metal sculpture *Two-Way Mirror Cylinder Inside Cube* (1981/1991), which, together with an accompanying rooftop video salon, morphs the role of the building itself into that of art. Although intended as an artwork, the piece is so architectural and extraordinarily revealing that it almost serves as an anagram for museum.

All these smaller-scale spaces have a symbiotic relationship with the artwork they contain (or encompass). They force the viewer to examine the surrounding interior environment, an objective reflected in the artwork itself. At the same time, it is the intimacy, the private quietude of these spaces, that is so engaging. While perhaps highly impractical, the fragmentation of the museum—individual displays dotted throughout the city— is a seductive idea. Intimate spaces within stores or subway stations, converted buildings, or free-standing structures could have rotating exhibits devoted to one or several (never many) pieces of art. Not dissimilar to a vastly expanded public art program, new and old culturally familiar spaces could be devoted to permanent and changing exhibits. This would not preclude the need for larger museums, but it could alleviate expansion issues and certainly reinforce public art education. One can begin to daydream, imagining a scheme of temporary mobile art exhibits driving around the city from location to location, like a library bus. These miniature traveling exhibitions would have no destination, only their mobile home. They would be a mutated microcosm of the traveling exhibit, an explosion out of the museum envelope.

TECHNOLOGY

Wandering around the exterior of the Bilbao Guggenheim offers a delicious slice of undirected discovery. One can walk up or down a variety of steps, contemplate the building's many intricate facades, watch the brown river, the bridge traffic, the gray city. This makes the offer of a handheld audio guide (as an aid in touring the building exterior) most disheartening. A ubiquitous fixture at all blockbuster exhibitions, this combination gadget, marketing tool, and informational device has transmutated experience in much the same way that the personal video recorder has replaced real-time experience. Do the tourists who video-record their own gondola rides down the Grand Canal in Venice really experience the ride, or do they experience the recording of the ride? Do those who approach art and architecture with a constant stream of aural information rushing into their ears have a different experience from those who rely purely on their own intuition? How can the users of this device possibly take in the pillowing texture of the titanium cladding, the smell of steam, the blend of Bilbao's noises: rain, traffic, flowing water? Our pragmatic, data-obsessed society consistently undervalues the sheer delight of personal discovery.

It is a commonplace that technology (the Internet in particular) has begun to remove architecture from the museum, to remove enclosure. In actuality, technology has been catalytic in catapulting the museum (as a physical destination place, therefore as real-time architecture) into a renaissance period. Many well-documented factors now draw people to museums: the blockbuster exhibition, marketing, a common interest in the visual, a dumbing-down of the exhibits. Digital connections and museum web sites are included as a positive influence on this draw. Rising attendance records are evidence that seeing an artwork on-line is an enticement, not a substitute, for seeing it in person. The human desire to gather, to mix and mingle, to engage in a collective activity in the same place, has ineluctably led to the museum's current success.

Now that our new media have made the museum the place to be, the real transformative power that technology can offer the museum is not flashy interactive amenities but technology as a resource for exciting new architectural possibilities. Scientific invention, including those of graphic techniques—such as Leon Battista Alberti's fifteenth-century rules of projecting a perspective, or the birth of photography in the nineteenth century—have historically expanded the vocabulary of the architect. The computer's capabilities are no different; as a new language of form evolves, the computer's influence on architecture is and will be tremendous.

Once again at the cutting edge, Gehry utilized computer software (programs common in aeronautics, shipbuilding, and bridge and highway construction) to generate form and to organize construction techniques when erecting the Bilbao Guggenheim. The computer as a design and building tool (rather than as a means of documentation) offers a design process divorced from traditional structural principles. Exploitation of the computer as a tool to generate form, in conjunction with ever-advancing construction techniques and new materials, is where technology will have a lasting impact on the museum— its physical presence, its architecture.

PROGRAM

Any particular building typology is primarily defined by its original program. Program, in turn, is shaped by the activities and events that are planned to occur within the building. As eloquently summed up by architect Bernard Tschumi, "There is no architecture without action, no architecture without events, no architecture without program."[27]

The word "museum" serves as a broad umbrella for a vast array of diverse kinds of programs; one can therefore find quite a variety of institutions and, hence, a variety of building types. What is contained in the San Francisco Museum of Modern Art is considerably different from the collection at the Japanese

American National Museum in Los Angeles, or the exhibition at the Museum of Natural History in Manhattan. These museums all have different displays, agendas, goals, and needs; all have different programs.

Over the last thirty years, traditional museums with familiar content (art, history, science) have been joined by institutions devoted to an enormously wide realm of subjects. Professions, industries, paraphernalia, regalia, natural disasters, man-made disasters, good happenings, horrific events—all have been subject to what Victoria Newhouse has referred to as "museumification."[28] Containing artifacts rather than art, these institutions include children's museums, ethnic museums, historical museums, remembrance museums, theme museums, and narrative museums.

The dichotomy of program between an art museum and an artifact museum, particularly a theme museum (the Louisville Slugger Museum [of baseball bats] or the Rock and Roll Hall of Fame and Museum in Cleveland), creates a very real formal architectural schism. As the program requirements mutate, architectural possibilities change, transforming the role of the architect. Is the architect responsible for creating an interactive drama, giving away subliminal cues? Conversely, is the architect responsible for designing a stage set—a platform for opportunity? Should the architect dictate an experience, a feeling, a reaction that would be universal for all visitors encountering a particular space or display? Or should the architect facilitate personal interpretation?

An illuminating comparison is that of the U.S. Holocaust Memorial Museum in Washington, D.C., designed by architect James Ingo Freed, an artifact museum, and the Felix Nussbaum Museum in Osnabrück, Germany, a museum that cannot decide whether it is an art or an artifact museum. The Holocaust Memorial Museum, a narrative museum with a mission devoted to raising social consciousness, architecturally manipulates the visitor's journey, enforcing an understanding of the gravity of particular historical events. To evoke the Nazi deportation of Jews, corridors are narrowed as the visitor gets closer to railcars. Air-conditioning vents were moved to the floor to make the space cooler. The architecture of the Holocaust Memorial Museum (as premeditated by Freed and the founding director of the museum, Arthur Rosenblatt), interlinked with the exhibition display, fortifies the museum's conjoined purposes—educational journey and built memorial. Emotional manipulation through spatial lexicon begins as soon as the visitor enters. The colossal four-story Hall of Witness, composed of red brick walls and dark gray steel structures capped with an off-kilter skylight, sets the visitor on edge. Material and form facsimiles, taken from the Auschwitz death camp, have been structurally incorporated; the arched gateway to the camp, the barracks' brick pattern, and four interlinked brick structures shaped like outsized Auschwitz watchtowers further disconcert the visitor. This is unabashedly didactic architecture that seems entirely appropriate.

The omnipotent, sensaround approach is questionable, however, in an art museum. The Felix Nussbaum Museum, designed by Daniel Libeskind and completed in 1998, attempts simultaneously to celebrate the work of one artist and also act as a Holocaust memorial. The main gallery and corridor is only 7.5 feet wide, an evocative recreation of the claustrophobic spaces Nussbaum, a German Jew, might have painted in while in hiding from the Nazis during World War II. Nussbaum was captured by the Gestapo in 1944 and sent to Auschwitz, where he died.[29] Such a narrow, unpleasant space intentionally manipulates the viewer, therefore trivializing the artwork. The paintings are not permitted to provoke individual responses and thoughts as the visitor is forced momentarily to become the artist. Here, architectural egotism dominates the art, creating a confusion as to the Nussbaum Museum's mission.

The Holocaust Memorial Museum very consciously does not include any artistic creations in its permanent exhibition. Concerned that symbolic or metaphoric exhibits might dilute narrative content or fuel those who deny the reality of the Holocaust, the displays are all narrative documentaries. The no-art restriction does not apply to the public spaces in the building, however, and the museum commissioned four site-specific works by the American artists Ellsworth Kelly, Sol LeWitt, Richard Serra, and Joel Shapiro.

It is worth noting that architect Daniel Libeskind's extension to the Jewish Museum in Berlin is also a programmatic hybrid. A museum dedicated to the cultural history of Berlin's Jews, the building opened in January of 1999 entirely empty, without a single object on display. An inhabitable concrete, steel, and zinc sculpture, the architecture is tremendously powerful on its own, sending the visitor through a series of expressive, evocative spaces. Here it is the architecture that inspires reflection, recollection, fear, and reverence. This building is a brilliant monument; it is not a museum, and would do best to remain empty.

The opposite situation exists at Bilbao, where chunks of the building were designed for site-specific artwork. A luxurious collaboration between artist and architect allowed the architecture to ally itself with particular works, creating the ideal spaces for viewing particular pieces. Comparing this to historical precedent, architectural critic Ada Louise Huxtable has pointed out the significance of these associative spaces: "They create a much more radical fusion of art and architecture than the traditional blank niches and walls reserved by architects of the classical tradition for sculptures, paintings and frescoes."[30] The result is a delightful strategy for a contemporary art museum with a permanent collection or commissioning endowment, but an impossible scenario for a historically based institution with a changing exhibition schedule.

Although all museums essentially serve as storytellers, blurring the distinction between the art museum and the artifact museum creates confusion. Any hierarchy elevating the art museum over the artifact/theme museum is completely outdated; yet it is essential when discussing potential architectures to differentiate clearly these two very different building types.

INHABITATION

Architecture is often misrepresented as merely packaging, wrapping, outerwear—a man-made skin that serves the same function as a coat preventing wetness or chill. But architecture is not merely a slipcover; it is the spatial definition, the structure, of our world. Interior and exterior are as inseparable as the various systems of anatomy.

This relationship between outside and inside is of paramount importance to the museum as a building typology, as museums exist in such an eclectic assortment of scale, settings, and contents: urban, suburban, and rural locales, public and private institutions, categorical and encyclopedic collections. Such diversity makes it impossible and undesirable to assign the museum a specific style of architecture.

The advent of "edutainment" has created a whole new set of criteria for most museums. The programmatic focus of many new narrative museums is interactive, multisensory exhibits. At Cleveland's Rock and Roll Hall of Fame and Museum the visitor can listen to over five hundred rock-n-roll classics by touching a screen; at the Newseum in Arlington, Virginia, the visitor can pretend to be a television broadcaster. Elements of "edutainment," and particularly the use of storytelling media, have infiltrated the art museum. Synonymous with issues of architectural influence over program, the narrative environment can detract from the objects on display and distract the viewer. The quest for jazzy information design has led to a clear design hierarchy within all types of museums. The architectural elements—including the gallery spaces, the exhibition display (graphics, signage, cabinetry), and accompanying interactive tools and materials—are usually designed independently. Information architects, those who design displays, are beginning to enjoy as much celebrity as our architectural heroes.[31] Ralph Appelbaum, architect and exhibit designer, believes that "Exhibits should be environments, not just furniture. Exhibits are marketplaces of ideas."[32]

A marketplace of ideas, or a marketplace in general? A clear area of programmatic crossover between the art museum and the artifact museum is that of the commercial insertion. Art museums have incorporated retail as a given, allocating prime architectural space to shops, restaurants, classrooms, lecture halls, and gardens. Appelbaum connects the two: "Leisure in America is fantasy-based, you learn about a world of fantasy creatures that are so engaging that you are prompted to take home little stuffed animals to remember the experience."[33]

Family activities, children's activities, singles' nights, and late opening hours all encourage human interaction at the museum. Romances begin and end, gift-shop presents are purchased, food and relaxation are enjoyed at restaurants and cafés. Very few cultural institutions are so effective in dissolving generational gaps. The contemporary museum is a place that reaffirms cultural values, generating our current rituals and myths. Much like the suburban mall, the museum has evolved into a place not just to see but a place to be seen. Seventy years ago Georges Bataille described the Louvre, identifying the true object of display as the visitor: "The museum is the colossal mirror in which man finally contemplates himself in every aspect, finds himself literally admirable, and abandons himself to the ecstasy expressed in all the art reviews."[34] Bataille's ideas are equally applicable today; museums of all stripes serve as our multicultural crossroads, drawing together a vast diversity of people to admire art, artifacts, themselves, and each other.

CONCLUSION

By its very nature the museum can be defined as a link between past and present. It is the museum's architecture that can best assist in successfully mediating that connection. This requires not only an understanding of the past but an openness to future possibilities. Rapidly advancing technology has made and will ultimately make its biggest contribution to the museum through enabling the use of new materials and new construction methods, and by serving as a design tool for innovative architectural forms.

All built form is representative of cultural ideologies and cultural status. Museum architecture is capable of altering a downtown cityscape—and therefore new museums have become a powerful tool for urban regeneration. Connection to a local neighborhood and relevance to a specific community begin with a building attentive to its surroundings. Responsible for reflecting a diversity of outlooks, the contemporary posturban museum must present an architecture that is substantive and welcoming. This museum may not look like anything we already know. Its architectural boundaries might encompass an entirely new building, take the shape of an addition to an existing building, or be a renovation, insertion, fragment, or collage. This diversity has a direct effect upon scale. There are small, medium, large, and extra-large museums; a condition that has enormous institutional and, therefore, architectural implications.[35]

Adding yet another layer of complexity to museum architecture is the vast variety of its potential contents. The relationship between art and architecture (specifically architecture as art) has always been and continues to be a subject of universal debate. The imaginary dividing line is excruciatingly elastic, mutating within the whims of fashion. The relationship between artifact and architecture is considerably more straightforward than between art and architecture. Artifact museums are creating their own rather literal path to narrative architectural articulation.

Yet, irrespective of a collection's content, a collection without a public viewing space is just a collection, and a public viewing space without a collection is just a public space. It is important to note that contemporary posturban museum architecture is similar to museum content, operating as an informant of society as well as a reflection of society. Museum architecture is both formed by culture and culturally formative. Occasionally applauded, often overlooked, frequently bemoaned— yet absolutely essential and always there—architecture is integral to the museum experience.

ENDNOTES

[1]Carol Duncan, *Civilizing Rituals: Inside Public Art Museums* (London: Routledge, 1995). Duncan explores the many layers of ritual that occur within the civic art museum. I am reminding us that all architecture, regardless of typology, embodies rituals and is in and of itself ritualistic.

[2]Neil Spiller, *Digital Dreams: Architecture and the New Alchemic Technologies* (New York: Whitney Library of Design, 1998), 23–24.

[3]"Posturban" is intended to categorize the current condition of our cities, recognizing that the boundaries between suburban and urban are dissolving. Despite the substantial shift of job centers and demographics to the suburbs, many city downtowns are experiencing a revitalization; indeed, there has been a recent renaissance of interest in the city. Conversely, many suburban ameni-

ties are creeping into city life, creating a disturbing blanket of visual and cultural homogenization.

⁴This organizational tool was inspired by the process in Charles and Ray Eames, *Powers of Ten*, vol. 1 (Santa Monica, Calif.: Pyramid Films, 1978).

⁵Walter Benjamin, "Pariser Passagen II," in *Das Passagen-Werk*, vol. I (Frankfurt: Suhrkamp Verlag, 1983), 1051–1052, translated in Christel Hollevoet, "Wandering in the City," in *The Power of the City/The City of Power* (New York: Whitney Museum of American Art, 1992), 53.

⁶Joseph Giovannini, "Gehry's Reign in Spain," *Architecture* (December 1997), 66.

⁷Robert Hughes, preface to *Barcelona* (New York: Vintage Books, 1993), ix.

⁸Victoria Newhouse, *Towards a New Museum* (New York: The Monacelli Press, 1998), 257–258.

⁹James Stewart Polshek, discussion with author, New York, 26 March 1999.

¹⁰Giovannini, "Gehry's Reign," 77. Giovannini writes that the exterior "gives visitors the confidence of their own intuitions, emotions, and senses."

¹¹Allan Schwartzman, "Art vs. Architecture," *Architecture* (December 1997), 58.

¹²Charles Jencks, *The Contemporary Museum*, ed. Maggie Toy, in *Architectural Design Profile* no. 130 (London: Academy Editions, 1997), 9.

¹³Newhouse, *Towards a New Museum*, 193–198.

¹⁴"Imagining the Future of the Museum of Modern Art," *Studies in Modern Art* 7, ed. John Elderfield (New York: Museum of Modern Art, 1998), 109–117. "The Museum and Society" Lecture Series, 3 December 1996. Janet Abrams comments on the experiential ramifications of technology within the museum and the danger of "being processed through an experience."

¹⁵Judith H. Dobryzynski, "They're Building a Lot More Than Their Collections," *New York Times*, 21 April 1999, special section on museums, 13.

¹⁶Charles Gwathmey, "On Wright's Foundations," *Architectural Record* (October 1992), 104.

¹⁷Susanna Sirefman, *New York: A Guide to Recent Architecture* (London: Ellipsis Koneman, 1997), 204–206.

¹⁸Thomas Krens, "Art Impresario: Interview with Thomas Krens," *Architecture* (December 1997), 50.

¹⁹Helen Searing, "The Brillo Box in the Warehouse: Museums of Contemporary Art and Industrial Conversions," *The Andy Warhol Museum* (New York: Distributed Art Publishers, Inc., 1994), 40.

²⁰Donald Martin Reynolds, *The Architecture of New York City: Histories and Views of Important Structures, Sites, and Symbols* (New York: John Wiley & Sons, Inc., 1994), 256.

²¹Stephen E. Weil, *Rethinking the Museum and other Meditations* (Washington and London: Smithsonian Institution Press, 1990), 27–41. In the included essay "A Meditation on Small and Large Museums," Weil explores many of

the conceptual and institutional differences between museums of different magnitudes, noting the "unavoidable interplay between organizational scale and the growth of bureaucracy."

[22]David B. Brownlee and David G. DeLong, *Louis I. Kahn: In the Realm of Architecture*, condensed ed. (New York: Universe Publishing, 1997), 212–223.

[23]Newhouse, *Towards a New Museum*, 20–22.

[24]Sirefman, *New York*, 76–77.

[25]Douglas Davis, *The Museum Transformed: Design and Culture in the Post Pompidou Age* (New York: Abbeville Press, 1990), 169.

[26]Richard Gluckman, interview with author, winter of 1997.

[27]Bernard Tschumi, *Architecture and Disjunction* (Cambridge, Mass.: MIT Press, 1994), 121.

[28]Newhouse, *Towards a New Museum*, 8.

[29]Ibid., 96.

[30]Ada Louise Huxtable, "Museums: Making It New" (review of *Towards a New Museum* by Victoria Newhouse), *New York Review of Books* (22 April 1999), 14–15.

[31]Rita Ciolli, "Stories at Exhibition," *Newsday*, 21 May 1997, B6. The phrase is attributed to Ralph Saul Wurman.

[32]Clifford A. Pearson, "Breaking Out of the Display Case, Exhibits Reach Out and Touch," *Architectural Record* (September 1994), 28.

[33]Ciolli, "Stories at Exhibition," B6.

[34]Georges Bataille, "Museum," in *Rethinking Architecture* (trans. of Bataille's entry "Musée" in the *Dictionnaire Critique* of 1930), trans. Paul Hegarty (London: Routledge, 1997), 5, 300.

[35]Ren Koolhaas and Bruce Mau, *Small, Medium, Large, and Extra-Large: Office for Metropolitan Architecture* (New York: Monacelli Press, 1995).

Victoria Newhouse

Is "The Idea of a Museum" Possible Today?

I N 1852, WHILE SERVING AS RECTOR of the new Catholic University in Dublin, John Henry Newman published his now-famous book *The Idea of a University*. In it he set forth a definition of higher education as its own object. For Newman knowledge was an end in itself, from which nothing—such as vocational considerations or even moral improvement—should detract. A similarly single-minded idea—the preservation and exhibition of a collection—inspired the first great public museums that were built in Europe and the United States throughout the nineteenth century. This initial wave of museums was intended specifically for the viewing of objects.

Just as today's pluralistic society has expanded the goals of higher education, so too have our museums exploded into a variety of functions. In addition to exhibiting art or natural history, museums now provide places for shopping, eating, performance, and community activities; they have also become an important urban-renewal opportunity for cities. Even the original prerequisite of an existing collection is being challenged by new museums focused on offering information (for example, the Glacier Museum in Norway and the Volcano Museum in France) rather than objects. Furthermore, what was primarily a celebratory environment (with the rare exception of unsettling medical museums) is now sometimes replaced by an intentionally disturbing experience. Witness, for example, the Holocaust Memorial Museum in Washington, D.C., (1993) by

Victoria Newhouse is the author of Towards a New Museum.

James Ingo Freed and the Jewish Museum in Berlin (1999) by Daniel Libeskind.

Clearly, the idea of the museum has changed. The hallowed precincts of yesterday's temples of culture are increasingly being replaced by lively environments that give equal importance to people-watching and entertainment as to the exhibits. A comparison of some contemporary examples with one of their most illustrious forebears, the Kunsthistorisches Museum in Vienna, provides some insights into the importance of historical museums and how they have evolved.

Paris's Centre Georges Pompidou (1977) includes a renowned museum of modern art, but its architects, Renzo Piano and Richard Rogers, have preferred to describe the facility as "a live center of information and entertainment." If this image differs from the serenity and seriousness usually associated with a museum, so does the Pompidou's role as the linchpin of a massive urban-renewal project in the Marais district. Increasingly, new museums are being used to revive neglected neighborhoods—as seen by Richard Meier's Museum of Contemporary Art (1995) in Barcelona and Frank Gehry's Guggenheim Museum (1997) in Bilbao.

And what about the idea of a museum as theme park? For a new building to house the Groninger Museum (1994) in the Netherlands, Frans Haks, then its director, cited the separate pavilions of Disneyland as the inspiration for a design by Alessandro Mendini and a team of high-profile architects. The resulting five pavilions have individualized interiors that suit their different contents; from the exterior, the colorful conglomeration calls to mind a trayful of the fancifully designed household utensils for which Mendini is famous.

The classic modernism of Richard Meier's J. Paul Getty Center in Los Angeles (1997) could not be more different from the Groninger's unorthodox design. And yet the Getty Museum also recalls the theme-park format: a tram regularly transports the public to five separate pavilions. Cafés and a restaurant are tucked into luxuriant landscaping, which includes a walk-in garden maze by the California artist Robert Irwin. The site's spectacular mountain, city, and ocean vistas are as much an attraction as the art (as views of Paris are at the Centre Pompidou).

The Getty's location on an acropolis-like hilltop is unusual. More commonly now, museums are woven into the urban fabric, plugging them into a neighborhood's circulation patterns. In 1982, Hans Hollein's Städtisches Museum in Mönchengladbach, Germany, was one of the first to do this, followed the next year by James Stirling's Neue Staatsgalerie in Stuttgart. Abandoning their former isolation within parks and behind fortress-like walls, museums have become an integral part of their communities; instead of being protected from the turmoil of their surroundings, they now acknowledge, and can even reflect, these complexities.

In contrast to traditional museums with their permanent collections, many new museums—Gehry's Guggenheim Museum in Bilbao, Spain, is one—function more as *Kunsthallen* for temporary exhibitions. The identification of museums by their most famous holding—the *Mona Lisa* for the Louvre, the *Demoiselles d'Avignon* for the Museum of Modern Art in New York—is being replaced by an association with their high-profile architects. And what these architects produce has a creative role of its own: unique forms such as those of Gehry's sculptural museums are meant to inspire artists to create site-specific work. (What would Cardinal Newman have said about this challenge to his stricture against the university's "advancement" of knowledge rather than its mere diffusion?)

While each generation of museums is valid for its own time, attempts to combine generations are often unsatisfactory. The successful grafting of contemporary structures onto older buildings seems to be more difficult for museums than for any other building type. The addition of massive modern wings to the Metropolitan Museum of Art in New York has deprived the building of its overall sense of place and procession, and the new glass and steel pyramid at the Louvre in Paris has sacrificed the elegance of a palace entrance to an anonymous commercial space. One of the few historic museums still free of such compromises is Vienna's Kunsthistorisches Museum; its purity can be used to point out some of the ways in which architectural alterations can completely change the character of an existing institution.

At the Kunsthistorisches Museum, no new glass and steel structures clash with the ornate masonry as they do at the Metropolitan's Temple of Dendur Hall and at the Louvre's pyramid entrance and skylights. Consequently, the clear paths established by the museum's architects—the famous German Gottfried Semper and his younger Austrian colleague, Carl Hasenauer—remain intact. The multicolored marble columns of a circular entrance lobby contribute to the sensuousness of a welcoming environment and, together with the monumental stairway (with a giant sculpture by Antonio Canova placed prominently on the landing), immediately announce the building's important cultural purpose. All of this also provides a clear orientation for gallery-goers. Designed for the Hapsburgs' vast collections, the building houses, among other things, Benvenuto Cellini's giant salt-cellar and some of the finest Pieter Brueghels and Titians anywhere.

In an hour or two visitors can see either the Flemish, Dutch, and German masterpieces in the second of three gallery levels at one side of the stairhall, or the Italian, Spanish, and French paintings on the other side. Large, skylit, richly articulated, and variously colored interior rooms accommodate overscaled paintings; smaller works hang on crescent-shaped partitions that create more intimate alcoves along peripheral walls opposite windows. Even the exceptional height of works by Rubens was taken into account by the architect, who designed taller galleries for them. This variety of conditions tailor-made for a specific collection provides an effective setting for art originally meant to be seen within the distinct framework of churches and palaces. The result is an intimate dialogue between container and contents, ideal for the exhibition of art. Such a dialogue is sadly lacking in many contemporary museum galleries (witness the cavernous Scaife Gallery at the Carnegie Museum of Art in Pittsburgh or the all-purpose spaces of the Museum of Contemporary Art in Barcelona).

The nature of Vienna's Old Master collection calls for quiet contemplation undisturbed by the concerns of daily life. Semper thus created a cultural enclave removed from the city's mundane activities. Instead of facing the newly-created Ringstrasse Boulevard, as do the other civic buildings erected there at the end of the nineteenth century, the art museum and its twin, the Naturhistorisches Museum, face each other across a landscaped esplanade.

Paradoxically, it was the calamitous breakup of the Austro-Hungarian Empire that deprived Vienna of the gifts and legacies that have traditionally augmented the holdings of major museums. (Now, even the few paintings that were added will in large part be removed by the government's decision to return art that was sequestered during World War II.) The positive effect of this collection's unchanging nature is the preservation of a distinct historical vision, which can be easily lost, often for the sake of a passing architectural fashion.

In the early 1920s, after the Imperial collections became the property of the newly created Austrian state, the Kunsthistorisches Museum—like many older museums at the time—was considered outdated. Consequently, there was talk of a new facility (and some departments, among them the splendid musical instrument collection, were spun off to other venues). Now, the museum's current director, Wilfried Seipel, is restoring the architecture as closely as possible to the original, updating the building only technologically and museologically (i.e., for climate control and hanging). It remains to be seen how the addition of a large new underground gallery envisioned by Dr. Seipel for temporary exhibitions might affect this historically correct building.

Standing still has not left Vienna behind; on the contrary, the contextual setting provided by this elaborate neo-Baroque structure is now emulated by some contemporary architecture. For example, elements of historic architecture were used within Richard Meier's crisp modern pavilions for the Getty Center to create a framework for Old Master painting and sculpture. Frank Gehry explains that he has tried to create a sense of movement in the Bilbao Guggenheim "as a replacement for the decorative vocabulary of cornices, moldings, and other details that architects in the nineteenth century and before could rely on to humanize space."

In the same way that the past provides lessons for the present, a museum's history is as important as the history of the objects it contains. This was acknowledged recently by Kevin Roche's renovation of the Greek and Roman galleries at the Metropolitan Museum. In a welcome change from its common practice of masking earlier designs, here the museum returned—as much as possible within the confines of a two-story addition—to the McKim, Mead, and White addition of 1917. Consequently, daylight now floods through windows and a skylight, which had been covered over for more than half a century. The galleries approximate the architects' original vision with the light-colored limestone wall-cladding they had designated (but did not install) as well as an abundance of natural light. The stunning result captures what could well be described as the museum's equivalent to Newman's "Idea of a University": a collection preserved and exhibited in galleries designed for it.

Charles Correa

Museums: An Alternate Typology

I N HIS MIT SEMINARS IN THE 1950S, Professor Gyorgy Kepes would discuss the notion of "museum fatigue": those feelings, ranging from ennui to fallen arches, that many museum-goers experience as they trudge through the Louvre or the Prado. He would then emphasize the need for contrapuntal areas, where the eye—and the mind—could rest.

This insight came vividly to mind when, as a young architect back in India, I was asked to design the Smarak Sangrahalaya for Mahatma Gandhi at the Sabarmnati Ashram in Ahmedabad. This memorial museum, to be located next to Gandhi's own house, would contain his letters, photographs, and other documentary material about his life and the freedom movement he headed. Since more such historic documents were sure to be identified and collected through the years, I realized that the museum itself would have to grow—in the process allowing each generation to pay its own respects to the Mahatma (an idea somewhat influenced by the Ise shrine in Japan).

A building in memory of Mahatma Gandhi cannot be the same as one to commemorate Charles de Gaulle—or Jawaharlal Nehru, for that matter. They were all very different individuals. And so this museum itself, through its intrinsic form, would have to express the message of the man: human-scaled, unpretentious, modest. With this as a starting point, the building very soon designed itself—as a series of pavilions, some open and some enclosed, interspersed with courtyards and a water pool. The mood is one of calmness and contemplation, qualities that

---

Charles Correa is the noted Indian architect, practicing in Bombay.

the Mahatma exemplified and that are essential to any scholar attempting to understand his ethos. Of decisive importance to the creation of this mood are, of course, the "rest" spaces—those open areas that interlock with the enclosed ones.

This question of the context we provide for the object (and the validation, or the distortion, it can cause) is central to any discussion of museum design. It has, of course, already been brilliantly articulated by the great scholar Ananda Coomaraswamy. Writing almost a century ago, he warned against the falsification inherent in the very act of putting any object "on display"—i.e., skewing it onto an antiseptic museum wall, far removed from its own natural context. Thus, the mud pot, used in an Egyptian village to draw water from the well, has completely different connotations when caught in a beam of halogen light at the Metropolitan Museum of Art. Regardless of our intentions, we have irrevocably changed its meaning.

The symbiotic relationship between container and contained was the key issue in the design of the National Crafts Museum in Delhi, built to house the finest examples of folk art and handicraft in India (figure 1). This includes, for instance, the magnificent mud horses that come from various villages in South India. Villagers make these horses neither for sale nor display, but as part of sacred rituals, which they perform on special festival days. How can one "show" them without falsifying their meaning? Here the client, Pupul Jayakar, came up with a simple, but brilliant, suggestion. Instead of arranging the thousands of items in the museum's collection chronologically, or by geographical location within India, or even by the materials and techniques used (all of which would serve to distance the viewer from the object), she came up with a marvelously simple structure. There would be just three categories: village crafts, sacred crafts, and court crafts. All three are vitally important to any understanding of India—in fact, they constitute a paradigm that can be used to comprehend many other crucial aspects of this country as well. From this *parti*, the design developed very easily. We created an open-to-sky pathway, a sort of meandering street that goes right down through the heart of the museum—from village to temple to palace. Off this street are the various galleries, which are also connected

Figure 1: National Crafts Museum, Delhi. Courtesy of Jyotindra Jain.

internally. Thus, you can either cover the whole museum at once, or visit only those galleries you wish to see, and in the order you prefer—so that the narrative is not proscribed and linear, but created anew each time. As in the Gandhi museum, the crucial element is the open-to-sky space—each time one emerges out into the street, the eye clears. Very soon the street, and one's progress down it from village to temple to palace, seems to become a metaphor for India herself.

Two other projects that make use of this typology (i.e., the disaggregation of the museum's intrinsic form and the movement through the open-to-sky spaces that lie between) are the Bharat Bhavan in Bhopal and the Jawahar Kala Kendra in Jaipur (figure 2). Both are art centers. The former is situated on a hillside that slopes gently down to the lake, setting up a series of descending courtyards and terraces, off of which are located various galleries and other facilities. The latter is an ambitious exercise, a metaphor for Nehru and for the city of Jaipur itself—an extraordinary creation by Maharaj Jai Singh based on the oldest myths of the *Navgraha* (the mandala of the nine

Figure 2: Jawahar Kala Kendra, Jaipur. Courtesy of Mahindra Sinh.

planets), as well as on the newest ones: Science and Rationality. In the Jawahar Kala Kendra, the client's brief was disaggregated into nine squares, each 100 feet by 100 feet, to correspond to the mythic qualities of these planets. Like Nehru himself, the building is double-coded, seeking simultaneously to rediscover India and to invent a new future for a new nation.

In all these examples, the contrapuntal open-to-sky areas are of primary importance—an approach that is perhaps somewhat more difficult to incorporate in a cold climate. It also complicates security systems for the institution, since the disaggregation of the intrinsic form necessitates that each subgroup has its own independent protection. But the rewards to the visitor can be considerable, and I was delighted to find these same principles at work in three different examples existing in quite diverse areas of the world. The first, about a decade ago, was a Howard Hodgkin exhibition at the Anthony D'Offray Gallery in London. The show was housed in three separate townhouses, each about a hundred yards apart, along a London street. They had to be visited in succession—and each time one returned to the street, one was back in the soft English rain. And then one stepped into the next townhouse and the magic started again. It was a wonderful way to view Hodgkin.

The second example is James Freed's unforgettable Holocaust Museum in Washington, where the excruciating experiences of the main galleries are interspersed with transitional areas that mark a clear change of rhythm. If these transitional spaces had not existed and the galleries flowed one into the next, the whole experience would have been fundamentally different. Here Freed is not using open-to-sky spaces, but he lets the harsh light falling on the grim vocabulary and construction materials of these transitional spaces transform them into the necessary punctuation points—a sort of architectural equivalent of Moussorgsky's *Pictures at an Exhibition*.

The third example is Ramirez Vazquez's wonderful National Museum of Anthropology in Mexico City. Here one enters into a large rectangular courtyard surrounded by various galleries, each showing a different period of Mexican culture. The galleries are magnificent, but what dominates is the huge courtyard, with its *axis mundi* at the center: a single column holding up a cantilevered slab, from which a sheet of water cascades down. Standing in the middle of this vast space, one feels that it takes on a primordial symbolism—especially so because of the open-to-sky context in which it exists. If Vazquez had built the same column within a covered air-conditioned space, it would resemble just another upscale hotel lobby. In fact, that is probably what is happening to many museum typologies—and for much the same reasons that it happened to hotels: It is easier to monitor and safeguard a cocoon. Thus, while the old Raffles Hotel in Singapore, like the ones in Bombay and Hawaii, had generous verandahs, the new hotels are fully air-conditioned sealed boxes.

Yet need this be so? Even today, a visit to the Topaki in Istanbul or the Red Fort in Agra—or, for that matter, the castle hovering above Edinburgh—involves a certain amount of moving through open-to-sky space. And in all sorts of weather. In fact, this movement, far from being a handicap, is essential to one's enjoyment of those experiences. Perhaps it is time we evolved alternate museum typologies—ones that take this fundamental truth into account.

Bernard Tschumi/Bernard Tschumi Architects

On the Museum of the Twenty-First Century: An Homage to Italo Calvino's *Invisible Cities*

THE MODEM MODERN (OR THE MUSEUM OF MODEM ART)

F OR A NOMINAL SITE-ENTRANCE FEE, the museum offers on-line exhibitions capable of allowing thousands more visitors (in the form of "hits" or virtual visits) per day than any physical museum structure could comfortably accommodate. The permanent collection is shown in its entirety at all times of day and night; a complex system of links and hot links allows a complete exposition of the diversity and complexity of the intertwined developments in the history of the modern art displayed. Special exhibitions are mounted and can remain available to the public for much longer time periods than traditional temporary exhibitions. Contemporary artworks can be displayed real-time in their native media—the digital realm.

Catalogs, monographs, and design store items are sold in the virtual bookstore and virtual design store. Bulletin boards on the current exhibitions and on a wide variety of art subjects stimulate intellectual discussion and social interaction. The museum library catalog and books are available on-line. Special members-only chat rooms foster networking. Without the need to accommodate visitors physically, the museum staff moves into several floors of any generic office building equipped to handle extensive computer cabling in any city in the world with sufficient computer hardware support services.

Bernard Tschumi is an architect and dean of the Graduate School of Architecture, Planning and Preservation at Columbia University in New York. This essay is an amended version of a text that was part of the submission of Bernard Tschumi Architects for the competition for the expansion of the Museum of Modern Art in New York.

MoMALL

The design store, bookstore, and eateries (Modern Meals) serve as the anchor stores in a new theme mall; they use the importance of the unparalleled collection of modern art to appeal to the throngs of people who already come to the area to shop. The museum becomes a brand name that is brandished on posters, books, and T-shirts. Name designers, promoted by shows in the museum, produce artworks in the form of garments and household items; these goods either are made to order for specific (member) clients or are available as off-the-shelf merchandise. The exhibition galleries are scattered throughout the mall behind retail storefronts; each is accessed and paid for independently as one more commodity in the mall. In this fashion, the exhibitions are able to draw a much larger diversity of visitors. Filled with picnic tables, the garden becomes the obligatory food court.

THE MODERN CLUB

Permanent Club

In addition to the usual public galleries, special museum galleries contain exhibitions reserved for contributing members. The members' restaurant becomes a social hub or club space from which the members' galleries can be accessed or in which the artworks are actually located. While advertised within the public section, these exclusive rooftop spaces are visually severed from the rest of the museum and remain invisible to the public.

Temporal Club

Certain sections of the museum accommodate social gatherings for openings or special celebrations (major financial contributions, art donations, museum anniversaries...). Spaces normally designated for other programs (lobby, hall, temporary exhibition, library reading room, performance space...) are designed to accommodate banquets, parties, or formal dances when necessary.

MORE MODERN THAN MODERN:
THE CONTEMPORARY ARTISTS' WORKSHOP

Actively promoting an artists-in-residence program, the museum commissions, exhibits, and collects works of contemporary art. Several large, unfinished spaces with rough, industrial detailing and layered traces of their own history provide unique environments in which artists can not only act but react to create site-specific installations. Extensive video and multimedia editing equipment, computer facilities with state-of-the-art graphics, and more traditional machine shops are both placed at the disposition of contemporary artists for the creation of new works and explained to the public to demystify contemporary art. An active artists-in-residence program provides an opportunity for several younger artists to gain exposure to how other artists are working. Some of the works produced in the museum are sold to pay the bills. In addition, the permanent collection of art from the nineteenth and twentieth centuries is actively maintained to provide the most complete historical framework available for contemporary production.

MODERN MULTIPLEX

To allow the museum to show its film collection to the ever-increasing art-film public, four cinemas are built underneath the sculpture garden. Screenings of modern classics from the museum archives are joined by viewings of contemporary art films and films on loan from other archives. Themed film festivals are accompanied by lectures, debates, and scholarly publications. By day, the museum lobby, bookstore, and restaurant serve the exhibition galleries; by night, they serve the cinemas. Popcorn, soda, and Jujubes are available specifically for the movie public.

THE MODERN PRESERVATION ARCHIVE

Given the extraordinary technical difficulties involved in preserving twentieth-century works of art, several large loft spaces are used as laboratories for experimentation. The fragility of many of the artworks created using techniques developed during the last century renders them demanding of immediate attention; the diversity of the techniques requires that multiple scientific possibilities be explored simultaneously. Works of art are loaned to the museum to be preserved, not to be placed on display. "Before and After" exhibitions, intended to spark debates over the role of preservation in the art world, often occupy the small public galleries.

THE MODERN UNIVERSITY

The museum offers three tiers of educational experience:

Self-guided: First-hand experience of the artworks is used as an educational tool; the permanent collection is organized to highlight the diverse and interconnected nature of the art historical developments of the late nineteenth and twentieth centuries. From "self-serve" computer terminals, visitors can access more complete historical documentation on the works that they find most interesting.

Classes and lectures: Lecture halls, conference rooms, and multimedia displays are liberally interspersed throughout the public gallery spaces. At night, weekly classes are offered to midtown professionals from other fields by the fellowship students and scholars. Daytime classes for primary and secondary school students offer a broader public outreach.

Scholarly research and symposia: Doctoral students and visiting scholars receive fellowships for one or two years of study during which time they live in apartments in the museum complex and do research in the museum library and study centers.

MODERN ART PUBLISHERS, INC.

Rather than creating exhibitions for display within the building, the curators create exhibitions primarily for publication.

MODERN ART WAREHOUSE/STOCKYARDS

The museum accumulates artwork from the nineteenth and twentieth centuries, but the exhibition is in chronological encyclopedic public storage. While the artworks are on display to the public, no curatorial efforts are made to contextualize or historicize the art. All of the art is hung in an identical manner. The gallery spaces occupy an enormous number of square feet to display all of the art in the collection, but the architecture is repetitive and banal.

MINI-MODERNS

Pressure for midtown space atomizes the museum, which opens a dozen branch museums around Manhattan and the outer boroughs. Traveling exhibitions move from Soho to Museum Mile to Harlem to Staten Island, touring New York City without leaving the museum.

THE MODERN SELF-SUSTAINING BUREAUCRACY

In a testament to that which is truly modern, all outwardly directed purposes of the institution will be halted. Every staff member will, however, remain equally as busy, as applied, and as serious about his or her work as before.

CODA: THE MUSEUM OF THE TWENTY-FIRST CENTURY

And so, as for Calvino, for whom all the future cities "are already present in this instant, wrapped one within the other, confined, crammed, inextricable," so the museum of the twenty-first century is not yet another institution different from all of those previously listed; it is the summation of all of them.

Most of the time, the museum is well balanced, with the different activities happening simultaneously and in proportion to each other. The museum also has the capacity to become any of these different museums, only to return to its balanced state shortly thereafter. The architecture of the museum of the twenty-first century must allow this transformation, this temporal change in the character of the institution from one museum to another.

DÆDALUS Issues in Print

The Next Generation: Work in Progress (Spring 1999)
Education Yesterday, Education Tomorrow (Fall 1998)
Early Modernities (Summer 1998)
The Brain (Spring 1998)
Science in Culture (Winter 1998)
The American Academic Profession (Fall 1997)
A New Europe for the Old? (Summer 1997)
Human Diversity (Spring 1997)
Books, Bricks, and Bytes (Fall 1996)
American Education: Still Separate, Still Unequal (Fall 1995)
The Quest for World Order (Summer 1995)
What Future for the State? (Spring 1995)
Health and Wealth (Fall 1994)
After Communism: What? (Summer 1994)
Europe Through a Glass Darkly (Spring 1994)
Reconstructing Nations and States (Summer 1993)
America's Childhood (Winter 1993)
Immobile Democracy? (Fall 1992)

* * *

Send $10.95 per issue
(Canadian residents send $12.50 per issue) to:

Dædalus Business Office
136 Irving Street
Cambridge, MA 02138

*For shipment outside the United States,
please add $4.00 for air-mail delivery.*